HEALING THE WOUND

HEALING THE WOUND

PERSONAL NARRATIVES ABOUT THE 2007 POST-ELECTION VIOLENCE IN KENYA

EDITED BY

KIMANI NJOGU

TWAWEZA
COMMUNICATIONS
"Working Towards a Better World"

Published in 2009 by:
Twaweza Communications Ltd.
P.O. Box 66872 - 00800 Westlands
Twaweza House, Parklands Road
Mpesi Lane, Nairobi Kenya
website: www.twawezacommunications.org
Tel: +(254) 020 375 2009
Fax: +(254) 020 375 3941

Design and Layout by Catherine Bosire
Cover design by Kolbe Press

With the support of The Ford Foundation, Office of Eastern Africa

ISBN: 9966-7244-5-1

Printed by Kolbe Press, P.O. Box 468 - 00217 Limuru, Kenya

DEDICATION

TO ALL THOSE WHO SHOWED MERCY AND GAVE
HOPE TO FELLOW KENYANS

CONTENTS

ACKNOWLEDGEMENTS

This publication brings together personal narratives of Kenyans who went through suffering, Kenyans who showed mercy and gave hope to fellow Kenyans at their moment of need and those who caused pain to fellow citizens. The narratives provide yet another account of what happened before and after the 2007 general elections.

We are immensely grateful to the Ford Foundation for supporting this important work and specifically to Dr. Willy Mutunga, the Regional Representative of the Ford Foundation Office of Eastern Africa and Dr. Joyce Nyairo, Program Officer in charge of Media, Arts and Culture and all the Ford Foundation staff for listening to us and supporting our work. Through their support it became possible for us to collect these narratives from around the country and preserve them for future generations. Even as we seek to reconcile and heal the country, it is imperative that the memory of the citizens be preserved.

We are also grateful to the researchers from around the country who collected the narratives on our behalf. The narrative collectors did the interviews at the community level and helped us understand some of the factors that may have contributed to the violence as well as how community members responded. The team at Twaweza Communications deserves gratitude for keying in the narratives, translating them into English, and editing them on our behalf. Catherine Bosire designed this publication and I am grateful to her.

Kimani Njogu

Nairobi.

ABBREVIATIONS

AGC   African Gospel Church

AIC   African Inland Church

AMREF   Africa Medical and Research Foundation

APHIA II The AIDS, Population and Health Integrated Assistance

ART   Antiretroviral Therapy

ARVs   Antiretroviral Drugs

CDF   Constituency Development Fund

CEO   Chief Executive Officer

CREAW   Centre for Rights Education and Awareness

CRECO   Constitution and Reform Education Consortium

DC   District Commissioner

DCIO   District Criminal Investigation Officer

DIO   District Information Officer

DO   District Officer

ECK   Electoral Commission of Kenya

FORD   Forum for Restoration of Democracy

GSU   General Service Unit

HIV   Human Immunodeficiency Virus

IDPs   Internally Displaced People

IRC   International Red Cross

KADU   Kenya African Democratic Union

KANU   Kenya Africa National Union

KBS   Kenya Bus Service

KCC   Kenya Cooperative Creameries

KCSE   Kenya Certificate of Secondary Education

KCT   Kenya Credit Traders

KHRC	Kenya Human Rights Commission
KICC	Kenya International Conference Centre
KRCS	Kenya Red Cross Society
LAP	Local Authorities Pension
MOH	Ministry of Health
MP	Member of Parliament
NADISGO	Naivasha Disadvantaged Support Group
NARC-K	National Alliance Rainbow Coalition of Kenya
NCCK	National Council of Churches of Kenya
NCEC	National Convention Executive Council
NSIS	National Security Intelligence Service
NSSF	National Social Security Fund
OB	Occurrence Book
OCPD	Officer Commanding the Police Division
OCS	Officer Commanding the Station
ODM	Orange Democratic Movement
PCEA	Presbyterian Church of East Africa
PEP	Post-Exposure Prophylaxis
PNU	Party of National Unity
RPP	Release Prisoners Pressure
RWPL	Rural Women Peace Link
UNICEF	United Nations Children's Education Funds
UT	Untrained Teacher
VCT	Voluntary Counseling and Testing
YMCA	Young Men Christian Association

INTRODUCTION

NARRATIVE AND MEMORY

If there is something that has been persistent and enduring as the human capacity to engage in violence and destruction, it is the tendency to make sense of such events through narrative. For every violent event there is a story told in varied ways from a range of angles before and after the event. The narratives collected by *Twaweza Communications* in this Volume tell yet another side of the story about the violence that engulfed Kenya towards the end of 2007 and the beginning of 2008. The narratives are part of a *Daraja Initiative* involving media monitoring, reflections and documentation of the traumatic post-election violence period often associated with the contested presidential results of 2007. The goal of the Project is to contribute to the protection of the constitutional rights of all Kenyans and to the development of a just and democratic country. Because violent conflicts constitute ruptures and continuities and are often preceded by tensions over the uncomfortable co-existence of political, economic, social and cultural systems and relations of power as well as what is perceived as valuable, mobilization for violence is driven by narratives of the legality and correctness of action such that notions of history, justice and memory are functions of narrative construction, power and authority. Narratives of violent conflict, such as happened in Kenya, are not absolute: they are contested, contradictory and incomplete. But they must be told so that the multiple voices from the citizens are heard. That is the purpose of this project. As we seek to reconcile and heal the country, we must record what happens around us.

The narratives show that the violence was not just about the presidential results. To understand it, one would need to examine long standing grievances related to land, access to pasture, political manipulation of ethnic difference, impunity among those identified as having organized political violence in the past, the winner-take-all political system, poverty and unemployment among the youth, the high stakes and closeness of the presidential race making it impossible to clearly 'see' a winner, the excessive powers of the presidency making the office immensely attractive to individuals and communities interested in controlling national resources, and the structural weaknesses of the Electoral Commission of Kenya (ECK). The character flaws of the ECK leadership were also contributors because what was said in just was poignant to viewers and listeners.

Politicians ignite mistrust among ethnic groups and encourage violence to reach their goals and maintain or acquire power. In certain cases, this means physically removing people from specific constituencies prior to the polling day, the denial of identification cards and voters cards and the manipulation of the voters register. Clearly, when the aspirations and objectives of politicians are locked firmly with the fears, anxieties and dreams of ordinary people in their quest for a better life, a recipe for violence becomes potent. This potency can be immensely increased by the existence of small arms, an inefficient and biased police force, an uninspiring judicial system and poor infrastructure. These factors have been in Kenya for a long time and must be addressed urgently and constitutionally to avoid a recurrence of election related violence.

At the peak of the violence captured in these narratives, about one thousand two hundred (1,200) lives were lost, thousands of people were injured, property worth billions of shillings was destroyed, houses were set on fire, over four hundred thousand (400,000) people were internally displaced and a large number sought refuge in neighbouring countries. The transnational transport system was disrupted through road blocks and uprooting of a railway line and there was overwhelming evidence of rape in the conflict areas. In internally displaced persons (IDP) camps the lives of women and children were in jeopardy due to rape, disease outbreak and hunger. Many families were suddenly rendered destitute.

The Kenya National Commission on Human Rights (KNCHR) published a report titled " *On the Brink of the Precipice: A Human Rights Account of Kenya's Post 2007 Election Violence*" (August 2009) detailing the mayhem unleashed on the Kenyan people by government forces and fellow citizens. In spite of its weaknesses, including the failure to capture the chronology of events leading to the post-election violence and inability to detail specific violence-related activities of national and local leaders as well as retired military and police officers during the carnage, it is an important document extensively used by the Waki Commission on Post-Election Violence. The Akiwumi Judicial Commission of Inquiry into Ethnic Violence, set up in 1998 had identified key politicians, civil servants and business people who may have been involved in the violence in certain parts of the country between 1991 and 1997. No action was taken on the recommendations of the report and therefore, the culture of impunity was entrenched.

Since the reintroduction of multi-party political participation in 1991, Kenya has experienced violence before, during, and after elections intended at times to ensure that sections of the electorate did not participate in the voting or to reshape demographic trends. The violence takes different forms such as disruptions of campaign rallies, eviction of citizens from their homes or constituencies, verbal threats and intimidations, looting, abductions, arson and destruction of property, torture, physical assault, obstruction of voting or nomination processes and death. In the 1992, 1997, 2002, and 2007 elections in Kenya citizens have been internally displaced and many have been injured or killed because they have dared to show support, associate or vote differently in areas seen as not ancestrally theirs. Over the years we have witnessed increasing intolerance of opponents in what is viewed to be strongholds of particular personalities or political parties which are also the ethnic bases from which political support is drawn. Termed as 'madoadoa' (blemishes), 'foreigners' are targetted for attack and their 'nests' (homes) are destroyed and they are displaced. Territorial exclusiveness is enforced under the guise of ancestral possession, at times misguided. Most violence is perpetrated by party supporters, political aspirants, organized groups and youth wingers.

Whereas between 1992 – 2002, most election related violence occurred during the pre-election phase at the time of voter registration, party campaigns and nominations, the 2007 elections were characterized by excessive violence, and crimes against humanity especially after the declaration of Mwai Kibaki of the Party of National Unity (PNU) as president in the contested results. Although according to the constitution, leaders of the Orange Democratic Movement (ODM) party under Raila Odinga, were supposed to go to court if they were dissatisfied with the results of the polls they refused to do so. This was mainly because the judiciary has over the years been perceived as not a true arbiter in electoral grievances. Attempts by presidential candidates in 1992 and 1997 to challenge the election of Daniel Arap Moi were not fruitful and over the years Kenyans have lost confidence in the judiciary, viewing it as corrupt and easy to manipulate by the state. This lack of confidence in the judicial system has accumulated since the 1960s and may be as a result of perceptions that it can be arm-twisted by the executive to give judgment in it's favour or other factors which lead to the circumvention of justice. The judiciary as an institution is not viewed as able to resolve contested presidential elections. Election petitions take too long to arbitrate and consequently, can be immensely frustrating for any agrieved party.

The narratives show (and this is attested by a wide range of reports including by the Human Rights Watch, the Kenya National Commission on Human Rights and the Commission on Post-Election Violence led by Judge Philip Waki) that whereas some of the post-election violence was spontaneous, much of it was organized and planned by political leaders and systematically targeted members of specific communities initially specifically the Gikuyu, Embu, Meru and Kisii communities seen to have voted for Mwai Kibaki and PNU. These communities were viewed as 'anti-change' and 'enemies of the nation' because they had voted for the *status quo*. Later towards the end of January 2008, organized angry Gikuyu youth fought back especially in Naivasha, Nakuru and parts of Nairobi in retaliatory and, the narratives claim, pre-emptive attacks. These reprisal attacks also took an ethnic dimension and the Luo and Kalenjin communities were targeted. In all cases, threats of possible attack were given to targetted communities beforehand. Disturbingly, national political leaders did not do enough to genuinely calm their followers in order to create a space for national dialogue and peace. There was evidence of doublespeak as they neither openly denounced the rampant violence nor purposefully addressed the issues that ignited violence in the first place rigorously.

On its part, the government under Mwai Kibaki who had been controversially declared winner by the Electoral Commission of Kenya and hurriedly sworn in by the Chief Justice initially took a hard-line position and rejected mediation efforts insisting that the legal and constitutional process be followed in coming up with a solution to the *impasse*. In early January 2008, the government temporarily banned live broadcasts and demonstrations organized by Orange Democratic Movement (ODM). ODM leadership constantly created the impression that the violence in the country was 'allowable' ostensibly because presidential elections had been rigged. Murder of voters was equated with the rigging of votes by a section of the political elite. Efforts by regional leaders and Committee of Eminent Persons under the Chairmanship of Kofi Annan eventually led to the formation of a Coalition Government and the introduction of a Prime Minister's post to be occupied by Raila Odinga, the leader of ODM when the National Dialogue and Reconciliation Accord was signed on 28th February 2008. Key players in the violence were incorporated in the government in order to create calmness. Later, they would attempt to entrench impunity and derail the reform agenda. The Coalition is still shaky and it is unclear what will happen once blanket amnesty to perpetrators of the violence is denied and senior politicians arrested and tried either by a local tribunal or at the International Criminal Court (ICC), at the Hague.

The emerging thread in these narratives is that violence must be understood as a historically situated phenomenon authorized politically, socially and culturally. It seems as if particular constellations of the political elite in the pursuit of the acquisition and/or retention of power will converge with a social memory of events about the cause of given predicaments expressed in a discourse of difference and buttressed by a biased and partisan mass media to disrupt the lives of citizens. Memory, individual and collective, is selective and changeable and undergoes processes of suppression or forgetting. It could also be shaped around silences and lies for fear of consequences or in order to protect or perpetuate specific interests. By capturing narratives about certain traumatic events we are able to provide an alternative view of understanding the violence that bedeviled Kenya.

The narratives link election related violence, negative ethnicity and multi-party politics. They also point to Kenya's voting pattern which demonstrates once more the primacy of individuals and ethnicity over policy, ideology and class in African politics. The primary objective of most political leaders continues to be personal gain and individual preservation as well as financial advantage. Few have shown political principle in addressing the needs of citizens. Instead, poverty and deprivation, political expediency and support from ethnic communities have been used to perpetuate self interest.

The 1992 elections could easily have seen the birth of a new Kenya considering that they came as a culmination of a tense and occasionally violent process in the pursuit of democracy and multi-party political participation that ended a 23-year period of single party rule. With the

1991 erasure of Section 2 (A) of the Constitution that had transformed Kenya into a one party state, the path to democratization was opened. Many political parties were registered, although hugely populated by remnants of the former single party-Kenya African National Union (KANU). Elections held on December 29th 1992 were expected to lead to a change of president and government. But predictably, they were characterized by allegations of fraud and irregularities, including the stuffing of ballot papers, the destruction of opposition votes and other forms of count rigging because the structural frame of government had not changed and neither had the values and attitudes of citizens. Africa Confidential reported in 1993 that '*Neither the foreign nor the local observer team had the capacity or resources to investigate comprehensively rigging allegations. Consequently, they reported only the most blatant and easily verifiable irregularities.*" It seems as if certain factors conspired to give KANU a win in the 1992 elections and to defeat the democracy movement. First, the opposition was unable to present a united front and a single candidate to face Daniel Arap Moi at the polls. Second, the elections took an ethnic and regional dimension and, third, the state's bias and electoral malpractice to the advantage of the incumbent. But elections were also characterized by killing, intimidation, and displacement of individuals and communities perceived as opposition supporters. Unlike the 2007/08 violence, the 1992 election related violence took place prior to the polling day.

Again predictably, the 1997 elections were violent, especially at the Coast where upcountry people especially the Luhya, Luo, Gikuyu and Kamba were intimidated and their property destroyed. Apparently, the 1997 election violence at the Coast had three aims. First, KANU wanted to break the dominance of the unregistered Islamic Party of Kenya (IPK) which had denied it important votes in 1992. Secondly, it wanted to break the Swahili-Arab and Mijikenda elite and thirdly it sought to dis-enfranchise upcountry people in Mombasa and Kwale. The 2002 elections were also violent although to a lesser degree. The relative peace that characterized the 2002 elections may be attributed to a number of things. First, Daniel Arap Moi had been barred by the Constitution from running for another term, relinquishing power to Mwai Kibaki who had won the election under the National Rainbow Coalition (NARC), a loose coalition of 14 opposition political parties. The common front ensured that the Coalition had support across the country and provided a formidable force to KANU. Second, different forums including the Electoral Commission of Kenya, Community Based Organizations, and Non-Governmental Organizations had undertaken massive civic education against electoral violence. Nonetheless, the Central Depository Unit monitors did report that 116 lives were lost in election related violence, while the media reported 209 deaths. Despite the relative peace, life was lost in 2002 elections.

But it is the 2007/08 post-election violence that shook the nation because of its spread, speed and ruthlessness. The closely contested presidential election was characterized by unrealistic promises, fragmentation, balkanization, media hype and strong expressions of ethnic nationalism. Inspired and propelled by the rejection of the 2005 Referendum on a government sponsored constitution, the main opposition party went full throttle to wrest power from the incumbent in the general elections. The possibility of a 'majimbo'(regional) political system promised by the Orange Democratic Movement (ODM) created anxiety in certain parts of the country because of its association with balkanization, ethnic cleansing, 'insiders' and 'outsiders', 'us' and 'them'. But the 'majimbo' concept also became a point of convergence among communities that have in the past supported it. To try to win even wider support ODM sought to replace the word 'majimbo' in view of its negative connotations and toyed with an alternative term *'ugatuzi'* (decentralization). The term did not, however, gain currency and was later ditched. In its public rhetoric while supporting some form of devolution, PNU expressed a distaste for majimbo because of its perceived potential to balkanize the country. Undoubtedly, both PNU and ODM supported some form of devolution during the campaigns but did not have the language to explain the system coherently to their supporters.

The narratives tell of how guns, arrows, machetes, spears, and other weapons were used to kill, maim and harm individuals who had no idea that casting a vote could lead to suffering. Although, it is often claimed that only the police had guns, there is a suggestion in the narratives that there were civilians who used guns on fellow citizens. Encouragingly, victims would like to forgive their attackers but the aggressors need to ask for forgiveness. Many victims believed that there were constitutional safeguards to their right to vote, even for an unpopular candidate, but by casting their votes they set themselves up for harm. In the 2007 elections, trust was destroyed and faith in institutions of governance, especially the Election Commission of Kenya (ECK) was shattered. Earlier, Kenyans had lost faith in the judiciary and did not see it as an objective arbiter of the presidential polls.

At this point, I need to say a few words about the lack of confidence in the institutions of governance. Although under Mwai Kibaki between 2003 and 2007, Kenyans experienced greater freedoms and there were clear economic changes with the country registering an impressive annual growth rate of around 7%, the nation was faced with challenges relating to the rule of law, control of corruption, government effectiveness and political stability made worse by ethnic tensions and inability to honour a Memorandum of Understanding between the 2002 election coalition partners and the rejection of a government supported constitution in a 2005 referendum. The flawed electoral process and weak institutions of governance including the judiciary contributed to the post-election mayhem. In order to build confidence among citizens, governance institutions ought to carry a number of key features: public participation and inclusiveness, transparency, effectiveness, efficiency and accountability. They must be guided by the rule of law and respect for human rights. Moreover, the institutions should be constitutionally protected so that they are able to function independently.

These narratives show that the violence was a convergence of many factors and that the Electoral Commission of Kenya was a significant contributor to the mess. Weaknesses in governance institutions including within the electoral process had been identified during the Constitution of Kenya Review (CKRC) process and it is quite likely that if a new constitution had been adopted before the December 2007 elections, the violence which we witnessed would not have occurred. It would appear that weaknesses in governance institutions made it virtually impossible to hold the country together. The voices in the narratives are crying for a national rebirth. They are saying that the country needs to build independent and strong institutions, transform those that are not working effectively and monitor all vital public governance and which control public resources.

How does Kenya proceed after listening to these voices? As Mr. Kofi Annan and the African Union Panel of Eminent African Personalities recognized in February 2008, conflicts in Africa cannot be explained only in terms of ethnic mistrust and deep-rooted hostilities. To understand them one would need to pay attention to the colonial legacy and state formation processes within ethno-regional diversity. It would also be critically important to pay attention to poverty and income distribution, access to natural resources including land, population density, institutions of governance and accountability among leaders. Of equal importance is the ability to adopt constitutions that cater for the diversity of interests within the nation-state and to reconsider the 'winner-take-all' electoral process. 'Insider representation' seems to be extremely important in Africa because the state has not been able to rise above ethnic interests.

Power sharing arrangements and coalition governments such as that brokered by Kofi Annan in Kenya are temporary measures. Long term strategies need to be put in place and these would include a review of how the democracy project can be actualized in ethnically diverse states. Democracy in Africa would have to incorporate the best in African culture such as consensus building in situations of conflict and a review of the constitution to recognize diversity and reduce ethnic fixation, address issues of representation in decision making and public affairs, inequality, land and human rights. It would also be necessary to develop national values which would be the pillars of public life and the conduct of national affairs as well as the development of a democratic culture. These values are best developed within families, households and communities. A nation that has no humanizing values is doomed to fail.

The media (the Fourth Estate) have an immensely important role to play. In a 2009 research Report " *Meddling with the Message? Kenyan Media Coverage of the 2007 Elections*" Twaweza Communications found out that certain sections of Kenyan media were unethical and unprofessional before, during and after the elections and they may have contributed to ethnic polarization and accentuated violence. While recognizing that the media must be free to 'decide for themselves what roles they choose to play of their own volition, they can play a key role in creating a vibrant space for citizen education, protection of rights and in the harnessing national integration.

Further, the media have a critical role to play before, during and after a conflict. They can contribute to, or conversely can challenge the (re)production of ethnic stereotypes and divisions in the nation-state. News media can function as a means of communication between elected governments and citizens. Secondly, they can act as guardians of accountable and transparent political engagement. The media can promote reconciliation, healing and long-term conflict management and societal development through provision of credible and balanced information and analysis. National media can encourage tolerance and a willingness to resolve conflict by providing background information and showing the multiplicity of factors that might create conflict. A healthy media environment is plural and diverse and able to carry a wide range of views, information and opinion that exists in society. These roles, when well played, can ensure justice and peace for all. But media must invest in training journalists on conflict reporting and ethics. The industry must recognize that in multi-ethnic settings, narratives that emphasize on difference rather than similarities can be disastrous.

In post conflict situations such as ours, independent media can contribute in transforming destructive conflicts into non-destructive debates through critical analysis of issues and choices. They can give voice to minorities, the vulnerable and those most affected by conflict. They can humanize opponents by bringing to the fore shared identities and downplaying differences. Political solutions are in most cases crafted by the elite but the media can ensure the participation of citizens in peace settlements through public debate. Yet for this to happen, greater professionalism and self regulation is needed in the sector.

The narratives provide a record, an archive which could inform future action and inspire further investigation by anyone interested in understanding the events related to the 2007 election. They spell out the difference between official state-inscribed versions of events and the people's history as it exists in popular memory. This memory is not simply limited to the telling collected here, it exists in the landscape of new donor-built homesteads and corrugated iron sheets freshly emblazoned with the names of the benefactors; it is carried in the scars, limbs, thoughts and reactions of all those who witnessed the violent events.

We also hope that these narratives can be used in the consolidation of citizen education. Institutions are vital for the consolidation of democracy, but citizens play an even bigger role. Quite often, the deficiencies we see in institutions are a mirror of our own weaknesses. Citizen education on the tenets of democratic practice including tolerance of difference, human rights, fairness in resource allocation, freedom of expression, ethical and professional reporting and the consolidation of other identities such as gender, and profession and the softening of ethnic fixation can contribute much in strengthening governance institutions. Citizen education would ensure that regions are not 'zoned off' for political competition and politicians should be told off when they attempt to do so. Electoral bodies do not work in isolation; they are buttressed by state and non-state forces and it is important to understand these actors in any future interventions in Kenya. These issues are of concern to us.

Twaweza collected these narratives from around the country – Mombasa, Eldoret, Naivasha, Kericho, Kisumu, Busia and Vihiga- but the number of stories (and the depth) depended on the willingness and comfort of citizens to come forth with their understanding of what happened. After recording the narratives sometimes more than once, they were transcribed, translated and minimally edited without changing the gist of the narrative. Occasionally, narrative sequencing was changed to allow for flow. The views expressed in these stories are not the only ones that help us understand what happened. They are only part of a complex story about a nation being born. But they are a vital contribution to the archive of information on Kenya. We recognize that meaning is never complete; it is always an approximation. Consequently, we encourage other researchers to collect additional narratives about the post-election violence and other national events. In the plethora of these stories, some with exaggerations and others with narrator censorship, lies a truth that might determine the future of Kenya. We are grateful to the researchers who worked with us to collect the narratives and to the respondents who accepted to share their experiences.

The narratives are divided into three sections: *narratives of pain, narratives of mercy and narratives of aggression.* For obvious reasons, the narratives of aggression are few. The names of the narrators have been changed, either at the point of narrative collection or in the editing process. Ours is just a humble contribution to the discourse on memory, history and violence and we are driven by the urge to create a nation where everyone of us will be at home.

REFERENCES

BBC World Service Trust. 2008. 'The Kenyan 2007 Elections and Their Aftermath: The Role of Media and Communication.' bbcworldservicetrust.org

Bratton, Michael & Mwangi S. Kimenyi. 2002. 'Voting in Kenya: Putting Ethnicity in Perspective'. In *Journal of Eastern African Studies* Vol. 2. No. 2, 165, July 2008 (Pp. 272-289).

Chege, Michael. 2008. 'Kenya: Back from the Brink?' In *Journal of Democracy* Vol, 19, No. 4. October 2008, National Endowment for Democracy and The Johns Hopkins University Press.

Elkins, Caroline. 2008. *'Divide and Rule: What is Tearing Kenya Apart? History, for One Thing'*. Washingtonpost.com/wp-dyn/content/article

Human Rights Watch. 2002. *Playing with Fire: Weapons Proliferation, Political Violence and Human Rights in Kenya.* New York.

International Crisis Group. 2008. *'Kenya in Crisis: Africa Report no. 137.'*

Jinadu, A. Adele. 2007. 'Explaining & Managing Ethnic Conflict in Africa: Towards a Cultural Theory of Democracy'. Claude Ake Memorial Papers No. 1. Uppsala. Department of Peace and Conflict Research, Uppsala University.

Kagwanja, Peter. 2001. 'Politics of Marionettes: Extra-legal Violence and the 1997 Elections in Kenya'. In Marcel Rutten, Alamin Mazrui and Francois Grignon (eds). *Out for the Count: The 1997 General Election and Prospects for Democracy in Kenya.* Kampala: Fountain Publishers, Pp. 72-100.

Kenya National Commission on Human Rights. 2008. On the Brink of the Precipice: A Human Rights Account of Kenya's Post 2007 Election Violence.

MacAurthur, Julie. 2002. 'How the West was Won: Regional Politics and Prophetic Promises in the 2007 Kenya Elections'. In *Journal of Eastern African Studies* Vol. 2. No. 2, 165, July 2008 (Pp. 227-241).

Mueller, Susanne. 2008. 'The Political economy of Kenya's Crisis.' In *Journal of Eastern African Studies* Vol. 2. No. 2, 165, July 2008 (Pp. 185-210).

Twaweza Communications. 2009. *Meddling with the Message? Kenyan Media Coverage of the 2007 Elections"*. A Research Report. Nairobi.

SECTION I

NARRATIVES OF PAIN

Congestion as IDPs seek safety in Naivasha. Photo by Antony Gitonga

I Sensed Something Would Happen

My name is Paul Mbugua and I live in Burnt Forest. Since late 1990s I have been living in this town centre. Burnt Forest being a business zone, we lived together with different communities doing a lot of businesses. We all had a good relationship; we interacted with the Kalenjin and helped each other in all ways as brothers.

During the referendum we started seeing differences emerging based on ethnic affiliations. The Kalenjin said that the Kikuyu supported the Banana whereas the Kalenjin supported the Orange. They also threatened us and said that if the Orange didn't win, they would chase us away to Othaya. However, the Banana didn't win and we were spared. So when the general election campaigns started, there were those who said that even if PNU or ODM won the elections, it was a must for Kikuyus to go to Othaya. Problems were experienced in business because the Kalenjin started separating themselves.

Some Members of Parliament moved around in this region preaching tribalism. They said that this election must be used to sweep away '*Madoadoa*' (blemishes) which was used to refer to the Kikuyu. The Kalenjin also have had a strong believe that this region (the Rift Valley) is theirs and no other tribe especially the Bantus should be seen here. At that time the government protected us and ensured that there was tight security. If the government had done this during elections I don't think fighting would have erupted. What I know is that the election was a reflection of what had happened during the referendum on the new constitution. The difference being that the security was enforced during the referendum but during campaigns and elections the government relaxed.

Even after the campaign we didn't think that clashes would erupt and change everything. Things changed immediately and the Kalenjin started talking about themselves and their leaders and the Kikuyu also behaved the same. When it came to voting, I was an agent and had to stay indoors to supervise the tallying of votes. During the process I realized that there was great difference between the agents. Whenever a certain vote was lifted from the ballot box, some agents would shout a lot making us fear. On my side, I thought they were joking and everything would go well. So I took the reports to the presiding officers and went home peacefully.

When the results were announced, everything changed. The Kalenjins started burning houses. While I went to Nakuru for a holiday, I knew almost everything that happened because my friends including the Kalenjins called me and advised me to look for another place to go because Burnt Forest was no longer safe. Though I was in Nakuru I didn't divulge my location. I remember someone called me on a private number to threaten me. He told me that he was seriously looking for me and I was next on line. He said that the moment I am dead, he would take over my business.

Although, I sensed something would happen I could not tell how intense it would be. My friends also told me to leave this place because all will not be right if the government won. I thought it would be something small. While away, my plot which I had fenced was destroyed. All the building materials I had bought were stolen and my house brought down.

Q: *Can you forgive the people who attacked you?*

A: Definitely, I have to forgive the perpetrators of violence because I am a staunch Christian and I believe there is power in forgiveness. If I meet them today, I would like to see them go down to their knees and repent so that God may also forgive them.

Q: *Is there anything that the government can do help?*

A: I don't think the government can do anything better than what they have already done. The problem here is not for the government to solve, but it is the duty and task of those who live around here. The residents should come together and talk so as to solve their differences.

Q: *Were you involved in the campaigns?*

A: I didn't take part in the campaigns because most of the time I was in my business premise.

Q: *Is there anything you would like to add?*

A: I would like to thank the government for the efforts it has made to take people back to their villages. I wish the government would have taken each individual to his or her farm. If a tent was pitched in the homesteads of the victims, it would be easier to heal and to interact with the Kalenjins. They would cultivate their farms. I would like the government to give people compensation because not all victims got the Kshs. 10,000 and Kshs. 25,000 that was being given. I would also like the government to quicken the rehabilitation of schools that were damaged because the children were highly affected and their education is now at risk.

IDPs reconstruct their lives in Kibunja, Molo. A new primary school under construction.
Photo by Kimani Njogu

IT WAS A SILENT MASSACRE...

My name is Mary. I am an Advocate of the High Court of Kenya. I did my studies at Moi University and eventually moved to Eldoret where I started practicing law in 2004. Life was normal before the elections. Eldoret was growing at a very high rate because of the activities that were going on there.

Eldoret is a multi-ethnic town. Though it is almost balanced but the majority groups are the local community (Nandi) and the Kikuyu. Beginning January to October 2007 life was normal; people were just campaigning. But towards December 2008 people started developing tensions. Divisiveness among the people started and some people claimed that some ethnic groups were not fit to stay in Eldoret. The Majimbo debate was the turning point. It even reached a point where buildings belonging to certain communities were marked and booked by the other community. They claimed they would possess them once they took over power.

There were also some rumors all over that some groups were organizing to carry out massacres on some communities. All of a sudden, the town was filled up with young men and local people did not know their origin. Local leaders would meet every weekend at some place but it was not for development purpose or campaigning. They would say they are holding party meetings in search of votes. But it was claimed that they were organizing some young men and giving them food and weapons. A local leader was said to hold tea parties at certain schools but every time he came he would dish out money and talk to people only from his community in pretence that he was conducting development issues.

Later on when things blew up people came to recognize that where the leader used to hold the parties is the same place where it was claimed weapons were kept and people also took oath from there. I was in Eldoret then at Huruma estate where the first spark of the violence started. On the Election Day it was fine. People were just tensed as they waited for the results. Huruma which is dominated by Kikuyu borders another estate called Kipkenyo which is dominated by Kalenjins. About ten minutes before the results were announced, we saw a group of young men at the other side of Kipkenyo and I got curious as to what they were doing. I told a friend of mine who happened to be a cop of our concern about the group but he said that we should not worry as those were young men from a circumcision ceremony who were just carrying out their rituals. Ten minutes after the results were announced we saw the first house belonging to a Kikuyu elder go up in flames. Around 7.00 pm there were almost ten houses burning on the side of Kipkenyo. Then the young men started crossing the river that separates the two estates. It was then that Huruma people realized what was happening but it was too late and they were caught by surprise.

These young men were armed. The entire night we spent in the cold because if you locked yourself in the house, they would break the windows and throw a petrol bomb while you were inside. Again being outside was not safe either because if they caught up with you, they would ask a question in their language. If you were not one of them, for a woman they would rape you, beat you up then take you to their camp so that you can be cooking for them. If you were a man they would force you to take an oath and pledge loyalty to their leaders. If the man refused to take the oath, they would kill him. Mostly it was the men who had married girls from their community. They were told that in order for their wives to be spared they had to take the oath. Most men declined and they were hacked to death.

We were chased from Huruma Estate where the battle began. We camped at a police station but later we were told to leave as the station was packed. Imagine being chased out of the police station! My dad was born and raised up in Turbo so he knows nowhere else. Also in the previous election his house had been burnt down. This time round they tried to kill my grandmother but she was saved by a nun and now she is at the Aga Khan hospital because she sort of ran mad. I also have two cousins who were living with my grandmother and now we have to get a place for them to stay because they are orphaned. We also suffered mental anguish because I could see bodies of men lying for four days outside until pigs were eating them. We could go nowhere until the police commissioner came. That is when things improved a little bit.

The same way the violence was conducted in Huruma is the same way it was carried out everywhere else. It reached a point where Eldoret residents called the police. The police responded but after seeing the mess they mockingly reiterated the Kibaki tena slogan "kazi iendelee" (let work continue). "So let it continue", they would say, encouraging the anarchists. They would then leave without helping victims. Also the people who were brought in by lorries were not talking they were just following orders given to them by the local young men. Those attackers were trained especially those that were brought in by lorries. You could tell by the way they coordinated the whole issue. Also they had a way of recognizing each other by applying white paint across their faces.

After 31st December 2007 and 1st January 2008 the attackers were burning the houses during the day actually at 8 am as people watched. I happened to be at the Moi Teaching and Referral hospital when the bodies of children who burned in the Kiambaa were brought in. The state was pathetic.

I can say for sure that had it not happened (*the burning of Kimbaa church*) people would not have known what was going on in Eldoret. It was a silent sort of massacre. Media was not there to cover the stories and when you ran to the police station you got no help. So that day people ran to that church to seek refuge. Being a holy place it was the safest place. Unfortunately, the young men followed them. It is claimed that women tried to save their children from the fire but the young men would grab and push them back into the fire. As a result they (*women*) too ended up burning as they tried to save their children. The bodies that were brought in were mainly women, children and the pastor of the church. In fact, their men had gone out to try and organize for security. They would take their families to police stations and be left behind guarding the area at night because the police had failed to protect them.

In my opinion, what was going on can be termed as ethnic cleansing because it was targeted at a particular ethnic group but somehow it failed. Our men were doing security patrols until the day the government posted the military.

My grandmother was held up at Turbo and there was no way out because they had barricaded the road with stones. In fact I had to pose like a Taita in order to get her out. I got away with it because they looked at me and said I am slim and brown so I passed for a Taita. If they doubted they would ask for your ID and if you did not have it, you would be killed. Women would be left behind and forced to cook for them. As for the men there was no discussion about it they were just hacked to death. It was rumoured that apart from blocking roads they wanted to destroy the bridges so that there would be no way out. An estate like Turbo borders Webuye that was peaceful but they wanted to destroy the bridge that connects Webuye and Turbo so that people could be locked in.

Tribalism is what motivated the attackers. Like there was a school that was burnt just because the headmaster was a Kikuyu. But all this was planned. It did not erupt because of elections. Somehow some ethnic groups had to shift from the Rift valley. There was a lot of coordination between the national leaders and the local leaders because whatever was organized at the national level was carried out by the local leaders. They would help in identifying which houses belonged to which community. We would see a lorry full of young men which was claimed to be from Pokot. But at the forefront were the local youths and leaders who would go pin-pointing the houses that would be burnt and those to be spared. A practical example is where a local leader came and identified our home because it was big and we had lots of farm machinery. He alerted his group to spare it as he would take it over. Since he did not know how to operate the machines he asked my parents to show him days before the violence. Unknowingly, my parents showed him how to operate the machines.

I also think that the church leaders were also involved because they didn't say a word when all this was going on. It was worse in a town called Turbo where my grandmother lived. Some people ran into a church to hide from the young men. But they followed them. They spoke to the priest in their language. He immediately chased out the group adding that his community was more important than their lives. Even the intellectuals were involved. At that time one's ethnicity was superior to all other factors and it didn't matter whether one was learned or not. Again these people had organized themselves because almost all the communities were fighting one community, especially in Eldoret. While the Luos would come beat up people and loot properties, the Kalenjins would later follow and burn anything that remained.

Land is the whole issue in Eldoret. The local leaders would come and tell the people that there were some communities who came and stole land that belonged to them. It was also claimed that the Rift valley and Nyanza should be on their own from the rest of the country. But that was difficult because people over the years had integrated. It would also be difficult to tell where the boundary would be enacted.

Q: *Would you go back to Eldoret?*

A: The issue of going back is tricky. However, circumstances can force you to go and work there but one does not feel safe at all. In order to restore peace in the country, there is need to talk to those people that were affected in order to heal the trauma. Then there should be the issue of truth and reconciliation. People should forgive each other though it is pretty hard. People should also forget the issue of tribalism.

Q: *On the issue of those houses that were identified and taken over, how do we ensure that they revert to their rightful owners?*

A: That is pretty hard because one cannot do anything about the issue of land for now. Maybe later on when one would sell it. In terms of movable property, how will one know who took what? So that makes it difficult.

Q: What would you like to tell our leaders?

A: Much as they are up there instructing people on what to do and not to, it's the common man who is suffering. After the military was deployed and calm was restored we saw some Kalenjin women demonstrating towards the leaders saying they wanted their children back. The looters, it was claimed, used to be paid one thousand shillings per day for the destruction and murder. Kenyans during the next elections should go for quality leaders. Not leaders who come promising small things and land that belongs to other people knowing very well there is a law that outlines the means of acquiring land and property.

Q: Did you hear of specific leaders who were involved in this violence?

A: A place like Eldoret it would be blamed squarely on a prominent politician and some tycoons who financed the young men. But unfortunately the tycoon died.

Q: The youth were so much involved in this violence everywhere; do you have a message for the youth in this country?

A: I would like to tell the youth not to let themselves be misused by selfish leaders.

OUR NEIGHBOURS HAD WARNED US...

My name is Annette Wairimu. I was born in 1976 and I live in Kuresoi. The town is inhabited by various communities – there are Kisiis, Kalenjins, Kikuyus, Luos, and Luhyas. We used to live peacefully with all these people without any problem whatsoever and interacted well with all of them. I went to school at a place called Kipkewa.

I went to school with Kalenjin children and there were no problems. After school I got married and we continued living peacefully. In 1992 our houses including property were burnt and cattle stolen by the Kalenjins. Generally, when we ask them why they burn our houses, they say that it is the devil who influences them. They always tell us to go back to our ancestral places like Murang'a because the land belongs to them. On our part we persevere because the land is rightfully ours. I have lived in Mwaragania farm since I was born. It has a good history. It only became bad after the 1992 clashes.

Mwaragania farm was bought by our parents though I cannot remember the year. They bought it from the white settlers. It was after this purchase that the land was subdivided to us – the children. We were then given our portions. We have therefore stayed in this place and our children were born here. Our children even inter-marry in these places. Therefore, it is not right to claim that non-Kalenjin communities grabbed land. There is nothing of that kind whatsoever. The same attack was unleashed on us in 1998 The Kalenjins are the people who attack us all the time. It normally starts with cattle rustling and then develops into clashes. Although there are claims that politics is a contributing factor, the 1998 conflict had no political connections. It is the recent one, the 2007 that had politics. In 1998 we still managed to go back to our farms and settled until this recent conflict.

In 1998 I lost one of my sons: a young boy who died because of staying out in the bush. I also lost five cows and eighteen sheep. In short, I was really affected because all my property was destroyed. Since 1992 our lives became that of being chased and then returning to our farms. We used to talk to our attackers and they would apologise to us. We would then forgive them. We then came to the latest conflict, that of 2007. In this case I can say that the conflict resulted from politics and not clashes as was previously the case. Our neighbours wanted us not to vote but we stayed put. I must say that there are Kalenjins who are kind hearted. They used to tell us not to go so that we can vote just like them. We nevertheless, moved out, everyone going his own way.

I went to Kinangop at a place called Engineer. In fact some of my children are still in that place. We were badly affected but despite this I praise God because even after all these, when our neighbours asked for forgiveness we gladly forgave them. We always hope that this conflict will end although they always blame it on Satan. We always forgive them and we will continue to do so because if you do not forgive you will not make any progress.

For now am living in Kahurura. I have an aunt who stays in John Muthama's place. She has a farm and therefore invited me to come and farm here. This place might be better than Kinangop. There were also prospects of being given fertilisers and seeds. From here I went to Kuresoi as word went round that victims and IDP's would be compensated. But I spent more time at John Muthama's, whose place neighbours Kahurura. My aunt's houses were burnt – she had four plots. The four houses that were not completely burnt are the ones we reconstructed and that is where I stay. We then started farming.

During the violence I suffered mainly while in Kuresoi. I was attacked, and my property looted. One house belonging to my sons was burnt. Although it was the Kalenjins who attacked us I will not blame all of them. Those who attacked us are those who stay in the forest. Those who are our neighbours normally warn us of attacks by phone. At home they call me Chepnondindet (Mnandi). They normally tell me "Mnandi, the attackers have reached this place please evacuate your children." They normally advise me not to think about property but instead save my children. Therefore, I can say that not all Kalenjins are bad. There are some good ones with humane hearts.

However, I cannot identify those who attacked us since we ran to Kuresoi centre. I do not know whether you know the centre? My home is near the route to Ogilge farm. When you are in the centre you can clearly see my place, but when you are at the centre you cannot identify people who are in my home. You cannot identify them even if you wanted to.

Q: What will you do when you meet those who attacked you?

A: When we meet we will greet each other warmly – what else can you do and you are living in their midst? You will not leave and they too will not. And it is your farm. About the issue of forgiveness, you cannot really know… *(laughs)* because a human being can say he has forgiven but deep in his heart he has not. But what I know of the Kalenjins is that they promise that they have finished the conflict but after a short while they start again. I cannot really know how their hearts are.

Q: Let us now focus on the government. What would you like the government to do to protect you?

A: I would really urge the government to remember those who were affected by the conflict; which left many of our people displaced. We only go there because we cannot get better places. We cannot fit in the new areas. The new places are not good for us. We always prefer our *shambas* but we have many problems. For instance, we have no roads. In the last one month the government had promised that food would be brought but to date that has not happened. Food does not reach us because of the bad roads. The road from Molo to Kuresoi all the way to Githima is impassable, and the alternative road is only through Chepsir (*on your way to Kericho*). Even with this, the food will only reach Githima but not to us. So that is one of our problems. The second problem that the government should address is peace and insecurity. Security is key to our lives. The government has tried but the security personnel are insufficient. Every time we ask for security they always tell us to be contented with what we have. They tell us that additional security is not available. We really urge the government to provide us with security.

Equally, they should urge the people to unite because even if the 'perceived enemy' went away, no one community can trade with itself. If all communities do not work closely together, they cannot engage in development. Only unity and working together can enable our children to learn (get education). No single community can progress alone. For instance, in the church I belonged to a women's group where we would engage in such social events as *Kibagenge* (working together). We would give gifts to other people. These groups collapsed when people moved away from Kuresoi.

Q: Did you actively participate in the campaigns?

A: I was an agent of a parliamentary candidate. This is somebody I did not really know. I had just been told to report at the polling station. He was a pastor. I cannot remember his name but he was not nominated.

Q: Because politics and land contribute to conflict between you and the Kalenjins, what can you say?

A: On that I can only say that let people unite. If they see that politics can bring conflict they should deal with this danger early enough so that it does not become a big problem. I will only say... what can I say (pause). In fact it was the political differences – those of ODM and PNU that brought conflict. If you see me with a PNU shirt you feel bad and vice versa. I would only say this – people should not focus too much on parties by saying I belong to ODM or PNU, because Raila was for ODM while Kibaki was PNU but it is us the citizens who suffer in the case of conflict. The two leaders can even sit on one table but we, the common people, are the ones who get hurt. Our children get hurt but Raila and Kibaki are comfortable. They laugh and eat together. They even have a common position at a given time.

Equally, I would say – as common people (raia) – we should stick together and ignore what takes place at the time of conflict because what took place is all folly. The common people are the ones whose children suffered and not those of the leaders. It is upto us as common people to resolve our conflict by deciding on how we want to live.

Q: What appeal would you make to the politicians, the likes of MPs and councillors?

A: As for councillors I would really urge them to interact with the common people so that they can hear the voices of the people. They should also listen to peoples' complaints. They should not always be listening to the top politicians and ignoring us. The councillors and the MPs are the ones making people fight each other. When we look at the specific case of Kuresoi they are the ones who used to make people fight each other. In fact, it was politicians like Mr. X *(name withheld)* who used to incite people against each other. During the campaign period the Kikuyus were associated with him. The Kalenjins used to say that they wanted to remove Mr. X from the seat and the Kikuyus agreed to join the Kalenjin in ousting him. In fact, we became the bridge for him to be removed so we do not understand why we were being attacked. When the clashes broke out we did not understand the reason because there was no single Kikuyu who had been elected as councillor nor did the Kisiis elect anybody except the Kalenjins. It was only when the results were announced that we experienced the war. We could not really understand what their problem was.

IT WAS VERY TERRIFYING

My name is Dr. Njoroge. I came to Kericho after graduating from Nairobi University in 1987. I was posted to the veterinary investigation laboratory where I worked for four years. After which I developed a desire of going into private practice and when I got a premise I decided to resign from government services. I didn't want to do my work as well as the governments' as I felt that my attention could be divided. The common thing now is for one to work in both government and private sectors which I felt would be robbing the government of its time and by giving more attention to my work and less to the government sector. I have been in Kericho all this time. I have got used to this place and made friends here. Farmers are my best friends.

I have travelled all over the greater Kericho and that has continued all through without any problems. The election campaigns ahead of the 2007 polls started very well and we used to comment that people are now mature and even when it came to voting time, we voted peacefully. After voting we went home to wait for the results. But everyone was aware that the results were not being announced promptly.

I voted in Kericho, Ainamoi County Council polling station, where I have always voted. The turnout was just wonderful. People arrived early and in big numbers. After voting, we went home to wait for the results. On the first day it was okay because we got to know the results of the members of parliament and the councillors, but for the presidential position, the results were delayed. By the third day we were all very anxious and afraid. But finally the results came in announcing that President Kibaki had won. Within no time we now started seeing fire in the town, people shouting and screaming and we could see smoke all over the town. We soon heard gunshots and this continued into the night. After that, things became tense. Many people were coming from reserves (villages). I remember seeing a large crowd coming from Kisumu road shouting "na tuuane" (let us kill). When they got to town we later understood that they started to break into supermarkets and even at the Equity Bank and there was a lot of shooting. After that we started seeing a lot of burning at Nyagacho. There was a lot of fire and smoke.

Things started to cool down in town but at the same time, we saw people coming from James Finlay Tea Estates. Kisiis and Kikuyus were being chased away from those sides. They were coming to camp at the DC's place. We were not operating our businesses. The whole town was closed. We did not even have food but I remember some friends from the church brought us sukuma wiki and some meat from the open butcheries. I also remember a guy who supplied us with milk from Kapcheptoror. He never failed to deliver milk even for a day and he even continued calling us and asking us how we were. I also had some friends from James Finlay, some were also calling. They used to inquire how things were – in fact we had thought of going there if things became worse.

After the first wave of violence, that is after two weeks since violence escalated, my landlord who is an Asian called me and told me that if he did not throw me out of his premises the whole of his premises would be burnt since I am a Kikuyu. This was because Kikuyus and Kisiis were being evicted from this place. We agreed with the landlord that I continue operating but be watchful.

In January 2008, we did business for a few days but towards the end i.e. on 31st January since my landlord was being threatened, he told me that we had to close for two weeks and see how things would go. I ended up closing for one week. I was just at home but, on 31st January somebody, came who wanted some vaccines. I came to open and after that I went home. Within half an hour, my caretaker came running and told us to shut the doors and close the curtains because news had come in that Ainamoi MP had been killed. Within a minute we heard war cries and shouts. We were very afraid.

My neighbour's wife, told us that things were not good. Ainamoi MP had been shot. She told us that she fears for us and did not know what to do. She didn't even know where to hide us as things got out of hand. I called somebody at James Finlay Estate; a white man who had promised to assist us if things got worse. I called and spoke with a man who said he was to call the James Finlay Managing Director. The CEO called me later. Since I usually treated his cattle, he asked me how he could assist and I told him that we wanted to move out of the place as we were hearing some shooting, a lot of commotion and burning had started. I requested him to send us a vehicle. He said he would send a tinted vehicle so that no one would be able to see inside.

When the driver was sent, he could not enter our gate as there were many men outside. Some of them wanted to kill our caretaker. We had to sneak out through our neighbour's gate. On reaching James Finlay the CEO told us that he had sent for an aircraft from Nairobi and if any of us wanted to go to Nairobi we could use the aircraft. We left for Nairobi.

On our way to Nairobi we called Mrs. Korir who told us that things were getting bad. She further said that several men had come with the intention of burning our house but she pleaded with them not to burn as we had left everything in the house and had left the keys with Dr. Audi. They decided to remove everything from the house and put into their houses so that if they burn at least they would have salvaged some things for us. We were in Nairobi for two weeks waiting for Koffi Annan to broker peace.

After two weeks we decided to return back for one week though Annan had not made peace and the place was so tense. But after staying for only one week we felt very much insecure. A politician's statement that there will be no way in Annan's meditation team and that there will be a call for *'civil disobedience'* made us think that if it will find us here then it will be disastrous. The country would just go to the dogs.

We looked for a lorry, parked out belongings and went to Nakuru. We stayed there for three weeks until when Annan's team agreed. Then people started telling us to come back and that is when we came back on March 15th 2008. Thank God because of that as some of us had thought of selling our businesses. In fact, some interested persons were calling me to inquire if I was selling. But after returning, things were still bad. People were threatening us. Infact it happened when a police inspector was inside here but they didn't know that he was a police officer. The inspector became harsh on that person and told him off saying, *"nyinyi ndio tukisema mambo ya amani mnarudi nyuma na kutisha watu"*. (You are the ones undermining our efforts of working for peace by threatening people). He told him that it is very wrong to threaten people.

Later, a colleague who works at the veterinary laboratory came and informed me that some of our colleagues were involved in the violence. I told him that may be it is competition and I thanked him for that information. Afterwards, another doctor called me telling me that someone had called him asking if he could be interested in my business. That doctor dismissed him. To me, the ordinary farmers have been friendly I have got no problem with anybody. When they heard that we had left, most of them were very sympathetic. They used to call and tell me to come back. I would say that those are some of the people who kept encouraging me. Actually I cannot say that people threatened me face to face, but they used to come through other people who relayed what they were being told. No one came directly to me. I have some friendly people in this community who were even feeding me, buying me meat and up to date I owe them so much for their assistance.

Q: Why do you think you were attacked?

A: Personally, I was not attacked maybe because where I stay I am the only Kikuyu. It's because it was perceived that Kibaki stole the votes and since I am a Kikuyu, I became a target.

Q: How do you feel about the whole issue?

A: It was very terrifying and painful in the sense that I knew there was nothing wrong I had done and knowing that it is my tribe that was being targeted. It was also more painful when I was informed that some of those involved were my colleagues. Otherwise the ordinary farmer had no problem. As a Christian there is one thing that impresses me in God: not to have any bitterness. I do not have any bitterness with anybody because I never got ill nor depressed and when I entered in the house I thanked God. Even if I would not have got anything I would still have thanked him.

I remember when I was in Kabazi (Nakuru), people greeted me and they were planning to go and attack people who live in Solai. I told them "Those are innocent people". I also remember them saying they went to another mzee in Moi's farm and slaughtered his cow. I told them that God would hold every person accountable, whether they did this because they were Kalenjin or any tribe. God would hold them accountable not as Kikuyus but as wrong-doers. When we went to our sons' home in Nairobi, I went to a barber who was trying to chase away people from other tribes from his salon. I advised him not to attack people because, whether they were Kalenjins or not, they could not carry the sins of their tribesmen.

I remember the government machinery that night when we left here. They gave me one OCPD. I called someone *(name withheld)* who in turn called that OCPD when people wanted to burn our houses. The OCPD sent some askaris twice to that area. They shot into the air to disperse the youth. They really assisted us. We also got some humanitarian assistance from our church leader Rev. Chumo. The AIC pastor went to the police station to help women and children who were coming from the estate. I decided to go to church on 31st January to thank God with some elders. Our pastor said that he will go to the DC's office to request for some people to come and stay in the church. We helped those people by contributing some money and even using the church get together money to cater for them. Personally, I didn't need any help from charity organizations and so I also participated in contributing some money. We contributed under the church so that the church could facilitate the distribution of the money.

Q: What recommendations will you make?

A: I don't know but the best approach is to involve our leaders. These are the candidates who were vying for both the parliamentary and presidential seats. There is this wrong assumption that the president usually assists his people and yet they have to work very hard for survival.

Q: Will you stay in Kericho?

A: I have made up my mind. I have always said *"ningetaka kunyolewa nywele nyeupe hapa"* (I want to grow old as a resident of Kericho). To date I have no thoughts of leaving Kericho. I have said this is my home. I came here in 1987, my children have grown up here and my best friends are here.

THE YOUTHS ASKED FOR A BULL...

I am Simon Lang'at. I was born in Roret village, in 1951. I schooled there till when I did my Form Four in Litein high school in 1971. In 1972, I was recruited as an Untrained Teacher in Kericho district. I taught in Keldet primary school for one week before I was transferred to Simbi for the rest of that year. In 1973 I went to Tonongoi primary school. It's called Sigowet, in Sigowet division, in Belgut. I taught there till the year 1981. Then I was transferred to Kipkelion division, a school called Momoniat. That's where I live now. I taught there till 1986 when I quit teaching. I started my own business and did farming for one year. Then in 1988 I started a business in Chesinende market and in 1990, I started an agro vet section in that same shop and I worked there for long.

In 1992, people (villagers) told me they wanted me to be a councillor having served them before in 1988 as a KANU delegate for the location and that is where people came to know me. In 1992 I had to compete with other candidates and by then KANU was the only party and I was elected as a councillor. I initiated and completed many projects which included four schools and I requested for a forest school called Killetien in a division that has no trees I wrote to the president and he agreed and we started a school that is there now. I started Kondamet primary, Sigowet primary school and Kamarus primary school. All these are in Chepseon location. As I continued we started a dispensary in Momoniat. It is still running to date but there is no other project that has been added. So in 1997, I contested but it was not possible because I had children in secondary school and all were in boarding schools. I saw that my opponents had a lot of money and my rival had just retired.

He was from African Highland. I preferred educating my children first. In 2002 I saw that the political arena was not good, so I quit. I was ready in 2007 to contest as a councilor again, and in August 2007 I got a call that I was needed in Kasarani, Nairobi. I did not know what was going on. When I reached Kasarani, I was told that I had been elected as one of President Kibaki's campaigners. As you know in government when one is called upon and given a responsibility you can't refuse. The Court of Arms is one so even if I tried to contest I would not succeed. I decided to work for the President. "If he succeeds he would see what to do with me," I thought. We were nine Kipsigis from Southern Rift who were campaigning. We campaigned from August 2007 and I told people that we were in multiparty country and everyone had a right to choose which candidate he/she wanted. I urged them by saying that whoever won would be a selection of the people and whoever lost it would be known since we were not a single party state. So they agreed and we campaigned in all the constituencies.

I went round the entire Kipkelion district speaking positively about President Kibaki and all what he had done which had helped this country. Even before we went for elections, we had been given a district as Kipkelion constituency and we were very grateful. So in November 2007 I noticed these people were not happy. After 20th December, someone told me that if PNU won I would not live in this area! I thought that they were just mere words. On 27th December we voted and I went round paying money to all the agents. I paid all of them and finished. On 28th

December 2007, before the final results were announced, we were through in Kipkelion and the presidents' agents had signed. Raila's and Kalonzo's agents had agreed. Raila was leading and in Kipkelion we got over 11,700 votes for the President. As the votes counting continued nationally on 29th I could see that people were not happy. They were saying the votes had been stolen, get ready. This was through the media, Kass FM station. On 30th Sunday, I was in church at 12 noon when I got a call from a good Samaritan who told me that my shop had been broken into.

"Everything has been taken, agro vet, and people are continuing with breaking", he said. I told them not to touch anyone but to let them loot so long as they don't burn the shop. At 2.00 pm I was called again and told that they wanted to come home. Then I said I will go nowhere because I had not stolen anything nor had I done anything wrong. I even got a call from the headquarters in Nairobi asking me where I was. I was advised to go away. I told them that I was just at home and that I was not going anywhere, until the DC's vehicle came. When the car arrived, the police took me to the DC's residence in Kipkelion at 5.00 pm. I had no objection but to leave because if I refused it would be an offence. I stayed there for about 4 days. On the fourth day, I went to the other home in Bureti. I used to stay in the forest and then come out to town to sleep at night and I would always hide while going down. They said I was in Bureti, as they looked for me in the evening. I was either in African Highlands or in town until the end of January 2008. In mid February, people started lamenting about my predicaments at home and said I had done no wrong. So why was I being chased from home (Kipkelion)?

Later, the elders talked and called me but I told them that I would not go until they agreed. When they agreed, the DC told me to go home because security was not bad. I went to Kipkelion together with the DC and the village elders and we held talks with the neighbours and the people who perceived me as an enemy due to my stand during the campaigns. To settle the scores, the youth asked for a bull to slaughter at home.

The bull was worth ten thousand. After taking it they said they would go and sell it. People were scared of coming to my place because they feared being victimised, however, many helped me. Those who came were courageous. The youth sold the bull and shared the money. We stayed for about two weeks then they came and burnt the AGC church where I worship. They also burnt Mile-nne town in Momoniat. They came and burnt the fence near my shop at home; they intended to pour paraffin so as to burn my house too! There were some youth sleeping there who heard the commotion and on coming out the arsonists ran away. We checked and found that it was really burnt and we put off fire. Then I reported to the police. Police came to investigate and I wrote a statement the following day. On that day we met with people. I told them, "If there is a crime Mr. Lang'at has committed, tell me. And if you wanted to kill Mr. Lang'at then kill him for this area to prosper because you want to kill him. Kill him!" The elders asked for forgiveness and said that they would deal with the case, we finished and stayed.

At least I knew one insider who broke my shop, a woman who is in Chepseon and a certain business broker. Those are the only ones I knew. I didn't know the rest. I was told that they were the leaders.

In my view these people were used politically by other people who I don't know yet. These people have a grudge against me as if I have taken something from them but I haven't. I don't owe them anything. I judge politics, using the analogy of how the whites came in 1904. They fought with Kalenjins here in Kipkelion. They fought for seven years, till the whites defeated Kalenjins. There was no peace until they identified their leader Koitalel arap Samoei and killed him. They later made a peace agreement and cut a dog in Kipkelion. Whites registered this land as Rupchan Rural Farm. Our people didn't understand about farms. They didn't think of what they could do to protect their lands.

In the following year, foreigners came to work for the whites as labourers. Sir Eliud was the Governor and they shared land with a person from World Vision called Dr. John Reckman. People were segmented into their elite. That was the cause of all these. After the whites came, the Kikuyu followed. They came for jobs and the governor told them they should not exceed five hundred. That is the largest number in an area or else they will be repatriated. So these people came and lived and after independence, President Kenyatta brought them and told them to live in Rift Valley knowing that they don't belong there.

The major problem which we have and which the government could solve is the land problem. People are saying their land was taken. I think we should know where the boundary is if we want to live together. For the Kisii its known, Luo is known, Maasai and Nandi is known but for the other side, it is not known. If we could know the boundary and we want to live together in mutual understanding, it could be good. But entering other peoples' territory one by one is not good. It's not real fighting. If they could eliminate the thing of killing people one by one then there could be peace Kipsigis are not bad, they agreed to live with anybody.

On the side of the Kisiis, they have their own evils the Kikuyu are better people to live with though there is a perception that they steal. But Kisiis practice witchcraft at night. There is a bicycle they use at night to travel which carries fire. Yes that is the problem. Is there anything else?

Q: In politics you have said you were in PNU and the majority here were supporters of ODM. What can be done to bring unity as there is no time people will agree on one party?

A: Yes, people will never agree but they have changed because some are coming to PNU. They are not deeply in ODM. Some have said that PNU was better because sharing of positions in ODM was not fair. These people were not given their rights. They were denied, especially the Kipsigis. There was the cutting of cake where only a few individuals got positions in government. The Kipsigis didn't get anything big and most of them see that if they were in PNU, it could have been better.

Q: How do you feel now that your property was destroyed and you had to run away from home?

A: Indeed it is painful though the Bible says that you should not keep anger until the sun sets. I lost my property but I remained strong and firm and left them to take. I will not investigate nor follow my property. My appeal to the government is that, if they can help me in any way, it will be welcomed. My property was worth Ksh. 2.6 million. I had an agro vet business but I can't follow the arsonists and the thieves. If the government wants to help me with anything, it is very welcomed so that I can start life. Then I can seek to make peace with my detractors. I will forgive my offenders. I always meet them and they are ashamed. They don't understand what was going on in the country. One can come and say an inciting word resulting in fights without knowing. Secondly, a woman was involved. Can I fight with a woman?

Q: No. And on the side of the government, what can it do to give you security?

A: Security is required. It is good to know that we are secure but am not saying that they come and guard me in my house. What is also needed is to ensure there is enough security in the country. They should also come down and meet people and know what is going on in the countryside. Some people who are working here do not take their work seriously. At times whatever information they are given is not taken seriously because the perceived offenders are their friends. Government agencies should be well established and if possible, they should have informers who were there before to enhance security. Secondly, chiefs were chased around and they are the people whom we ran to for help. They should be given security. There should be a strong security team so that people can realize there is a government.

Q: What about NGOs? How can they help in what we have been talking about?

A: NGOs can help people to invest in terms of projects to avoid people loitering. If they are grouped and work on projects like bee-keeping and farming, or 4K club which existed earlier, it would help these people to start doing their own work. This will avoid idleness. I am urging the government to use LAP tax to see if they can join institutions like polytechnics to train people as drivers. Likewise Form Four leavers who failed their national exams, can be trained in various areas so as avoid idleness and this will encourage others to work hard. But if they come home and stay jobless they will perceive education as useless.

Q: Since the church has its own specific role, what can it do in such things?

A: I agree, it has a lot to do since it helps in spreading good news and it teaches on how to live. The word of the Lord is clear on how man should behave even when Jesus was preaching to the world, he said; "I have come to warn you those who hear let them hear..." But people are difficult to reform because it is written that it's a mistake to steal someone's property but they don't listen. They have to be told again and again. Churches and NGO's have many projects thus they can help the community. We have many children who are orphans and they need to be helped. For instance, in this location, we have come up with a project called Greenhouse Community sponsored by Tenwek Community Healthcare. We have more than a hundred children whom we have helped. We now request Red Cross and AMREF to join us so that we can work together towards a new project called Chepseon Greenhouse where we have been able to help 10 children! We have bought a cow for another family, which they are now milking.

Q: In conclusion what would you like to say?

A: I want to tell the government to get ten leaders from the Kisiis, the Kikuyus and the Kipsigis as well as youths and women to go and discuss with the president about their problems. This will help the president to understand what problems to address when he is talking to his people.

There are high levels of poverty and the taxes are high. Money from service charge should be channelled to the grassroots where people can access the money and be able to put up small businesses which can help them meet their daily needs.

My Community Referred to Me as a Traitor

Call me a Peace Ambassador or a human rights activist (*name withheld*). I was born in 1960 in Lesirwo in Kipkelion. I went to school around the same place in 1968 and then in 1969, I transferred to Londiani in a place called Jubert. It is a forest station and my father was working with Kenya Railways, East African Railways then.

In the Forest camp we were mixed ethnic groups. We had Luos, Luhyas, a few Kalenjins, 1 or 2 Kikuyu and therefore in the camp we were exposed to other languages. I managed to pick Luo and therefore I came to understand the language fairly well. In school the majority of the students were Kikuyu about 90%. Therefore, in school I managed to pick substantial part of the language until I was fluent in the language. In 1970 third term, my father was transferred to a place called Thiyobei where I went to school from Std. 2 to Std. 7. I sat for my Std. 7 exams and went to Londiani secondary school from 1976 to 1979. I then joined St. Patrick's High School in 1980 and completed my high school education in 1981. I joined University of Nairobi and studied law in 1983. In between I taught as an untrained teacher at a place called Rongai. I stayed in the

University for 1½ years through which I got involved in students politics and unfortunately was expelled from the university. After expulsion we tried to continue with our education.

We were expelled for engaging in student's politics and specifically in the students' leadership. We were betrayed to the government. There was students' politics to do with learning, academic affairs, politics of the country and so on. After expulsion we spent one year outside trying to look for avenues to continue with our studies but unfortunately I did not succeed. Around this time there was a movement fighting for alternative political organisation which came to be called multipartism and I got in touch with other former students of Nairobi University. We were arrested the following year in 1986 and jailed. I was jailed for 15 years together with my other colleagues.

We were charged for sedition, malicious damage of property and so on and jailed in Naivasha, I spent six years there. We were released in 1992 as a result of pressure from mothers of political prisoners and Release Political Prisoners Pressure Group (RPP). On our release we joined the Pressure Group. We became active members and fought for the release of others. After that in 1993 I began to look for work in civil society organisations. In 1993 I worked with Kituo cha Sheria as a paralegal assistant and was posted to work in Korogocho. Later I worked in Mombasa then I was put in charge of School Programs on Civic Education. That was between 1993 and 1996. In 1996, RPP managed to secure funding for the first time and I was requested to come and head the secretariat as a Coordinator of Programmes. That is where I stayed for about 5 years, from 1997 to 2002. Some of the programs focused on civic education, workshops, helping communities to organise themselves to secure the rights of prisoners, meeting prisoners and so on.

In 2002 I decided to go and contest for a parliamentary seat in my home constituency. I got registered as a member of Ford People and campaigned for sometime. I tried to get nominated but I was not successful. Therefore, I didn't go to the polls.

I think the main reason for not succeeding was due to the issue of the parties. You know parties are not democratic. There are issues of hand picking of candidates without subjecting them to fair nomination process. I didn't succeed therefore we waited for the general elections. It took place in 2002 and NARC carried the day. In 2003, there were several

Committees and Task Forces to look into issues that were pressing at that time. One of them was establishment of Truth, Justice and Reconciliation Commission and I was appointed to be a member of that Task Force. The Task Force was headed by Prof. Makau Mutua. Our work entailed sampling views from around the country on the need to establish a Commission of that kind.

Over 80% of the people wanted the Truth commission to be formed. They gave us the time frame, the mandate of that Commission and we wrote the Report and presented it to the then Minister for Justice and Constitutional Affairs, Hon. Kiraitu Murungi. The Government pledged to implement the Report.

Immediately after we completed work in the Task Force I was appointed as a Commissioner of Kenya National Commission on Human Rights, a newly established body by the government with the view of promoting and protecting human rights. I was one of the nine Commissioners. I came from Rift Valley and our chairperson was Maina Kiai. I worked in that Commission for four years. My docket handled issues of prisons whereby I visited and inspected prisoners. I was also in charge of what was called Rapid Response where we could go to conflict stricken areas to try to intervene and ensure that people's rights were not violated. I was also in a programme called Social Economic Program – an economic and social affairs programme. This is the work that I did for four years. After 4 years we were supposed to seek reappointment. I tried to but I was not reappointed. Therefore I left the Commission. That marked the end of my life in civil society.

Now came the period leading to the general elections of 2007. I was fortunate to be in Kericho during this time because my constituency is Kipkelion. I saw what was taking place in terms of campaigns, mobilisation of people and to some extent incitement of people. What I can say was that there were two main trends. The government and the PNU were using the provincial administration to mobilise people, take them to places like Kapkatet and generally using the provincial administration to campaign for their party. On the other hand ODM was engaged in mobilising people but unfortunately on very narrow spaces because there was an ongoing discussion of 'it is our turn'. There was a discussion of "us, the Kalenjin" against "other communities" since it was claimed the Kikuyus had taken all the important positions. There was a lot of tribal talk and the Kipsigis were supposed to vote as a block. If you were not in that block then you were counted as an enemy.

The majimbo debate really contributed to the violence. The reality of the majimbo on the ground was that this land, the Rift Valley, was going to be for the Kipsigis, Kalenjin, Maasais, and may be the Turkana and all the other communities were supposed to be thrown out. But when the politicians explained it in the media they were simply saying 'we are talking of devolution, we are talking of people in the grassroots organising themselves, getting their resources and so on'. So what you could see here is kinds of double speak. Speaking to the ordinary people in the grassroots you tell them, 'it means we are going to do away with these people who are finishing you' but when you come to the national level (media) you explain it as devolution and even as what the CDF was doing. So this kind of double speak was what was to wreck havoc. So as I said those were the two main trends but there were problems if you were not in either of the two camps. In fact a number of us felt that we were orphans of some sort because we didn't believe that PNU had a right of using state resources like the provincial administration and using them to mobilise people. On the other hand we did not support ODM's preaching of majimbo which was poison since we were going to end up with a country composed of various ethnic groups and each group saying this is our area. So we were kind of sidelined.

Personally, for some time I didn't know which party to support and when the voting day came because I had to make a choice, I went and voted for whichever party. As we were coming out of the local polling station after the counting of the votes, I met young men who were talking openly of having voted more than once. There was a young man who said he had voted five times and I asked him why he engaged in such an illegal thing and he said, "You see if I do not vote five times, there is somebody probably a Kikuyu who would have voted even 10 times." I told them "The two of you are thieves; you are both stealing the votes because you have voted five times yet I have voted only once."

ODM was leading and its supporters were very happy. They were sure Raila was to become the president. Now when things began to change in terms of the presidential votes, tension began to rise. When the politicians went to KICC and started disputing results, they were actually inciting people without necessarily intending to do so. I remember by Sunday mid-day there was so much tension that people were not engaging in any other business, and for the first time, people usually associated with peace like women were seen taking sides. Shortly before the elections were announced that must have been on a Sunday you would come across women saying that if the votes are stolen it will be very bad. Some were even saying 'I would better die' and so on. So this created an atmosphere for the youth who went to the streets to burn property and chase people since there was nobody to restrain them. The women were not there, the old men were few in number and may be they had voted for another party so they were ineffective.

I do remember that on Sunday shortly before election results were announced we heard that violence had broken out in a place called Junction, (the junction from the main Nakuru- Kericho highway to Londiani). There was fire and youths had barricaded the road. We went there with one of my neighbours and when we got there, we found that the police had come and dispersed the youths. But there was still a group of youth around that place. We talked to the OCS and told him, 'If you have managed to stop people from the violent activities, why don't you have the fire put off?' He said that he had done so but it was only that nobody had taken any step to put off the fire. Remember when the smoke rose, it was seen from far away and people were running away from Junction. I must explain that Junction was the convergence place for Kikuyu and the Kipsigis and they are on both sides of the road. We talked to the OCS and he told us to get some water and put off the fire which we did. Then he requested me to talk to the youths so that they can disperse, which I did. I thought a better idea was to ask one of the people who had been elected councillor to talk to the youths. Unfortunately this man refused and he in fact ran away so I had no option but to talk to the youth and when I did talk to them I asked what the problem was and they said one of their young men had been beaten at Junction.

We went round with a few friends to try and discuss the problem. This took place where the Kipsigis and the Kikuyu lived together and where there was a fair degree of calmness. Later, I went back to my home.

The following day, I received information that in Londiani town there was so much violence and tension, and that a number of people were moving out of the town so one of my neighbours asked me to go and help him remove some of his items from the town. I went there with a pickup and got his items. He was shifting from Londiani town to his home which is a short distance from where I live. We found the chief of that area who asked us to give him a lift so that he could monitor the violence. We came with him and stopped at Kahurura which is about 3km away from Londiani. We stopped there, talked to the people and he told them to be peaceful. We moved from there to Junction where the violence had started and we found some Kipsigis youths having grouped themselves some distance away. They were discussing what will happen because these youths came from about 3 farms i.e. Tegunot, Chebewor and Kipkoiyo. Thus this was a big meeting. The problem was that the youths were coming from far, bypassing the people who were near the Junction bordering the Kikuyus and going directly to attack them. The people who were neighbours to Kikuyus were not happy, they were saying, "People should first come and ask us whether there is a problem between us and the Kikuyus before attacking." But unfortunately those with that point of view were the minority. Majority were saying, "We as the Kipsigis should be one regardless of where you come from and if one of us is attacked by Kikuyu they all have a right to revenge."

I was surprised that when the Chief was given the opportunity to address, he never told them, that was wrong. Instead, he told them that if they hear of any incident he wanted them to group in one place and then send a representative to him before they decide the next cause of action. Basically it was like he allowed them to come organise and continue with the violence. I left my neighbour with the pickup to proceed to his house. I must say that during that week, the Chief tried to ask me to speak to the youth to calm them down because they were really in a violent mood. I declined to speak to them judging from the experience of the previous day.

They were armed with bows and arrows so I did not speak to them. The Chief spoke and explained what I have just told you. After that meeting we decided to go round again in a peace mission with the Chief and one other elder from that place who is a Kipsigis. We talked to the people we had spoken to the previous day asking them to maintain peace, and if there were incidences we were ready to become ambassadors of peace. We completed our mission at around 5.30 pm and walked back. At the place where we were then, the Kipsigis were on one side and across a very small stream, were the Kikuyus. Before we could reach Junction – we were in between the two communities – presidential results were finally announced and Mwai Kibaki had been declared the winner. The first people we heard were the Kikuyus at Kahurura village celebrating and my recollection was that the celebration was by young fellows, boys, girls and so on. You couldn't hear adults. On the other side of the junction where the Kipsigis lived, it was quiet. I told the old man that I sensed things were not going to be good and I wanted to get back to my home and rest. I had been holding peace meetings for two days without any rest.

I went home and the old man went to his house too. On my way, I decided to go back to Junction to buy some items. On reaching there, the place was quiet and I saw a police vehicle with some people. I bought what I needed and went to my home but on the way I found a number of youths running from Junction to their homes and one of them said, 'Sasa tunaenda kuchukua silaha tuanze kazi' (we are now going to collect weapons to start work). Remember there was some tension even before this announcement was made and subsequently the Kikuyus had celebrated. This therefore must have been a reaction to that. All this was happening barely ten minutes after the results were announced. I was really disturbed by that kind of approach because I even talked to my neighbour's son and I asked him why he would want to do that kind of thing. But by then, they were out of control. So they ran. I proceeded on and I met with a number of people moving towards Junction. Remember Junction is going to be a kind of a theatre because it is the convergence point between the Kikuyu and the Kipsigis, Kahurura village specifically. I met a number of people, elderly men and women. I tried to reason out with them. I asked them why they cannot restrain their young men. They answered that votes had been stolen.

In one incident I asked one woman why she was encouraging people to go and fight and yet they might get killed and she asked me how I knew that those other people had weapons. Very many people were by this time moving out of Junction to our farms called Cheberon. This farm extends from the Junction all the way upto the forest. After the first incident there was a plan to invade Kahurura village from three different directions. The first direction was Londiani junction, there would be other people from Kamara and the third group was from Kedowa on the other side. So the Kikuyu in Kahurura about 5,000 or 10,000 people were really going to be sandwiched and crushed in the process. I called the DO and explained what was happening.

Out of my intervention the village was not burnt that night and the place was condoned off. Young men could not have access to Kahurura. Unfortunately somebody overheard me calling an administrator and that made me a traitor. Later on the town was burnt. Nobody can say who burnt it because it is inhabited by the Kikuyu and the Kalenjin among other communities. What happened is that there was some *tit for tat* burning of houses and by the end of the day the whole town was razed and you cannot blame this or that group. There were claims that the police could tell people to go and burn houses by giving some signals like, for example, if he shot in the air it was safe to continue burning but when he shot on the ground it was not safe. There was an incident where the Kalenjin youths surrounded a police officer whom they wanted to kill with arrows. The OCS was quick enough as he shot some of those young men in the legs. I remember taking one to the hospital and people started saying that the OCS was a bad man.

I also remember when I made efforts to visit the IDPs at the Catholic Church, I passed through the Forest station and found some armed officers. We discussed the whole issue of the election. I asked them why people were so mad about stealing of the election in Nairobi and not interested with the rigging at the local level. They refused to escort me thereafter because of what I asked.

In Murenduko, IDPs were not interested in taking any blankets. The place had been razed to the ground. People of Murenduko had been resisting resettlement and usually said that they could not go anywhere even if they were attacked many times. When we moved from Murenduko to Londiani to drop a Catholic Sister, we met some youths going to invade Kahurura village. I knew one man and I asked him, 'why are you screaming and why do you want to fight instead of talking to these youths?' A very agitated young lady came and questioned me and the others who were in the car. She asked, 'Why are you stopping these young men from going to attack the Kikuyus yet they have been disturbing us for a very long time?' She picked a stone and threw it at me and then the boys now started throwing stones at us. Luckily I was not hit and we sped off towards Nakuru.

Police came to Junction and shot two people dead. And a story was told of how I called the police to kill people. They went to burn my home. My daughter called me and told me about it. I made some phone calls I talked to the DO, my brother and my uncle and explained to them what had happened.

During the burial of one of the people who had been shot, a friend of this lady who had stoned me asked for some time to speak. She claimed that I had summoned the police to come and shoot people and afterwards I jumped into a government vehicle and went to Nairobi. She told the people to go to my house and loot.

Q: How do you identify the people who bear the biggest responsibility?

A: There is a way of identifying them by starting with the Waki Commission and then at the local level the CID can be used. There should be a mechanism. I know suspects were arrested but they were later released. Even in the village people can identify the ring leaders. At the national level of course those who masterminded the chaos should be investigated. They should be put on their defence. They usually claim that the person who should be investigated should be Kivuitu. There should be a form of punishment.

The issue of Kenya as a nation needs to be revisited because there are so many people who think that you can talk of your region, you can talk of your district and forget the rest of the country. The same people who are talking have their sons, daughters, friends, relatives in other parts of the country. I find the issue of saying that the Rift Valley is for Kalenjins very ridiculous because there are many Kalenjins outside the Rift Valley than those who are in Rift Valley. Of course it happens that Rift Valley has more land than other provinces but that should not make us arrogant and chase away other people. We all need one another; we need some things from other people. If everybody was to say this is my region, then there will be no Kenya. People living at the Coast will start saying the port is theirs, the coastline is theirs. You have Central Kenya which may claim Nairobi, and Rift Valley may claim the land in between and the food production there. Then the Nyanza people would say that all the fish is theirs and the water in the lake; Western would claim the sugarcane. There would be nothing left.

Q: (Interjection) a big part of Rift Valley belongs to the Maasai, isn't it?

A: Even in terms of names, most of the names are Maasai and the Kipsigis for instance who are my community have gone to other places. Even if we were to say that Rift Valley belongs to one community, Maasai, Kalenjin, or Turkana, there will be a big problem between the Maasai and the Kalenjin because the Kipsigis have gone to places where Maasai consider their own like Narok and Transmara. Yet majority of the people in Transmara are Kipsigis. The Maasai will start fighting the Kipsigis in Transmara. They will start fighting with the Kipsigis in Narok also and there will be no end.

In addition in Kitale you would be talking of Bukusus, Sabaot and Pokot. But again you see we have to get out of the land issue. There are things which can be done but not necessarily as we are talking about. My view is that so many people have raised the issue of land and even at the national dialogue we accept that if you are going to other people's land other people can also come to yours, I don't think there will be a land problem because most of the farms belong to the Kipsigis. Infact Kikuyu farms are less than ten, out of maybe 20 or 30 farms. So to me I don't see the land problem as a major issue. I know for a fact that there are many Kipsigis who are land owners and the land that the Kikuyu have taken is not so big to warrant people to rise up and chase them so that we can get land. Actually Kahurura is a slum. Most of the people who were going to attack Kahurura are from families who have got 5 to 10 acres each whereas Kahurura is a plot. Even if you are to throw people out of Kahurura, there will be no land.

Q: What do you think of these people saying foreigners have taken over land whereas there are huge white farms and they never talk about them?

A: You see this is the twisted kind of thing. What they are talking about is not land reforms, it is just some territorial kind of thing. That is our territory. Now that a number of those Kikuyu people have been forced to flee from their land, it doesn't mean that it is for any other person. If they do not have money, they will not be able to buy the land. The youths who were burning houses will not be in a position to buy that land unless they have the money.

Q: Would you say these are land politics perpetuated in the country by people who have vested interests?

A: Yes. Particularly the politicians are guilty of the land issue problem. Indeed there is a land problem in the country but not in the way it is normally discussed. There is need for land reforms but we cannot achieve it by saying so and so or certain communities should not have land while we should have land. We need land reforms so that if you want to farm you have access to that land.

I AM ROAMING ALL OVER LIKE A BIRD...

My name is Rispa Wanjiru Waihata. I am 74 years old. I was born in Wanjohi in Ol Kalau. During the war of Kenyatta (Mau Mau War) we were arrested and deported to the Reserves – in Fort Hall in Kikuyuland (Murang'a). We stayed there for some time. When Kenyatta was arrested we were in Murang'a. It was during this time that White men (settlers) said that they wanted people to go and pick coffee in these sides (Rift Valley). We were therefore transported by train to the Rift Valley. The train belonged to the Labour department. We were offloaded at Kipkelion Railway Station.

From Kipkelion, the White people took us to Kericho and we were placed before some government officials. From here each white settler would come and pick the labourers that he needed. The number was either four or five– he would then take them to his farm. In our case we were taken to a farm called Mutaragon in Kipkelion. We stayed there for some time, until we got tired with the place- tired with picking coffee for the white man.

It was at this time that Kenya got independence (1963). Kenyatta then allocated people land in Shauri Yako in Kipkelion Town. We then came to live in Shauri Yako. The District Commissioner (DC) is the one who allocated us the plots to live in and he would instruct the chief to show one where to build their house. The chief of the area by then was Mr. Kenduiywo, the Senior Chief (Retired). He is the one who showed us where to build our houses.

We stayed peacefully in this new area. We used to keep cattle and sheep. In fact those days we used to stay with Mr. Geoffrey; the one you are calling Njogu. We stayed peacefully until God took away Kenyatta in 1978. We were still in Shauri Yako Village. Shortly after this the next president of Kenya Mr. Moi came to power. He took the place of Kenyatta. It was then that things got bad in our Shauri Yako.

Houses were pulled down and we began to disperse. Some people went to look for rental houses. We went to rent a house near the Water supply area in Kipkelion. We stayed in that place up to now. The recent post-election violence found us there, even this neighbour of mine knows. I will now try to tell you what brought about the recent problems of 2007.

The problem resulted from the disputed poll results. It was alleged that Mzee (Kibaki) stole Raila's votes. Then the burning started. We were chased all over the place. Kiosks belonging to the Kikuyus were burnt down. The kiosks were located near the main bus stage in Kipkelion Town. We then discovered that they were going to invade all the places, including where I was staying. They were going to burn down our houses. It was then that our youths (Kikuyu) decided to repulse them. They did not fight them as such – they just scared them away. The invading youth's then disappeared to a nearby farm where they burnt down Kisii and Luhya houses.

We were all told by the District Officer of Kipkelion that we all camp at Water supply where we stayed for some time but we were congested so we moved to Kipkelion Police Station. After a short stay in the new place we were given tents, which we put up behind the police station. We stayed here for a long period and as you have been told by Mrs. Nyaboke we left there on May 2008. We used to be given relief supplies–food and other items, including soap. In fact the government helped us and even now, it has not deserted us. It still remembers us. What we do not get these days is soap – for washing our clothes –even this old man neighbour of mine can at least attest to that. We get food and cooking oil in plenty, but we do not get salt - sometimes we sell the food so as to get money to buy salt and soap in order to get clean. The government still takes good care of us even after we left the tents.

Q: Why do you think these things (violence) take place?

A: These things? I do not know why despite my age. These things normally start with our leaders (the big ones) when they compete over votes we become victims, and not this year alone. I see as if this violence has occurred three times. The first time it also involved the burning of people's houses and property. That was the time of Matiba, Kibaki and Moi – in 1992 and then there was another round of house and property burning. We were really unable to comprehend this problem the second time – when Kibaki had also contested the presidency – the violence was not that much – in fact nobody relocated from Kipkelion. There were no problems when Kibaki was elected the first time in 2002.

The 2007 violence was on a higher scale, in fact people spent nights in the bush, others got killed. We almost went mad. In fact you do not have to look far – the Kisiis and the Kikuyus were the target – they were in real danger.

Q: What did they say you had done?

A: I will not hide it from you. They claimed that our Kibaki had stolen the votes. As for the Kisiis they fought Ruto, led by Mr. Nyachae, using the Chinkororo. I will not hide it from you – my son. We were in real danger – Kisiis and Kikuyus. We could not step into Kalenjin areas, even now as we are here. But Maragolis (Luhyia) and Luos would go. They can even farm there. Not so for Kikuyus and Kisiis – we can't plant even vegetables.

Q: What was the situation before the violence –between you and the Kalenjins?

A: It was good – we used to live together peacefully – even sharing meals. They would even invite us to their ceremonies. We on our part would also invite them to our homes and functions. I do not know where this Satan came from.

Q: Do you, Grandmother, have children? How many?

A: I have. But a number of them are dead. So far four are dead. I have only two sons left and a daughter who is married. They live in Nakuru, at a place called Mbaruku. I only have those two sons and one daughter.

Q: So you are still here at Kipkelion?

A: I am still here – I have not left. I am roaming all over the place like a bird (laughter) I have no means of getting out of here.

Q: Do you plan to stay here?

A: I do not prefer to stay here – if I can get the means I will leave. If I stay here and I have nowhere to farm what sense does it make? The Kalenjins have not changed their attitude towards us although I am old. There are some bad feelings remaining.

Q: What is this bitterness about?

A: I do not know. But I told you that it is about power struggles by our leaders. And these leadership struggles have no meaning tous, the ordinary people. Both Raila and Kibaki co-exist peacefully; together with Kalonzo Musyoka and Uhuru Kenyatta. It is we the ordinary people who kill each other for no reason.

Q: What advice would you give to our people?

A: I would advise people to love one another. I pray that God hears this. We should stay peacefully as we used to. We should stay like brothers and sisters. Like we used to hire farms from the Kalenjins, plant our crops, harvest, and take them to our homes. We pray that this situation is restored. We do not want war. War is a bad thing. If I despise you it is also bad. Let us live as brothers and sisters.

Q: What about politics?

A: Which politics? The present or the future one?

Q: The coming one.

A: We will pray to God seriously that people will not fight each other. Prayers come first. You know I am saved. I go to the Worship Centre here in Kipkelion. That is why I have no grudge against anybody. I pray to God that we will become united.

Q: Thank you Grandmother – we have finished. Or would you like to speak in Gikuyu?

A: What do I say?

Q: Pass one message.

A: In Gikuyu – I am saying – God help us so that we stay as one like brothers and sisters. We should not despise each other. We should eat from one plate.

I DEAL WITH MOTOR VEHICLES

My name is Joel Cheruiyot. I reside at Kapsoit. I was born in April 1965. I schooled at Kaptoboti primary school then I proceeded to Cheptenye high school. I stayed home briefly as I farmed then I went to Nairobi. I got a job at Kenya Credit Traders as a salesman. I then moved from KCT to Credit Africa to become a manager. In the year 2002, I came home to start my own business; a hardware shop, which I have up to now and I am in the transport business.

Currently, I live and run a business in Kapsoit. What happened in the post election violence is that we voted very well expecting good things. Kapsoit was ODM; people were anticipating Raila to be announced as president. In the morning people were happy. By 2.00 pm, Raila was still ahead. When it reached 4.00 pm, the gap became closer between Raila and Kibaki. Kivuitu had earlier on claimed that there were some people who were "cooking..." somewhere. What were they cooking? People started saying that votes were being stolen because Kivuitu had claimed that votes from Central Kenya had been hidden. The results being announced were from outside Central. People started to suspect that something fishy was happening because Kivuitu was saying that. Leaders like Ruto, Martha Karua, Nyong'o and Orengo were heard complaining. People became furious when it was announced that Raila had been defeated. Processions started, nobody told them to do anything and police did not appear on that day. They protested then they went home.

The worst happened when the Ainamoi MP was killed on 3rd February 2008. Kapsoit borders Belgut and Ainamoi but the large part is in Ainamoi. Screams were heard coming right from Ainamoi towards Kapsoit. When news reached Ainamoi that the MP had been killed, people started to burn vehicles, lorries and Easy coach buses. I was there when the Easy coach buses were burnt. Passengers were told to alight and offload luggage. It was burnt because people believed that the retired President (Moi) had an interest in the bus company. The passengers who knew the place walked to town and were directed to the Administration Police Camp at Kapsoit where they were assisted. While the vehicle was burning, it blocked the road and people now started burning several other vehicles.

A Ugandan vehicle carrying fish and an Akamba bus were burnt near Grassland Academy. While all these buses were being burnt, the innocent passengers were being assisted by residents; some were taken to the residents' homes but most of them were taken to the police station. Many of the passengers were from Western Kenya where my wife comes from. In that case I took four passengers to my home. The following day I escorted them to go back to their homes.

Later, there was a lorry carrying fish which was burnt and since people from the village were hungry, they came to get fish. I came with my family to see what was going on and I was informed that a lorry had been burnt. Thereafter, police came in a government vehicle (white land rover) followed by a GSU lorry. This is when a cyclist not involved in the chaos was shot dead. After that I drove to Kapsoit and on reaching there I told the locals that some people had been killed at Grassland so they should all disperse and get out of town. Some left but others remained. Within a duration of 30 minutes, a number of people had been hacked with some sustaining serious injuries and others dying at the shopping centre. One man who was cut on the right hand lost 80,000 shillings in the house! My wife treated that man together with another one shot at Kapsoit who was in my house. There was shooting and one bullet killed a man who was in his house alone! His house is not far from Kapsoit shopping centre. The body stayed there for one day without anyone knowing that he had died as everyone had fled from the shopping centre. The following day police came to pick the body, post-mortem was done then the body later buried.

I think that the government used excessive force even on innocent people who were going about their own business. The shops remained open in town. Infact the police used to force people to close their shops by using live bullets or by beating people. There are ladies who were raped but are silent. They only say that their houses were broken into. There are some people whose houses were destroyed. A man who was coming from the hospital was shot while sitting under a shade. He was shot on the leg by police on a mobile vehicle despite having his papers and being peacefully seated alone.

Q: What might have caused all these problems?

A: It was brought about when Raila was defeated. When Were, Embakasi MP was killed, rumours spread that the government wanted to kill all the ODM MPs. It was only after the killing of the Ainamoi MP that we saw the government as determined to kill because they had already killed two! This is when screams and violence erupted until a police officer was killed in Ainamoi. People broke into the armoury but the guns were later returned. In contrast, the police officers at Kapsoit were not touched, as they were good. No police officer engaged in shooting as they were seeing that there was no violence. Policemen who came from Ainamoi to work in Kapsoit are the ones who shot people.

Q: What recommendations can you give?

A: I do not know what was in the mind of the Administration Police Commandant when he said Fire! Fire! as if people were armed. The APs should be prosecuted especially the ones who shot and killed people and they should be taken to court. The other thing that contributed to this violence is the media. For example, a radio local station would use provocative words. They were not neutral as they were on the side of PNU and our side was ODM. First, a local radio station presented started by ridiculing KANU; secondly, he criticized the former president seriously; but even if someone is bad, if he is your relative, he will remain your relative. You ask yourself, why criticize one person all the time? Why not mention their people as well? Was there no mistake committed by Kenyatta? Or has Kibaki committed no mistake in the past four years? As much as Kass FM was talking, there is no time they told us to go to the road to protest or do anything.

Because of the political situation at the time, if Raila had been announced as the president, people could have celebrated and there could be a lot of happiness in Rift Valley particularly Kericho as it was like 100% ODM supporters.

People should be taught and accorded their human rights like in America. Democracy should be followed. When I vote that vote should not remain in the polling station but be taken to the headquarters. Leadership will come whether people like it or not, it will come to a person who is chosen to lead. Kivuitu made a mistake of telling people that there was something cooking because that was poisonous to people.

Usually there are rumours that a sitting president will rig elections, so what Kivuitu was saying was just a confirmation. Kivuitu should now be taken to court to explain because if he had kept quiet, we couldn't have known what was going on. Look at Kamukunji and Embakasi which are barely 5 kilometres from KICC but the results delayed. People were wondering why within Nairobi, results had to be delayed as opposed to places like Elwak and Mandera where communication can be a problem.

The best way forward is to reconcile and accept that a problem arose. For instance, this year the business environment is bad for everybody. Everyone is sick. People like Kikuyus usually know where to get cheaper goods of which we don't and if we are to get the goods, then we get them at a higher price. What we are asking is for people to come together and be united as one Kenya not Central province or Rift Valley. There can be democracy like what is happening in America. We can have two parties and we vote somebody on policies and not on ethnicity. We can even have Elmolo to lead Kenya as long as the policies are within the constitution. All these tribes like the Masai, Pokot or Mijikenda can give us a president. That can help.

The other problem is our constitution. We have been talking about reviewing it since 1992. It is now 20 years and yet we are still looking at it and yet the Lancaster constitution took only one week to be reviewed.

Q: Did you contest?

A: Yes I did. I was vying as a councillor at Kaptoboti ward in Belgut constituency. The rigging was there even during the ODM nomination. There was no proper method of nomination as people were just writing names on papers. We paid the nomination fee in Nairobi but you could still find your name missing. Rigging started from the nominations to the real election. I was number 2 and I just decided to support the party I wanted myself.

I AM A BOOK SELLER

My name is Reuben Cheruiyot. My home is in Fort-Tenan. I schooled at Kiptens Primary School. Thereafter, I went to Taita Towett secondary school in 1980-1983 when I cleared my form four exams. I became a UT teacher for 3 years at Chepkechei location then I moved to the National Cereals and Produce Board where I worked for ten years. When I was affected by retrenchment, the money I received allowed me to move to Londiani in 1991 where I opened a bookshop and called it Londiani

Modern bookshop. The reason why I came to this place is because of the big exposure due to the high population unlike our place that is still underdeveloped. I moved here, got a shop, stocked books and by the time of the elections I was doing well.

In 1992, there were chaos but I was not affected so much. In 1997 I was also not so much affected as my neighbours' businesses which were burnt. I decided to relocate my stock to another building and that is the time good and bad Samaritans were seen. I could pack books in sacks and instead of people helping to transport the books, some would pick the sacks and go to sell the books in places like Makutano and Total. It was hard to identify my books are similar. The estimate of the lost stock was about Kshs 50,000.

In the year 2007, there was a problem of which I cannot say its cause. What I know are only two things; everybody picked their Identity Cards and the voters cards, everybody voted and the results were passed on to wherever. When the results were out, we became enemies with our neighbours of which I do not know the reason.

The strange thing which happened and I have never seen this in history is the burning of Londiani town. Houses were burnt and people were hurt. My house got burnt mysteriously. I decided to save my life when I saw things were getting worse. When we heard bullet shots, my *shamba* boy and I ran away. I have some cattle and as you know Kalenjins keep cattle close to their heart. I decided to close the business and I went home to see the cattle. The following day I was told that I no longer had stock. I thought of going there but it was difficult since the Kalenjins were not allowed to go into town. The bookshop had already been burnt though it had earlier been spared when chaos broke out before the first of January.

It started in the village when the election results were announced in Nairobi. The person I blame is Kivuitu and I call him a bad referee. When he said a goal was scored and yet it was never scored that must have sparked the chaos. There was a lot of hatred when Kibaki was announced the winner.

There were problems even in Farmers farm. I went to Road unit where there were forest guards and stayed there. In the morning a boy whose parents are a Kalenjin and a Kikuyu came and told me not to go to town. He was one of the watchmen I had left to guard my business. He told me that the business and the adjacent store were on fire. I tried to go but it was very difficult and it made me sick. Though it was cold, I started sweating as I remembered what I had lost ranging from household property to the business that I had struggled to build. I wondered how I would cater for my family needs.

I have a family of five children. I decided to send my family to Fort Tenan so I remained alone here. It could not be possible to transport a large number of cattle so I decided to remain here with the cattle. I tried to go and see my burnt business and I requested two forest guards to take me to the police station to record a statement. I had sixty bags of maize, a generator, car engine and a stock of timber. All these burnt in two days. I saw it all and I have to live with that memory but since I am a Christian I comforted myself. I can't compare myself with Job in the Bible whose problems were extensive and more than mine. You know even Jobs' children were killed! I then decided to go to the Catholic Church to register my loss. While there, I met some catholic officials who were Kikuyu. One asked me, "Why are you coming yet I am not the one who burnt your house?" I left him and went to Catholic Fathers where I was given two blankets after being registered.

I was so traumatized but my brothers-in-law assisted me and they still assist me to date. I lost everything. People donated some money; some gave 5,000 shillings, others 3,000 shillings and others 4,000 shillings etc. and that is what I survived on. At least I bought some clothes and some other basic necessities. The building belonged to a Mr. Rotich. I bet he is currently building it. I am ready to go back to business next year January.

Chaos in Londiani started due to the elections. This place was an ODM zone. The rest of these people (Kikuyus) are small in number. The referee announced the results without knowledge of repercussions. There was hatred and even incitements before elections through sms (short messages). There were a lot of rumours in the villages and the Kikuyu homes were burnt down so they had to come to town hence they didn't want to see any Kalenjin businesses.

In my view the government was biased because the OCS is a Kamba. My shop was just 50 meters from the police station. Our people were chased away from town as it was suspected that they came to town with bows and arrows. In contrast, the other people had pangas. People like

DOs and chiefs etc were all sent away. For example, Lilan who is a Kalenjin was chased away and infact there was also a time Mr. Rono who was a chief was nearly attacked by the Kikuyus.

The church, NGOs and friends in Londiani tried very much to assist us. The Catholic helped to a certain level. Both the Catholic Church and the AIC were biased on ethnic grounds to some extent. Kikuyus were assisted very well. Imagine when my house was burning someone photographed it and claimed that it was his house. These people can do anything to be assisted.

Q: What can the government do to stop chaos from recurring?

A: First the MPs should get saved and try to embrace the human spirit. They should give money to the poor. For somebody to get a political seat, they use dirty language on others. Our politicians were emphasizing on negative issues for example saying that the Mumbi house will never hold power for ever, because of the Goldenberg. There were also rumours that these individuals wanted to develop processing industry to be processing our maize in Nairobi and selling it. It was also alleged that a certain politician and others were interested in taking over pyrethrum as an organization. Politicians usually incite others so much that if you do not think logically you will cause a lot of problems.

There is also something else. Other possible ways include:

- People were very exposed

- Loss of rights –when the ECK announced the unconvincing results.

- Disputed results – Kikuyus could not have voted a Kikuyu to win. It was not possible.

- Land issue is not well addressed. In Israel, there are families of Jacob, Benjamin etc. it comes to 12 families. Likewise, in this country it was divided into provinces; Luos belong to Nyanza, Luhyas to Western, Kikuyus to Central etc.

When the white man came, he pushed our people to marginal lands. Our people never went to school and they refused to buy land despite having cows and other properties. The Kikuyus came and bought the land because they were exposed.

There was no transparency in the election. Bias was evident in employment and several of our people were sacked. If it were possible, they could have employed their people to lead us like chiefs and even sub chiefs. There was also bad language in politics. Incitement on phones, sms etc. contributed immensely.

Lastly, if it were possible we should have an institution for training politicians on good leadership. Distribution of national cake should be even and there should be respect for one another.

People should be assisted by the government at least to keep them busy. Imagine I was just given 10,000 shillings. I have not seen the 25,000 shillings which is said to be coming. I lost a business worth 2.5 million shillings. God helped me because I am a Christian.

THEY FOUGHT US FOR THREE CONTINUOUS DAYS...

My name is Henry Inyambula. I was born here in Kipkelion town in 1968. My father came to Kipkelion in 1948 to work for a white man in the white highland. I am the seventh born in a family of ten children. I started school in 1975 at Kipkelion Township. I finished schooling at a secondary school called Taita Towett in 1987. I have therefore lived here for a long time and I have seen a lot of things. We have lived closely with our brothers who are Kalenjins, Kikuyus, Luos, and Luhyas.

Right from the years 1985 and 1986, politics took center stage. Our village which was called "Shauri" was demolished because of politics. Those days it was seen like the other communities were more than the Kalenjin so we were forced to move out of Shauri which was a farm belonging to the Town Council. We were thus chased out because of politics. Since then we have all along been renting houses in the town. Politics continued especially when it reached the era of multipartism. It brought with it enmity between the Kikuyus, the Luos and the Kalenjins because those days President Moi was in power and the Kalenjin were seeing as if one of their own was being persecuted so that he can stop ruling the country. These politics continued up to 1992 where there were serious land clashes. People were killed and others were chased away from their own farms on those sides of Nyagacho but in town nobody was touched.

In the year 1997 likewise, there was a problem of tribal clashes but it was not severe because President Moi won the seat. Most Kikuyu who were there had already moved to other places. In the year 2002, there were no clashes. When Kibaki beat Uhuru it was so easy because nobody was attacked and we were very happy. In 2007, since I have been a committee member of Constituency Development Fund (CDF) and I also participated in the Board of Schools and any development activities especially in youth groups, the youth asked me to contest for a seat as a councilor on a PNU ticket. We contested seriously with my colleagues. By then we had PNU and ODM as strong parties. PNU was made up of several parties and there was a lot of bad blood; Kikuyus and Kisiis were seen as leaning towards PNU. We used to meet in Kipkelion town and other times at Kapkatet and Fort-Tenan. Our opponents were not happy about the meetings because most of the time the rallies were being organized by the office of the DC in conjunction with chiefs and their assistants and some money was also being given.

PNU were thinking that they would pull people to vote through that kind of approach. In spite of all these, ODM was the most popular party. Even some of us who were PNU aspirants were never happy because we were being denied money by PNU – money was given through the DO's and the DC's offices. The Chiefs used to collect people, hire a van and take them to places like Kapkatet. The van would cost 10,000 shillings and everybody in the van would receive 1,000 shillings. You cannot tell how much the leaders pocketed!

For those who were in the opposition, the ODM, were not happy because they were not receiving any money. The chief and everybody else who was in the government was campaigning for the government. Every time we got to the village, we would be asked whether we were to vote for Odinga or not. I used to tell them that they should vote for whoever they liked. There was no democracy in doing these politics. Also ODM used to have meetings secretly at night. We had informers there who would brief us on what was going on. It was like they were planning something.

After that, Kibaki came to campaign in Kipkelion. They did their things and the people were there listening without showing any anger. ODM as well usually came and campaigned mostly on majimbo kind of politics and many people living around Kipkelion were not happy because they came from different tribes. This was because they have lived here and have bought the farms. The most contested thing was about land and how this thing called majimbo was going to do. That is how the Kalenjin used to think. Some of us feared for our property. It was like majimbo was to force people back to their original homes. On 18th December 2007, some leaders (names withheld) came to Kipkelion to say that there would be a huge rally at Kapkatet on the 22nd December 07. The rally was to determine where the Kalenjin vote was to go. In that meeting the people who had attended called us and informed us that the leaders who addressed them said that there would be clashes and if ODM won majimbo would be implemented. So the politics were very tense.

When the Voting Day dawned on 27th December 2007, there were threats and I even did not see the agent who was to represent me. Furthermore, the presidential agent was not there as most of them were sent away. We were very suspicious. After voting, I went to Kipkelion county hall and conceded defeat to our councilor, Mr. Cheruiyot from the ODM. That time presidential votes were being tallied. Magerer had won the MP seat with a big margin. That time Raila was leading and on our PNU side we were very sad. After sometime, Kibaki closed in on Raila and people started saying if votes were stolen, fighting would break out. On 30th, Kibaki seemed to have led in the votes tallying. Everybody was now listening to radios and nobody was saying anything. Signs of war were in the air. I called my sister who was in Chepseon telling her to start preparing for any eventuality. She had told me about people there running around singing war songs.

Immediately Hon. Kibaki was announced the winner, the fighting started immediately. Some people who were at a hotel were being guided by a tout; they started burning Ndung'u's shop. They were many. It started in town with the people shouting. Others were also heard shouting in the villages and up the hills like Laibons and Blue Hills. They then started coming to town from as far as Soil Conservation. The whole night they tried fighting us but the police assisted us. They fought us for three continuous days. They were fighting the people living in town. You know in Kipkelion, President Kibaki got 362 votes in the town polling station called Mjini where most people were Kikuyus. When we were campaigning, the people supporting Kibaki were from Mjini. They were chased away by police. We were told by the OCS to leave our homes and go to the nearest field belonging to the County Council. Around that time, in Kasheen area people were fighting. We came to learn that the fighting was caused by somebody who was killed while stealing maize from a granary belonging to a Kisii. The violence spread to Lelu, Tinga Farm and the Monastery. Subsequently, the displaced people from those areas came to join us at the camp that we had already established and we stayed together.

The clashes continued until one time when Rashid Irungu a villager went to collect his maize but he was killed. He was the son of Ismael Wachira. People started moving out especially when ODM announced mass protests. People were saying that if their leaders would tell them to stop fighting then they would stop. People lost lives and property. I also lost a Video deck, Samsung TV and a generator. Generally, I lost things amounting to Kshs. 108,000. This is because I also had a business in Chepseon. I might have lost some other things as I was moving out but nothing was burnt.

Q: *How do you feel since you lost your property?*

A: The government had said that it would give us at least some money to assist us to pick up but we got only 10,000 shillings which cannot even buy a TV screen unless on hire purchase. The people in the village had been promised that homes would be constructed. Atleast the process is on. We were also to be paid 25,000 shillings. The violence affected everybody from the farmers to the businessmen in town. Nothing has been given to the businessmen. I fall under that category and 10,000 shillings cannot assist me much. But we thank the Red Cross, who have given us food right from January up to September. The government abandoned us right from the time we left the camp and very few people were paid the 10,000 shillings. The government has not done its part in helping us.

Q: *What are your feelings about the perpetrators of these problems?*

A: Some believe that the devil invaded their minds. Some are asking for forgiveness and some are just dumbfounded because they did not benefit in any way. I don't know if most of them would not participate in violence if the political clashes returned.

Q: Have you forgiven them?

A: Yes, I have forgiven them because I still want to live with them, especially since I was contesting for a councilor position. I still need them.

Q: Will you contest again?

A: It will depend because I am still an assistant secretary for PNU. I will weigh my options first. I have to rebuild my business. Considering that most of my supporters migrated to other areas it will depend on the response of the people that we will be living together with.

Q: What is your last take?

A: The government should remember the Internally Displaced People (IDPs) and to bring us together and find out what the main problem was because it is said that the land issue caused all these problems. Kalenjins are saying Kenyatta gave Kikuyus land and some Kikuyus are saying that they bought the land with their money.

The government should address the land issue seriously and give everybody enough share. The people will live well if they are taught about democracy and the process of electing leaders.

I HAVE LIVED IN KIPKELION FOR 85 YEARS...

My names are Charles Maigwa Kibe and I was born in Kipkelion in the year 1924. My father was working with the Milk Creamery. We stayed there upto 1938 when we moved to a farm called Kamachungwa. It belonged to a white man known as Mr. Smith and it is not far from Mambwa. Actually, it is between Leperer and Mambwa. It was a small farm of about 260 acres. They were an old white couple. After staying there for a while the white man (Smith) died and the farm was taken over by the government. From there we moved to a farm belonging to a Bwana (Mr.) Lucky where I left my parents and went to school in Nyeri. I joined a school called Ireri primary school, then Othaya Intermediate School where I studied there for seven years then came back home. When I came back my father was still here but he decided to go back to Nyeri. That was around 1950. I remained here and started to teach at a PCEA church. I started teaching in 1943 upto 1950 when the school was taken over by the government.

In 1953, Township Primary was built. Then there was the emergency and the Kikuyu teachers were not liked because the Inspector of Schools belonged to AIC and this church was not in good books with the PCEA. Consequently, the PCEA teachers were sacked. This was done by a white man who came from Kijabe called 'Jambo' by the people because he was bad and every time he came around he would say' Jambo! Jambo.'

We were four Kikuyu teachers: one from Londiani, myself and two others. They created some rumours that we had introduced students to oath taking. We were stopped from teaching. We stayed on because the white man who enrolled me into teaching was still around but living in Nairobi. He used to visit on Saturdays since the church was his. He said that I was not supposed to be dropped, and he took me to the mission where I became a religious teacher. The Emergency was still on so he used to be disturbed especially by the screening which was happening in Kericho. Those who were found to have taken the oath were taken to Manyani or detained.

I had no problems. We were given something called a Movement pass written Kikuyu, Embu and Meru. So I was given one and I stayed for sometime. By now, the white man had become very old and he transferred us back to PCEA. He was called Mr. Anderson. Those days PCEA was called Kenya Siplestician Association Mission. I started to preach until 1960. That is the time when blacks started to acquire land. The issue of land allocation was done by the ministry and the whites were the ones giving direction. Mr. Anderson called a Mr. Kiprogony to come and take me to be enrolled with the Ministry of Agriculture. In total I taught for 11 years and then worked from 1964 to 1980 when I retired.

People started coming to this place after independence and buying land from white farmers. I also bought my *shamba* (land) at Momoniat then I was to buy another piece in Nakuru in an area called Wanyororo but I decided not to because I lived in the church compound. I have lived here until recently when politics started to crop in and the Kipsigis were saying, 'Why are these people not going back to their homes?' This started in 1988. People were moved but the DC a Mr. Sirma told me not to leave the church. I stayed but people went. During the 1992 election there were clashes but people in town had no problems but in 2007, it became a problem. We used to hear some kind of jokes especially with the youth saying that whether Kibaki won or not, us people (Kikuyus) would have to leave. The election was done very well but during the campaigns we saw that these threats were real. People were coming: Raila, Kibaki and several others, they were going as far as a place called Kapkatet.

After voting, the results were not announced immediately. They were delayed for some days and there was a lot of tension. We were watching the tallying process on the TV and only five minutes after Hon. Kibaki was announced the winner, we heard a lot of noise. On coming out, we saw smoke from a distance. We stayed awake the whole night and the following day was worse because the whole place was on fire. On Tuesday, we heard that people had been killed and this was scary. The DC called for a meeting. When we were at the meeting the youth continued to attack. The DC had to call for more security. People were moving out in large numbers.

I was left here alone with my son who refused to go to the police station. We stayed in this tense environment day and night until the peace mediation started. People were killed especially at Kasheen; about 16 people were killed; 2 of them were from our church and were brothers. Here, in town, they killed one man called Rashid Irungu who was a good man. That is when we got to know that it had become bad. There is one house around the corner belonging to a young man called Nyaga that was burnt the same day. We stayed here as enemies as there was nobody crossing the territories of the "other" community.

Q: *According to you, what caused the problem?*

A: The way I see it is that we do not usually like to talk the truth. We had a meeting at the DC's office and people were asked the same question that you have just asked me. Some people alleged that the Kisiis and the Kikuyus are living in the Kipsigis' land. One group said that these people had inherited the farms from the white farmers. Another group said they wanted the boundary with the the Kikuyu to be around Nakuru. Some people said that the Kikuyus are very bad: they are greedy and they want everything. They said that the Kisiis are liars, they are night runners and introduced drugs to our children. Some said it was because Kibaki stole something which was not his and they did not want any other community to lead. That was one meeting and they were told to go home and come back on Monday with a solution. For us, we were asked what the cause of the problem was. I was the one asked that question. I said that it arose from two things: one is that the old men have abandoned the youth. Secondly, these youth were poisoned by the leaders. When there was such a problem, old men should have come around and called the government to address the land issue. Those were my observations.

On Monday we met again and they were asked what they had found out. About three or four people answered that their opinion was for these people to go and another said they should go until a solution was found and another said the Kisiis should go but the Kikuyus could remain because they are not much of a problem. Some were saying they needed us to stay the way we were before. Hence, we continued with such peace meetings. Infact, at one time we held a meeting in our church and all of us, including the DC were there. Old men were about 160 people. One old man said the Kikuyus did something wrong but we needed to remain as one.

They took the bows and arrows and pangas which were being used in the violence and burnt them, then we prayed and asked people to go back to their farms. The DC said the camp near the road was to be closed the following week. People went back to their farms and the peace meetings have continued since then even here at the church.

Q: *What do you think is the solution to this problem?*

A: My brother, what I can say is that, if there is a problem, instead of people going to fight they should start by holding meetings to talk. We have a lot of leaders; chiefs, headmen, church elders and we should involve all these leaders; they should always be consulted.

Q: *What of forgiveness?*

A: That is where there was a problem but I stood and said that the Bible says we should look for peace and pursue it. We should forget what has happened and move forward. For instance, we have been hearing a comment like; "My cow is being milked by somebody else". We have to forgive. We said that people should return what they had taken through the chief. I never lost anything. It is only that I incurred a lot of expenses due to the people who were coming here. For three months I never sold my milk. I had sixteen people here to feed. We are still engaging in talks at least to live peacefully but it is not easy.

THE YOUTHS WERE SO MANY...

My name is Michael Waweru Mwangi. I was born in North Kinangop in 1934. I started schooling in Magogo. In 1945, I went to a school in Central Province where I continued until 1957 when I did the Common Entrance Exams. In 1952, I did KAPE in a school called Marira. After I completed my KAPE, a State of Emergency was declared that day. By then, my parents lived in Kinangop and it was hard getting home but after some struggle I managed to get home on foot from Central Province. After that, things got tough because they said that everybody who was working had to be photographed. We refused and they arrested us and took us to Naivasha detention camp. Later, we were loaded into a train and taken to Central Province.

Things were tough and I decided to join the Mau Mau who were fighting the colonialists in Nyandarua. We fought all through 1953-1954 when I left to join others in a village called Mwarano in 1955. We continued to work though with difficulties.

In 1960, my brother and I came to the Rift Valley and joined Sorget which was a forest station. I was employed as a teacher in 1962. I worked as a teacher until 1963 when I joined a teaching college in St. Joseph's Kitale. I was brought to Londiani and worked as a headmaster. It was very calm because there was no tribalism. We worked with Luos, Kalenjins, Kikuyus and all were fine. In 1980, I was transferred to Kamwingi because I had bought some land there. I continued being a headmaster until I retired in 1992.

When I retired on 15th April 1992, tribal clashes started the next day and we did not know what was going on. I tried to speak with people and suggested we talk about it because I thought it was just a small conflict. Later on, I read in the newspaper that my head was wanted by Kalenjins. After some time the chaos died out and normalcy returned. We have been helping each other with Kalenjins in farming and in the church where I was a leader in Londiani parish.

In 2007 everything was okay, even in the voting we were together and there was no sign of violence. After 30th December 2007 which was on a Sunday, we had arranged to go to Sorget as a whole parish on 1st January 2008. When in church, we heard screams from a farm neighboring the church called Kivuno.

We heard that some people had attacked residents there. I called the priest and told him that we could not go to Sorget because there were signs of bad things to happen. Burning of houses started on the night of 31st December 2007 and on 1st January 2008 things became very difficult. Kamwingi 1, Kivuno and Kwitu farms were attacked.

We had very few policemen and were not prepared for war. Some of the policemen were ODM supporters and were even communicating with the attackers on mobile phones. We realized it was a war between ODM and PNU supporters. We tried to speak to the D.O. and the OCS and were given GSU policemen.

The GSU police camped at the Catholic Church for a while, but when things got too bad in Mugumoini, they were all taken there. That is when we were attacked and the army came and said everybody had to go to the police station. Houses were burning while the police just watched. We got tents and the Catholic Church brought us polythene bags. Later on, the Red Cross came and brought us tents. The problem was that the army was too far to come and protect people outside the camp. I once asked a Mr. Onyango why people were being killed in the full view of police and he told me to go ask the people who were killing us. How do you speak with murderers?

Things got worse and people were told to leave their houses and camp at the police station. The attackers were burning and looting. All this time I was still at home. Towards the end of the month of January, at about 4.00 am we were completely surrounded from Kivuno, Kwito and every other side.

In my compound alone, there were about 500 men. I was so scared. I locked myself in the house and called the OCS, chief and the military but they were all busy because the youths were so many. They took about 150 sheep and 20 cows from my home.

When they were busy running after the cows, some policemen came from Jambo side. They shot in the air and scared them away. I opened the door and the police saw me. By now my house was all on fire. They took me with them to Kamwingi centre.

Homes destroyed around the country. Photo by Kimani Njogu.

The problem was that all these people who were attacking us were not our enemies. We have lived with them, worked with them and co-existed peacefully for a long time. Here we are surrounded by farms owned by Kalenjins like Itoik, Cheres, Kiplokyit. We have never had any problems with them. All we think is that the violence was ignited by politicians.

We also fought for the multi party system together because we thought that the one party system was dictatorial. The multiparty system looked like it would bring freedom of voting. Personally, I feel neglected by the government because we suffered so much as if there was no government. It looked like the government had been overthrown. Three quarters of the policemen were on the ODM side.

The role of the government is to protect every citizen regardless of their ethnicity; whether Luo, Kalenjin or Kikuyu. It is calm now and we are being provided with foodstuff and other things. Nobody has a problem with their neighbours. No one is insulting the other. The only problem we have is that the refund or Compensation Fund that the government has offered is not sufficient to rebuild our lives.

The compensation is not enough. For example, my house had 11 rooms and staff quarters. The cow sheds and the sheep shed were all burnt down. All my livestock was stolen so the Kshs. 25,000 I got is not even enough to buy iron sheets for the store. I had a silo for my 400-500 bags of maize which was burnt. The only silo I have now can only take about 60-100 bags. I have not farmed as I always do. Even though peace has been restored, I cannot farm because the fertilizer is too expensive. The Agriculture Minister says it has been subsided to Kshs. 4,000 a bag, but where do I get the Kshs. 4,000? I can't even hire a tractor to prepare the land. The only thing we can celebrate is that we have peace again. I don't know if peace will last for another five years then the war starts again. I have started rebuilding my home and I am staying there, but facing many problems. There is no milk, no food aid anymore and no tractors as promised. We are not even sure about the seeds. We are now wondering what the future holds for us. We hear the constitution will be amended, but we don't know if that will change our lives.

The government should take care of all its citizens and protect them. Some politicians will always incite people so as to get to parliament. Such politicians should be discouraged and we should hold them accountable.

Q: Can you forgive those who attacked you?

A: I am a Christian and I have no hard feelings even though all my property was destroyed. I pray that those people find it in their hearts to know that they hurt us. It is written in the Book of Isaiah that if we repent and come back to God, our sins will be forgiven and we will be as white as snow. So if they repent and never do that again, I have no problem with them. I did not burn anyone's house. I didn't insult anyone and I do not understand how we can restore peace without them returning my livestock and the things they looted. How can I forgive someone yet they are milking my cow and selling me the milk? Let's forget that these things ever happened. That is why we have two eyes in the fore head because God doesn't want us to see behind like chameleons. It's not good to keep seeing our neighbours using our property which we can even identify. For example the iron sheets they stole and don't want to return. But I know God will repay me. I am now 74 years old and my life maybe short. As I told you I took part in the Mau Mau rebellion. The Bible says that everyone who was born of a woman lives for 70 years and the rest is a bonus. So I don't want burdens to prevent me from going to heaven. All those we were working with should come so that we help each other as usual. I won't ask them what they did to us. God will repay me. Jesus said that he left us his peace. I would like the whole of Kenya to be peaceful and no one should think of killing the other. No one should ever think of stealing from the other and all the things that have passed should be buried in the past. With those few remarks, may God give us peace so that we can live as brothers and sisters.

THERE WERE SIGNS...

My name is Michael Gachiri Munga. I was born in 1973 in Shauri Yako village. I am the second born in a family of seven- six boys and a girl. We have no father. I went to Furaha School from class 1 to 8. Then I joined Wamishida School from Form 1 to Form 4. I completed school in 1994. I started casual labour in various sectors such as construction. I left Shauri Yako in 1998. I was in class 8 and one day after school we found notices on the door. We had two weeks to vacate the village after which the government brought the bull dozer to pull down all the structures.

I heard it was a DC called Sirma who did this. We left Shauri and went to town where we rented a house because we did not have a plot. I had been working as a casual labourer until the post election violence. The violence was also there in 1992, but that was the normal tribal clashes. We don't know what causes the clashes. It just happens. We cannot say it is caused by elections. One tribe suddenly rises against another and there is loss of life and property. The most recent clashes started during the counting of votes. There was tension all over. Taxis from Junction came with warnings that the place is not safe and the youth were warned not to go there. There were signs that violence could occur. It was on Saturday night when we heard that war had erupted in Ndiwa. When we went there we found badly injured people who were mainly Kikuyus and Kisiis. Their houses had also been burnt. It was claimed that the people who were burning houses were Kalenjins from Ndiwa. We came to the Catholic Church the following day and there was still tension.

We noticed that there was a problem because the Kalenjins did not attend mass as usual. After mass we went to town where tension reigned but the Kalenjins kept assuring us that it was peaceful and everything was alright though they did not sound genuine. They were just trying to keep calm. That same day the war started.

There were rumours that the town would be burnt down which turned out to be true because they came at 1.00 am in big numbers and overcame the watching youth. They came with arrows and we only had pangas so the arrows would be shot from far and they overpowered us. We fought for sometime and then they started burning houses and running away. On reporting to the police, they took more than thirty minutes to arrive and shoot in the air to scare the youths away. That is when families started camping in the church, police stations and others went to the railway station and things kept getting worse. I remember a certain Ndirangu who was shot with arrows. He was taken to the hospital and later passed away. That is when we realized things were very bad and we started arming ourselves with pangas and keeping watch. We did not kill anyone because the Kalenjins would sell us milk during the day and turn into enemies at night. They killed a woman by hacking her head with an axe and we found her dead in the morning. The woman was a Kikuyu called Ng'endo.

The fighters were coming from nearby farms like United, Chebewor, Masaita, Ndiwa and so on. They were saying that the town must be flat. Kahurura must be flat and that they were reclaiming their land. We cannot tell the land history very well because we were born and brought up here and we went to school with all these people. They just turned nasty and became our enemies overnight. They told us to go to our ancestral land and we did not know any other place. My grandfather used to be a foreman at the United farm near Londiani back in 1960s. It is not known very well what else he was doing here. He later died and he was buried at Londiani cemetery. My mother was born here and we were also born here. We are told we came from Central province but we even don't know where in Central province.

The rental house I was staying in was among the plots that were burnt but we had to vacate for safety reasons. People started getting sick because of the cold. I also got sick because I was not used to the cold. From that time I suffer from pneumonia and I have been in and out of hospital and I have to keep warm. Some people were able to relocate, but majority lost property. If not to the fire, it was looted. We camped at the church, the Chief's compound and police station. Back in 1992 during the tribal clashes, people slept inside the church and after 2-3 weeks we went back to our homes. In 2007, when we were planning to make ourselves comfortable in the church, we got news that people had been burnt inside a church in Eldoret. Out of fear, we couldn't sleep inside the church, we stayed outside. All the aid was provided outside the church and we stayed there for about five months. When we left the church, we went to the stadium where we stayed for 1-2 months before we were told to go back home. Organisations like the Red Cross, Goal, Fadhili and others came and helped us with tents. Each family got one tent. A church was put up, a police camp and chief's camp. People were overcrowded and hygiene was a problem. We formed cleaning groups to prevent disease outbreaks and I was the secretary. After the camp, I went back to town and rented a house.

Q: What do you think the government should do to improve security in this area?

A: Well, we have enough security officers in this area and even during the post election violence, they were still around. But they did not help much. When we were attacked on Sunday the administration government was aware. The OCS and the DO knew about it. They only responded to our distress calls after 30 minutes of attack. We were confronting the attackers with pangas and they had arrows. We only had homemade shields for protection. We were preventing them from entering into the town and burning houses using petrol. We would also scare them off by screaming hard. As for the government, we hear that it cannot protect everybody, but even the police officers and other security forces seemed divided because when they identified the attackers who were armed with arrows, they only shot in the air to scare them. But I think we don't know the meaning of weapons. You would find someone coming with the weapons to your house telling you to vacate but no one told them that they were breaking any law. I don't think it is lawful for anyone to tell another Kenyan to go back home because all Kenyans can stay anywhere they choose. We don't know any other home.

Q: How do you think other organisations can do to help you?

We have had different organisations visiting us. Like the Red Cross, Goal, San volunteers, banks like the Kenya Commercial Bank etc. Goal registered people for fertilizer supply because most of us are farmers. They took our names and they forwarded them to the Ministry of Agriculture but unfortunately there was no transparency in the distribution. Most of us did not get any but most Kalenjins did, even the ones who were not displaced. The same case applies to the funds. The Kshs.10,000 fund that was set aside by the government, some of us never got it. We are even tired of filling out forms. Even though there is a committee that manages the fund, they never seem tog et our names in the list. The same case applies to the food rations that benefit non-IDPs more than the real IDPs. However, some organisations do help us especially the Red Cross. Even at the camp we had to take names at night so as to identify genuine IDPs and give them to Goal. If the names did not match with the list with the agriculture people, the people would miss out on aid.

Q: What would you say about people who forced you out of your homes?

A: Well, those are very different people because we had been friends for more than 35 years but surprisingly, they changed so much such that we don't even greet each other. According to me, one day elders have to be put together from all these communities and they should talk to a neutral person who won't favour any side. The leadership e.g. the chiefs and sub chiefs favour their communities here in Londiani. For instance, people were accusing a local leader during the violence because he could be seen in town and houses would be burnt that day. We had a meeting with the Kipkelion DC at the social hall and many people were pointing fingers at him. The new DO was also warned against the senior chief.

Q: Do you forgive the people who did this to you?

A: At times it's hard. I am a Christian yes, but the loss was great. Where I am now is not where I would be because I had plans to go to college – teaching college in Nyeri. I don't have the address of the college anymore. Up to now, my heart is not at peace because some of my important documents are missing. I do not have my school leaving certificate. My original ID, voters card and many other things. I replaced my driving license the other day. My education and nationality has no proof anymore and all my plans were messed up. I no longer farm as I used to. We might face food problems next year because people no longer farm in the county council land which we used to lease for Kshs. 2,400 per acre. I would like to forgive them but my conscience tells me that they are my enemies.

Right now I am many steps backwards yet I should be far. Even the aid we get should be of help to other people elsewhere. Peace is not bought and it cannot come from anywhere else. It is for you to be peaceful and me to be peaceful and come together for life to go on.

I SAW MANY ASTONISHING THINGS

My name is Grace Matia. I live here in Vihiga. I was still living here in 2007 selling cereals at Nyata estate. We have different ethnic groups living here. They include the Kikuyus, the Kisiis and the Luhyas. There are those who work as civil servants, farmers and also business people.

On the material day *(when Kibaki was declared the winner)* as I was going to open my business, I heard a lot of commotion. When I arrived there, I found the police throwing tear gas at people who were breaking into people's shops and looting. One police officer told me to go back home and sleep. But I asked him, "How can I do that when my property was being stolen?" That night, at around 10.00 pm, my husband called me from Njoro-Njokerio farm where he lives with our last born son. They wanted me to go there earlier, but I could not go immediately because of financial constraints. So on this day, I was travelling from home in Western Kenya to Njoro but on reaching Majengo there were no matatus because there was violence at Burnt forest and Kericho. The drivers advised me to try the following day.

I started off at 5.00 am. I woke up my neighbour called Gradre who escorted me to Majengo stage where I boarded a matatu. On arrival at Kisumu, we found things were not good and so we were forced to take the Eldoret route. At Kapsabet, we found stones which had been thrown on the road and some people armed with bows and arrows. The driver was forced to go back to Kakamega and take another route via Chavakali. At Shamahoho we found another group with pangas, bows and arrows.

Although our driver was a Kikuyu it reached a point where even cars that were being driven by 'other' ethnic groups could not pass in some areas. Out of the driver's courage, who talked with them, we were allowed to pass but on condition of putting tree branches on it.

In Eldoret, we found houses burning. In Molo we saw the same thing and also at Salgaa the situation was the same but now all the PSV vehicles were stopped. We were sandwiched between trailers – one in front and another trailer at the back - we had nowhere to pass. The driver tried to persuade them in Kikuyu then they removed one trailer for us to pass. When we arrived at Nakuru we found that the situation was the same and that it was also burning. Gun shots and tear gas rent the air over the town. We couldn't go anywhere. We took the State House route towards the show ground. It was very hard to pass because only women and children were allowed while men were stopped and held there. People had to crawl on their knees while passing because a stray bullet could hit you if you stood up. At the showground, we found people from Burnt forest and various parts of Rift Valley. The first night we slept in the cold. We were not regarded as human beings in any way and priority was given to those people who had gotten there earlier and only if you spoke in Kikuyu. By the third day, I talked in Kikuyu because my mother is a Kikuyu. It's only my father who is a Maragoli. I was brought up at Njoro and I speak Kikuyu very well. I managed to get a mattress and blanket but with food it was a must for you to be known first to receive any food. People queued for food and others even fainted because they were too weak to withstand the hunger after going without food for several days.

We faced many difficulties, more so the elderly people. The place was dusty all over and many people got a lot of infections. At some point there were fights in the camp between the Kikuyu, the Kamba and other ethnic groups from Nyanza and Western. It was then decided that the Kisiis, the Luos and the Luhyas be shifted to the stadium whereas the Kikuyus and the Kambas would remain at the showground where I happened to remain.

I tried to call my husband but he could not be reached on phone. I tried my brother who was also unreachable. I was really worried more so because I was so near my husband and yet I could not see him nor the son I had gone to collect. Luckily, I talked to my brother who works at

Egerton and I told him I was at the showground. He organized with his boss to allow him to come with an ambulance to pick me up as a sick person. This was also a way of avoiding a lot of road blocks on the way.

On arrival my brother talked with the policemen at the gate because there was an identity card given to me. The rule was if you were going out for good one had to return it but if it was for a short while, it was to be rubber stamped. I gave out the card because I was going for good. I later learnt that where we were going in Njoro was worse. It was about 6.00 pm when we alighted, screams filled the air. Moments later people emerged with bows and arrows and it happened to be the Kalenjins and Dorobos fighting the Kikuyus. I found my mother's timber house burnt down with everything in it. I went to my brother's place where I rested for a while as he went to look for her. I was happy to see her with my son.

Fighting was the order of the day for the period that I stayed there. I saw many astonishing things. I saw a pregnant woman with arrows in her body protruding from the other side. The arrows were poisonous, one could not pull them because they had hooks so if one attempted, they would come out with flesh. We sought refuge at Egerton University. When things cooled down, we set off with my husband to western Kenya. When we arrived at Salgaa they were asking for our ID's and based on the name one passenger was forced out of the car and slashed with pangas. I saw a lot of things which I would never ever want to recall in my life.

Q: In 1992 and 1997 there were clashes, were you affected that time?

A: No. I was in primary school that time.

Q: Were you involved in the campaigns?

A: I wasn't at all but I was a PNU agent. Even my husband was not involved because he works at Njoro.

Q: Why do you think you were attacked?

A: It was just specific communities who were fighting. If you could talk Kikuyu you could have been killed and the other way round was also true. All this happened after the elections and especially after the announcement of the results.

Q: Do you know those who attacked you?

A: They were total strangers to me. I didn't know them.

Q: Can you forgive those who attacked and did all sorts of evil?

A: I will forgive because the Bible says we forgive and God has taught us to forgive.

Q: Are there any conditions you set for them for you to forgive them?

A: I just want the government to solve the issue of IDP's first by at least giving them something to survive on or to start projects with. Right now most people have become very poor due to this violence.

THE CHILD DIED IN MY HANDS

My name is Jane Wangari Maina, a farmer here at Majengo and a Red Cross volunteer. I am a Kikuyu and I have been married here for close to twenty years. I was at home on 31st December 2007 when the chairman of Red Cross called and informed me to be on standby because I was a member of the Red Cross. I wondered what the chairman wanted from me. Before long, I started hearing gun shots and I assumed that those were just policemen carrying out their duties.

I wore the Red Cross emblem and left. My child asked me, "Mum where are you going, and can you hear gunshots?" I told her that I was invited by my friend to travel to Nyagogi and that was where I was going. When I arrived at Mdasa I saw tyres being burnt on the road and people looting shops. I just wondered what was happening but I proceeded to the function and then came back. When I was returning, at Eludu I saw corpses and that is where I started carrying out my life saving duties. I am a first aider. I first took someone who had been shot and put her in the ambulance. That woman was so terrified but I assured her not to be worried at all.

The police by that time had put road blocks to prevent movements from either side. I told the police that I was a Red Cross worker and that is when they allowed me to pass. At Mugoda, we found other people who had been shot. We also saved a small child and laid him in a shade;

the child had been shot in the leg. I could not go home so I asked the Red Cross chairman to send me more people to help because things were getting out of hand. He sent me Lumadede and Chally Inoda whom I told to go and get a stretcher to start evacuating people. We took the child to Vihiga health centre but unfortunately the child passed on later in the night in my hands.

Unfortunately, on 9th February 2008, people broke into my house and stole everything: household items, money, my phone and even my livestock were not spared. I felt bitter but I just asked God to forgive them. Before the elections, people were optimistic that ODM would win these elections. You dared not say that PNU would win even by fluke because you could have received a thorough beating. Before the elections, people lived very peacefully as brothers and sisters. We used to help one another by *doing merry go rounds* (coming together in social groups). During the elections, things changed. The ODM supporters could not see eye to eye with PNU supporters and vice versa. I used to ask them why we should fight each other and even kill one another and yet we were common *wananchi*. I told them that no one would be employed by the politicians and that it was them and their families who would benefit and not the common person. People used to think that if Raila takes over as president they would personally benefit a lot.

Q: Do you know the people who attacked you?

A: I know just a few of the people who attacked me because I ran to my bedroom to hide. I can forgive them because God says we should forgive them. They were incited, due to their arrogance and peer influence. I will forgive them unconditionally. They were also affected because even their houses and other effects were burnt.

Q: Were you involved in the campaigns?

A: I wasn't involved in the campaigns at all. As Red Cross members we don't involve ourselves in campaigns because we are life savers. I think I was attacked because I am a Kikuyu and people thought that I was on the PNU side. It was automatic that if you were a Kikuyu, the assumption was that you belonged to PNU. Being a Kikuyu was enough reason to warrant an attack.

Q: *What do you think the government can do to unite people?*

A: The government should work really hard to unite these communities. The MPs incited people by telling them that the Kikuyus who live there are given money by Kibaki to run their businesses. They planted a misconception in them. I think it is the government and the MPs who can bring peace in this area. They should enlighten people by telling them that a person can get rich through hard work not by stealing or getting unconditional monetary help from somewhere.

Q: *What can you do to promote peace as a citizen?*

A: As a citizen, I urge everyone to uphold peace because if we fight, we are the ones who suffer in the long run. The leaders will still stay in comfort, meeting to make merry at their undisclosed venues. We are the ones who will buy sugar and other commodities at very high prices. We fought to give the politicians jobs at the expense of hard work. I also urge everyone to love one another and help each other irrespective of community differences.

I HAVE FORGIVEN THEM

My name is Mbiro Muiah and my husband's name is Josephat Muiah and we live here in Nguu Tatu. After retiring from my employment, we came here, bought land and started developing it. We found many people of diverse ethnicity such as Giriamas, Luos, and Kambas. The local community welcomed us very well and we felt this was an ideal place for us to build our home because the locals were very welcoming.

In 2007 I was still living here, but by the time the election results were being announced, I had travelled to Bamburi to take my husband to hospital because he was unwell and we had to stay in Bamburi as he got medical attention. We had lived here peacefully with the local people who included the Wagiriamas, Rabais and the Mijikenda community. Although there are many different tribes here, we have always lived in harmony until the election period when things changed.

Life changed during the Referendum when people started taking sides, some saying that they were in ODM, while others supported PNU. Discrimination on the basis of what group one supported started and they didn't need proof of your support to the opposing a party – mere speculation was enough for you to be discriminated against. Until after the election results were announced, I had not actively supported any political party but I knew that voting was my constitutional right. I used to advice them to vote for a person whom they knew would meet their expectations. I started noticing changes because even my employees didn't look happy and on questioning them, they would brush me aside. I did not know that our MPs were planting seeds of discord amongst us.

In 1992, I was still living here in Mombasa and I was not affected by the clashes but in 1997, it was bad. We were stoned when we went farming in Kadzandani and our house broken into and all our property looted. That was very shocking, more so because I had witnessed such an incident before.

What befell me in 2007 was worse, as I had told you before, I had taken my husband to hospital and that is when I received a call that my hotel here in Nguu Tatu had been burnt down and no one dared to help. This was on 30th December 2007 immediately after the presidential results were announced. I couldn't understand this as this is a peaceful place. Little did I know that it would be the boiling point of the clashes. They burnt down Turkey Base, they torched everything: our goats were slaughtered and some driven away; they chased our Giriama workmen escorting them far away. We had one young man whose bride was viciously attacked and raped and this really hurts.

There was a time we thought of travelling from Mombasa but my husband's health condition held us back. It was a very harrowing experience and very shocking considering that these were people who a day before were our friends. We walked together as we went to cast our votes. It shocks me because it was the result of my refusal to say I supported ODM.

My children are scared of going to our farm which is called '*Mzee Poa Farm*'. They say they will not go to the farm because ODM supporters attack people there. Later on when I inquired, I was told that the youth had been paid to carry out the attacks against non-coastal people. I couldn't understand the logic considering that I got married to a man from Shimba Hills in 1970 and my children can't speak Kiembu my mother tongue. They all speak Kiswahili because they were all born here and furthermore, they don't know any other home apart from here.

We never received any warning either by pamphlets, calls or verbally about the clashes. The most surprising thing that occurred was what a young Giriama man whom we had sponsored for a driving course told me. He informed me that an aspiring MP had approached him and other young men for recruitment and taken to Kashani where they were going to be given monthly payment. He really wanted to go but I pleaded with him advising him that it was not right for him to abandon his course midway. He insisted that they were going to be compensated fully and I found this to be abnormal since it is not usual for one to abscond a paid-for course.

Later, some people came surveying and on enquiring whose premises this was, they were told it was Baraka Children Home. Then they asked about the house next to the home which was magnificently built which they were told, "It belongs to Mzee Poa who had also built the children's home and so if you torch the home, what will happen to our children?" That is what saved the home from being torched. The Giriama young men who were on motor-bikes went past the children's ome and set our house on fire. Our house being stone-built was the only one burnt down in the whole area. Based on reliable information, this attack was planned because the person carrying out the survey wanted to be shown houses belonging to Kikuyus and infact pointed at our house identifying it as a too well-built to belong to a Giriama, thus it had to belong to a Kikuyu. It is hard to identify the perpetrators but the politicians were the force behind these 'projects'.

Those involved were local youth who were recruited and put together elsewhere because I know some of the youth who burnt down my property. Even those who raped were later identified because they were people who used to do casual construction jobs at my place. A large number of the marauding youth came from Mishomoroni and Kashani and these chaos were undertaken by youth who planned to do it that week under a certain politician, because previously we had lived with some of these youth peacefully.

All this was done in the presence of the police who were just watching. After burning down my house, they stole my goats and went to celebrate at my elderly neighbour's compound. The old man was arrested and taken to Bamburi Police station but after one week he was released. When I was asked to go to the police station and see the one who was in charge of looting of my animals, I was surprised and I asked him why he did it and he said he did not understand why he did it. I asked the Inspector of Police to set him free so that they could go and finish eating whatever had remained of my goats. I said that if they had asked me to give them the animals, I would have freely done so because missing my livestock would not have hurt me as much as burning my home. One can easily get more livestock but building a home is not an easy task. Even before the issue of forgiveness and reconciliation was flouted, I forgave the old man and had him released from the police, fed him at a hotel and gave him enough fare to get him to his home. I knew that he was just influenced by someone. How naïve could they be that they could not reflect on how we had lived together peacefully and that I had even facilitated the piping of clean water and here they were biting the hand that had fed them! If they valued all that, they would not have done this. This was sheer stupidity and I don't visualize them planning this. It had to be someone else.

I have not gone back to my home since the day when Bamburi OCS went and saw how everything had been burnt, looted and he recorded everything. The OCS called me and told me that he had seen and recorded everything and that investigations would be carried out. No one has been seen there upto today.

Q: What would you want the government to do?

A: I would advice the government to give people civic education about political groups and personal accountability in the political group and as a Kenyan. I wish they knew that we do not elect a person because of the political party, neither on empty promises nor promises that after being elected they would chase away certain communities. I pray that they realize it is not right to attack someone they have lived with peacefully together for over 20 years, and not listen to people who wake up one morning telling them to harm others. It is sad that hungry people were used to perpetrate violence in exchange for money to buy flour for a day. Just a day's meal! It hurts because if only they knew that after that day that inciter will just disappear, not to be seen again. He would not help them yet they have bitten the hand that feeds them.

In my case, for example, I am the only person in this area with clean drinking water after spending over Kshs. 200,000 to make it possible. I freely give them drinking water without any discrimination yet even the group water project which started a long time ago has not succeeded. I can never be inhuman to them and yet they dared destroy my property. Let us just take it that hunger pushed these youth to that extent because if you kill the goose that lays the golden egg for you what will you do tomorrow?

Q: Did you participate in the campaigns?

A: I was not an active participant in the political activities but I advised people to vote wisely as voting is everyone's right and it is a personal secret. Everyone voted alone and didn't divulge whom they voted for. I would advise them to vote wisely and not be bribed with two kilos of sugar or one packet of maize meal nor two hundred shillings because if you did and the person got elected, that would be the last time you would see him until after five years. Thus I was not involved and furthermore, I am a Christian and I don't like involving myself in politics.

Q: Why do you think you were attacked?

A: I was attacked because of tribalism. Later, some young men came apologizing and we have now given them casual jobs at home so that they can be able to buy school uniform for the children. I have even had to give food to the hungry ones. One cant really understand these people because they like us and even call my husband *"Mzee Poa"* (Good Gentleman) for he is a very understanding person. Some of these youths feel uncomfortable because of what they did to us but we continue educating them on issues pertaining to peace and co-existence; that discriminative tribalism is not good. For example, my husband is not from my tribe. He is a Kamba from Shimba Hills who arrived at the coast in 1954 and I am a Meru. I have lived here since 1970.

I was attacked on 31-12-2007 and I know those attackers even some by their names. I even know where some of them live so at times I also ask them why they destroyed my property. I know them so well even the one who was their ring leader had worked for me for five years and had even married while still working for me. I know this young man so well as he is my neigbour, yet he led others to burn up my place. I don't want to prosecute them though they wronged me. I have forgiven them and I pray that God blesses them. I pray that those clashes should never happen again and tribalism should not emerge for it is deadly.

Police Shot my Husband Dead

My name is Rose Gathoni Mathenge and I live in Mishomoroni and this has been my home for the last twenty years. People from different ethnic groups live here as brothers and sisters. We do not know tribalism. But after the elections, problems arose. During the elections in 2007, life underwent changes. People alleged that the announcement of the presidential results was delayed and this stirred up negative tribalism. In 1992 and 1997, I was not affected but when the results were announced on 30th December 2007, I was really affected. My husband and I were at home the whole day until the results were announced that Kibaki was the winner. That is when we saw many youth from the southern end of the main road – I live next to the main road - carrying luggage and then going back for more. We stayed indoors with my husband until 8.00 pm when all the ferrying of goods stopped. I think they had looted everything.

When all was quiet, my husband, an old man, who had been indoors through out the day told me that he needed to buy some cigarettes. The distance from my home to the shop is about 100 yards and that is when he met with policemen who shot him dead, at the mosque near where I lived. That evening, they stormed my kiosk and looted everything. I used to sell paraffin, flour and other small household items. From that time, I have suffered a lot having lost my 25 year old son, who used to help me in February 2007 and now my husband. I have really suffered with no one to help me. My husband was killed by policemen who met with him and shot him in the stomach and the back. Earlier, we had received warnings from one ethnic group saying that if Kibaki refused to go back to Othaya, we, the Kikuyus would be in danger. They warned us even before the election results were announced but we didn't take the warnings seriously because we took these threats to be just campaign tactics.

Q: Can you forgive them?

A: They will be forgiven for we have no alternative. But just consider me. For example, think about the pain I feel and the suffering I go through because my husband, my provider, the one who used to pay house rent for me, is no more. I am really suffering.

Q: As a citizen who loves and respects nationalism, unity and peace what advice would you give to the government to help Kenyans live in peace and harmony?

A: Yes the government can protect its citizens and I would urge the government to ensure that election campaigns are carried out without intimidations because these intimidations are the beginnings of violence. When political leaders hurl accusations at each other, the people also begin to hate one another. Some even go as far as killing others. As this goes on, the politicians are in their homes safe and sound.

Q: Did you participate in the campaigns?

A: I did not participate in the 2007 election campaigns. I stayed at home going about my business but I voted because that is my constitutional right.

Q: You have lived here for a long time and your neigbours are like your relatives for you know all of them both young and the old, men and women. Why were you attacked and your property looted and your husband killed?

A: I was attacked because of tribalism. We had lived together for a long time in peace. These politicians planted disunity and tribalism between us and this led to me being attacked. This attack happened on 30th December 2007 immediately after the announcement of the presidential elections. As soon as Kibaki was announced the winner, my kiosk was broken into and looted and it is on that very same day, that my husband was killed by the policemen.

I do not know the people who attacked me but they were young people. As a Kenyan, my wish and plea is that we should forgive and forget the past, because whatever happened will never be erased. Let us forgive each other so that we can live in peace like in the past and be able to continue with our lives.

I SAW PEOPLE WITH DEEP CUTS

My name is Christine Mwaka Nyawa. I live in Maweni Estate in Likoni. Most people who live around here come from the Digo, and Nduruma communities. There are also a few Kikuyu, Luhya, Kamba, Chonyi and

Luo. We have been living well with these people and businesses have grown. I have been living in Maweni for several years and during the 2007 general elections, I was still here.

To be precise, violence started in the coast in October 1997 during the campaigns. I cannot quite remember the date, but it was on a night at around 8.00 pm when chaos broke out. The first thing I heard was commotions as people ran up and down. So, I ran towards where people board the ferry. On reaching there, I was shocked to find the police booth on fire and several Kenya Bus Service (KBS) passenger service vehicles were also burning. I also saw people with deep cuts, property and money strewn all over. Bonfires lit the roads.

This was the time that local residents were chasing away people who were not indigenous residents of Coast Province. The locals referred to them as 'watu wa Bara' (upcountry people) and never wanted them to vote in Coast Province. The "unwanted" communities then (1997) were the Luos, Luhyas, Kambas and Kikuyus. The situation remained tense for weeks, and businesses were badly affected. I decided to move to my rural home in Kwale.

However, the government responded by deploying officers from the General Service Unit who restored calm. But it was not until December, that same year when I went back to Maweni. Unfortunately, I found that my house had been broken into and all my property gone. This pushed me back to starting life at a very low level. With the help of the GSU officers, we managed to vote peacefully and we lived peacefully thereafter.

During the 2007 general elections, again the situation degenerated to the worst. This time, there was much more hatred than in 1997. Violence broke out on the night of 30th December 2007 immediately after Kivuitu announced that Hon. Kibaki, who was contesting on the Party of National Unity (PNU) ticket had won. That night, chaos started in the same manner that it did in October 1997. I could hear commotion sounds of gunshots and shouts. I was too scared and so I locked my self inside the house. Youths were demonstrating, they claimed that the votes had been stolen. They lit bonfires on roads and marked their houses with ODM initials to indicate that they were supporters of the party. The youths would then attack any unmarked house. They perceived the owner to be a supporter of 'other party'.

Q. *Did you loose any property?*

A. Yes. I thought the situation would get out of hand and so I moved again to Mwanguta the next morning. While, I was away some demonstrators broke into my house and stole all household items. They also vandalized my house and stole the roof and all doors. They also stole a lorry worth of charcoal.

Q. *Are you willing to forgive those who offended you?*

A. Yes, I have forgiven them. I cannot say that I will revenge or hold grudges against those people. If I met with them on the road I would sincerely do nothing. They are in hundreds while I am alone. I can only ask God to make them see their mistakes and know that doing evil doesn't pay.

Q. *Were you involved in the campaigns?*

A. No, I wasn't. I think the reason why I was attacked was because I am half Duruma and half Kamba. I am married to a Kamba and the local residents were chasing away Kambas too.

Q. *What action do you think the government should take to ensure that peace prevails?*

A: Though the President, Vice President and the Prime minister are in the same government, we are aware they belong to different political parties. Whatever they do, the party difference is what is reflected on the electorate and Kenyans at large. I would urge the three leaders to sit on one table and decide which way they should best lead the country.

STOLEN PROPERTY WAS LOADED INTO POLICE VANS

My name is Joseph and I live in Likoni flats. I was still living in this place during and after the 2007 general elections. Likoni is cosmopolitan and residents had coexisted well before the 2007 polls. The environment was conducive for business and more and more traders moved in. However, after the 2007 elections, the situation turned ugly. Most of the businessmen lost their property. Nowadays those who used to drive have been reduced to trekking, as those who rented big homes have been forced to live in small flats. In general, the standards of living have become harsh.

During election campaigns, I witnessed neighbours take arms against each other. It was at this time that one would distant himself or herself from a long time friend, based on tribal lines. The Luos identified themselves as supporters of ODM, while Kikuyus and Kambas branded themselves as supporters of PNU. The situation degenerated to a point that one could not dare ask for any assistance from a neighbor who did not belong to his or her ethnic community.

Trouble started on the night of 31st December 2007 after the presidential poll results were announced. Local residents announced that it was time to get rid of Kikuyus and Kambas from Coast Province. Some youths went round labelling homes ODM, and they would attack any house that did not bear the acronym ODM. Personally I did not label my house. It started with commotions and sounds of people shouting while running. By then I had gone to a nearby town called Kigogo. I quickly but cautiously went back home only to find that a handful of young men had broken into my house and were looting. At that very moment I saw a police Land rover approaching, and on taking a closer look, I saw the area Officer Commanding Police Station (OCS) inside. I pleaded with him to intervene and stop the stealing, but he instead urged me to walk away and let the looting continue provided I was safe. The OCS asked the youth to touch and take anything on their reach but not to harm anyone. I witnessed stolen property being loaded onto police cars and taken away. On the next morning, the attackers broke into my two pubs, stole all the stocks and burnt the premises. They then turned their wrath on my car which was parked outside and stole the battery and all the tyres. They also vandalised my other car that was parked at home.

Frankly speaking I don't know why I was attacked since I have never been involved in active politics neither was I involved in the heated 2007 elections campaigns. I only voted.

I perceived all this as the aftermath of hate campaigns and tribal politics. That's why I have chosen to forgive all those who offended me. Infact some have approached me asking for forgiveness. Recently one of the youths brought me a crate full of empty bottles. He excused himself saying he was sorry that he had drunk my beers and was asking for forgiveness since he had made efforts to return the empty bottles. Indeed, if at all the attackers have seen their mistakes, then I can forgive them.

Q: Now that you are willing to forgive them, what do you want them to do first so that you reconcile fully?

A: I don't have anything much to ask for. Most of the attackers did not know what they were doing. They cannot explain the circumstances that made them act the way they did.

Q: What would you tell them if you come face to face with them?

A: It is not a big deal whether or not I come face to face with them because after all we go out to night clubs with most of my attackers. We often meet at leisure spots.

Q: What do you think the government should do to foster peace?

A: The government should come out to help those who registered their names as victims of post election violence. The Government should assist those who were affected and had taken loans from banks to repay them. This is because many have defaulted in servicing the loans and their property is being auctioned. I witnessed today a vehicle belonging to a victim of post election violence being towed away by auctioneers because of an unserviced bank loan.

Q: Would you like the government to assist you personally in any way?

A: I don't have any special requests to the government or favours to be offered to me personally. This is because I have not seen them assisting citizens at individual levels. For instance, I cannot demand compensation from the government for my stolen beers. I think people should be helped collectively in Sacco's or unions through affordable loans.

Q: Why do you think you were attacked?

A: In my view, business rivalry was a contributing factor to the violence. I overheard a neighbour say that he had been sent to destroy my business because it was thriving extra ordinarily. My Landlord claimed that I had better customer relations than my competitors. I can testify that many Landlords, who did not like their tenants took advantage during the electioneering period to throw them out. Most of the business premises that were vandalized belonged to people who did not have ancestral homes within coast province. However, shops belonging to the Somalis and Dholuos were spared. There were claims that Administration Police officers had been deployed to guard them. Security was provided on tribal basis.

Q: In your opinion, what measures do you think the Government should undertake to avert such chaos in future?

A: First of all, the government should put in place stringent rules prohibiting any holder of an administrative office like a District Officer (DO) or Officer Commanding a Station (OCS) from being partisan in politics. If the law enforcers were non-partisan in politics, then I think the problem would have been of a smaller magnitude.

LIFE WAS BETTER BEFORE THE 2007 ELECTIONS

My name is Ndegwa Duka and I live at Ukunda. In 2007, I was still living here at Ukunda with people of diverse ethnic communities but the majority being the Mijikenda. Generally, the living conditions are hard here in Ukunda especially after the post election violence when everything was destroyed. People depend on tourism here but the sector was negatively affected by the violence. Businesses were also not spared.

Life was better before the 2007 elections because people used to do their businesses freely. But after 2007 life has become hard and this has made me contemplate on going back home to carry out farming. I used to engage in small scale business before 2007, whereby I used to buy and sell charcoal, to be precise a minimum of two bags and a maximum of a lorry when I received a loan. I am sad that we left our businesses for safety's sake after voting peacefully. Chaos broke out on the evening that the president was sworn in. We locked ourselves in our houses that evening when chaos broke out. From far, our business premises could be seen engulfed in fire. We were really terrified because we could not step outside our doors; sounds of gunshots rent the air that evening. We couldn't do anything but sleep until the next morning when we got courage to visit our premises and maybe to salvage what could have been left behind. Actually, I had just brought in a whole lorry of charcoal and I had sold only about three sacks, the rest (120 sacks) were burnt in that store. No one got the opportunity to save or put out the fire, everything in the store was burnt.

I was not affected during the 1992 and 1997 clashes. I don't know any of our attackers. We are now used to this kind of life. It makes no difference whether or not I knew them because a normal human being should forgive. I am therefore obliged to forgive my attackers, we will forgive and live with them as we used to before. I am also ready to forgive unconditionally whoever burnt my charcoal store. I know they are just petty offenders and so they cannot even afford to compensate for anything. If I met them coincidentally, I would not question them because I will flashback bad memories. I would not like the post election events to haunt me forever, I want to be free.

I watched my charcoal store burning into ashes, as friends and neighbors watched helplessly. The only thing I managed to do was to take a photo of the dramatic fire, the onlookers and a photo of my wife near the fire. I took the photos as evidence to present it to the chairperson where I took the loan from. The loan was under my wife's name and so I had to do everything possible to get all the possible evidence which I presented to the chairperson of that society. We also recorded statements with the chief and police, it's very sad that nothing has taken effect up to this minute. No help has come our way, even the society where we had taken the loan from could not believe our story. With the little saving I had, I was forced to pay that loan to avoid seizure of my household items which were the surety of that loan. It was through God's grace that I managed to pay that loan. I have concluded that the society was never beneficial to me during that trying moment. I am now suffering since I have no source of income to keep me going. I feed my children with whatever little I get, it's just a hand to mouth ordeal.

Q: What do you think the government can do to help people live peacefully?

A: The government should rectify all the errors that occurred in the 2007 elections to avoid a repeat of the same in future. It is not our making because we used to coexist harmoniously with all the ethnic communities before the 2007 elections. It is this government that made us feel that we belonged to a certain community. They made us feel that someone stole the votes and this was the cause of the conflict. If the government fails to deal with this problem no one will vote in the near future.

Q: Were you involved in the campaigns?

A: I was not involved at all, I just voted because it is a constitutional right. I have never involved myself in any politics in.

Q: Why do you think your charcoal store was burnt?

A: It was because a certain party won elections in this area, some people thought that their votes were stolen and so the only way they had of venting out anger was through destroying people's property. I tend to think that it was their way of expressing anger. It was a pity because that wasn't the right channel. All these events happened soon after the president was declared winner.

Q: Did you identify those who attacked you?

A: I didn't identify any of them. Our businesses are located approximately 200 meters from the stage. I only heard gunshots and commotion as people ran from that stage to our premises. It was not safe at all; we all fled the scene in fear. Other gangs had also taken advantage of the situation to loot other shops.

THEY DISLOCATED MY ARM...

My name is Samuel Maina and I live in Maweni Estate in Likoni. I have lived here for close to thirty years now. Over the years people have been living peacefully as brothers and sisters. I have seen many people born and raised here and later intermarry.

After the 2007 elections, life drastically changed without residents understanding what was happening. A group of youths started looting goods from shops at Nafuu trading centre. They mostly went for television sets and video decoders. I heard them say that they were taking property that belonged to them.

However, the situation was calm before the elections. I was a staunch supporter of PNU but I would still face and chat with an ODM supporter. There was relative calm until when people cast their votes. I think trouble started after residents saw on television what was happening in Nairobi. People had been monitoring the events via television. They could see

Members of Parliament arguing with the then Chairman of the Electoral Commission of Kenya (ECK), Samuel Kivuitu. Residents here believed what the legislators alleged about favouritism and vote rigging. They believed and spread that message to others.

After the final results were announced, the next day violence, robbery and arson erupted. The most targeted people were those from the GEMA communities as it was said that the GEMA had voted for PNU candidates. GEMA are the Gikuyu, Embu, Meru and Akamba. In fact, supporters of ODM were not only targeting individuals from these communities but also their property. Demonstrators broke into their business premises and stole goods. I believe business rivalry also contributed to the violence.

When I saw that the situation had gotten out of hand, I rushed to the ferry to try and save my hand carts. I wanted to bring them home in order to save the metal bars in case they were set ablaze. But by bad luck after I had pulled one hand-cart halfway, rowdy youth emerged and surrounded me. What ensued was a total struggle. They wanted to take away my handcarts but I could not let go since I had worked so hard to have them. While one was pulling the cart the others were ransacking me. Finally, they overpowered me. That is when they took away my phone and a 1,000 shillings that I had. I also found out later that they had taken the remaining three handcarts that I had left behind.

Indeed, the post election violence affected people directly and indirectly. In my case I lost the four handcarts that I relied on to run my business near Likoni Ferry. It was unfortunate because I also dislocated my arm during the struggle. I suffered silently as my arm continued to swell because after chaos erupted, town was a no-go zone. The only option was to treat it using hot water. It was only after a week that I was able to access the hospital. I did an x-ray which showed where the problem was and it was plastered. Despite that nothing was destroyed in my home and it was a sigh of relief.

Q: *Can you forgive those who attacked you?*

A: How can you forgive a person you do not know? Was that person aware he was committing a crime? Or did someone send him to commit the crime? In the end he will be judged according to his deeds but not someone else's. If you killed someone without intent it is understandable but there is no room for those who kill on purpose.

Q: Do you know the people that attacked you?

A: No. I just saw a big group coming towards me and I paid no attention to them. What was in my mind then, was to take my hand carts home for safety. But that did not happen because I was attacked. Though these guys were armed I did not give up easily. However, even if I was attacked by my brother I would not tell because it was indeed a massive group of about fifty to a hundred people.

Q: What if somebody showed you those who attacked you?

A: If I met with them and they are more than five to fifty people, I would not really tell who among them beat me up. May be their intention was to take what I had but I resisted and that's how I got hurt. I would not ask them anything.

Q: Were you involved in the campaigns?

A: I was not involved in any way although I voted. After the elections I had to protect my business by avoiding party politics. I deal with people from different ethnic affiliations including the Luos, Digos and the Kikuyus. If you mix your business with party politics you will definitely loose customers. For instance, there were claims that one was given 100 shillings after campaigning. How long can this sustain you? Party politics is dangerous to one's business thus I played neutral.

Q: Why do you think you were attacked?

A: I think I was attacked because of my ethnic affiliation. There were claims that all the Kikuyus would vacate and leave their properties behind. Their properties would be inherited by the Coastal people because they *(Kikuyu)* had accumulated it from the region.

Q: In your view what should the Government do to restore peace in the area?

A: That's a very good question. The government is to blame for what happened. This is because this government started all this in 1992, then came ninety seven and two thousand and seven. If one had killed during the previous elections and nothing was done to him, what would prevent him from killing again in two thousand and seven? They should have dealt with the perpetrators of violence long time ago to avoid a repeat.

The common man is only incited by the leaders. If they stopped calling for mass action the youth would not have done it on their own. The government should arrest all those responsible despite their status. Discrimination will only make things worse.

ENCOUNTER WITH SABAOT LAND DEFENCE FORCE

My name is Nyota Mwero and I reside in Magongo Bokole area. I live with my wife and children in a rented house. We have neighbors who belong to various ethnic communities like the Luos, Luhyas, and Digos. Generally it is an area which is comprised of a mixture of various ethnic groups. We have good people here; they live cordially and mostly carry out their daily chores without bothering anyone.

Before 2007, everything was smooth and people lived harmoniously. Everyone travelled where they wanted to go. My life was good simply because I could get my daily bread with ease. I used to work in a certain company called ISRI star as a *turn boy*. We used to travel widely to Kakuma, Lodwar with our semi-trailer KAX 133C.

Things changed to the worst during and after the elections. We were attacked regularly during our travels, for instance, when we used the route via Salgaa. Groups of young people with guns and other crude weapons used to block the roads and attack motorists. It was during this ordeal that I was shot in my right hand and thigh.

In 1992 I was not affected in any way, and so was in 1997. It's only this time round that I was caught up in the skirmishes. It all started during the campaigns, where everyone supported his or her preferred candidates. However during the campaigns life was smooth and normal till when people started expressing their choice of candidates openly. People did that until they voted and when the results started trickling in, that was the time when the situation changed. By the time the Electoral Commission of Kenya was announcing the presidential winner, there were no vehicles on the roads.

I vividly remember the events that transpired on 5th January when we left Mombasa and headed for Mariakani Weigh Bridge to weigh our lorry. On our way we heard that the roads were impassable forcing us to make numerous stops. We did not relent on the journey and struggled up to Kitale. In Kitale, things were getting out of hand. Armed groups started attacking us but we managed to leave the town without any major incidents. This was a noble exercise since we were transporting relief food to Lodwar.

We had just left Kakuma camp when a group of men armed with guns attacked us near Marashi police station about 5 kilometers from Marashi Centre. When we enquired, we were told that it was a group called Sabaot who had ambushed people, broke into people's houses and pelted motorists with stones. That's how I happened to be one of those being attacked by the Sabaots.

Talking of forgiveness, surely even if I forgive them, where will I get my daily bread? That was my only source of income which I depended on before chaos broke out. I am asking the government to find a way to help us because presently we don't have any means of earning our daily bread. I have children and I don't know what they will eat or where I will get money to cater for their school fees.

After the attack, we were taken to Ortum hospital where they performed a first aid on me before being taken to Voi where I was admitted for one month, waiting for a surgery to remove the bullet in my thigh. The scar on rekindles bad memories and this really pains me. It is no longer business as usual for me. I am just looking up on God for divine help.

Q: In your opinion, what do you think the government can do to help people live in peace?

A: No option rather than preaching peace. Everyone should take that responsibility because this is our country which needs development and not war.

Q: were you involved in the campaigns?

A: I voted. I just voted nothing else.

Q: Why do you think you were attacked?

A: I don't know for sure and neither do I know those who attacked me.

THEY THOUGHT I WAS DEAD...

My name is Charles Nkando. I was born and brought up in Meru. Currently, I reside in Changamwe which is part of Kilindini constituency. I came here in 1993 and this is where I went to school. After completing my college studies, I got a job here in Mombasa. I worked and saved money which enabled me to start my business. I started business in Changamwe at a place called Magongo Mwisho, Portreitz Location and that's where I was living in 2007. We coexisted well with all the ethnic communities that lived there. Almost all the 42 ethnic groups of Kenya live in Changamwe.

Before 2007, life was normal and everyone carried his/her business as usual but the situation changed drastically. After the announcement of the presidential results, people emerged from all corners chanting ODM songs. They continued singing as they looted my businesses (a cosmetic shop and a chemist). I used to live behind the shops.

During the 1992 elections I was not affected but in 1997 my shops were burnt. My six-roomed building was burnt together with my property. I didn't manage to save anything. After the announcement that the current president was the winner, chaos erupted instantly. In Changamwe, they chanted ODM songs saying they wanted their property and justice to prevail. While doing that they identified all the Kikuyu, Meru and Kamba houses. They first started with Kikuyus and Merus claiming that the votes had been stolen by Kikuyus and Merus. They came into my shop, broke the doors and stole everything then set the shops ablaze. Later on they came to my house and broke the gate and the fence. They spent about twenty minutes to break the gate. When they were breaking it, ten of us including my sick mother were in the house.

We didn't know where to run to. We were forced to climb on the wall that had pieces of glass on top one after the other. I was the only man in that group of ten. The others could not climb the wall and so I had no option but to help them jump over one by one. Meanwhile, the attackers were struggling to break the gate as they chanted songs. Miraculously, they slowed down for ten minutes until I finished helping my entire family to jump over the wall. When we got to the other side of the wall, they entered my house and carried everything. Since it was on a Sunday

I had worn a T-shirt and shorts. I did not carry anything so I lost an estimated property worth almost four million Kenya shillings. I was left with nothing. As a young man aged 32 years, after struggling with my wife for almost ten years to accumulate wealth, it disappeared within ten minutes.

We ran to our neighbours (the Luos) but they chased us away. By bad luck, when we were jumping over the wall, my wife broke her arm and neighbours could not give us a piece of cloth to wrap the arm. I had no option but to tear my T-shirt and wrap her until the following day. My wife is a nurse. She works at Portreitz district hospital. We tried to call for at least an ambulance but the hospital could not provide one because of the chaos. We called the police and sadly they acknowledged they belonged to ODM so they could not come to our rescue. We managed to call one of our friends in Nairobi and asked him to call anyone he knew in Mombasa to bring us an ambulance and he did. Unfortunately, when the ambulance approached where we were, there was too much chaos which forced the ambulance to go back. We were left with no means of leaving there.

Since my wife was sick and we could not get help, we decided to run towards the Mombasa International Airport which was nearer. We tried to evade the estates while fleeing but luck was not on our side as the rowdy youths saw us. We ran through the estate using 'panya' (short-cut) routes as they followed us behind shouting, "There they are. They are the ones who stole our votes". God is great as we came across two girls fighting and tearing each other's clothes. The youths chasing us got amused by the act and stopped to watch and we got a chance to escape to the airport. I was able to save my family as I had all the proceeds I had sold that weekend totaling to about Kshs. 200,000 in my pocket. I bought tickets worth Kshs. 90,000 and boarded a plane to Nairobi. When we arrived in Nairobi, I met a police officer who happened to be a former schoolmate. He took me and my family and accommodated us until the following day. Nairobi was also chaotic so he got us a vehicle which cost me Kshs. 7,500 to ferry us home. He also organized for police escort to Thika though I paid for the escort services. From Thika onwards there was no problem so the escort returned to Nairobi as we proceeded to Meru.

I stayed in Meru for three weeks and then went back to Mombasa. When I got there, I realized that I had nothing at all except the little I had carried. People said they would inherit whatever that was left since they assumed I had died. Later on I reported to the police when I realized most of my property was within the estate. However, the police warned me against mentioning anything because it would spark off the violence again. I was told to wait and leave the matter to the police to get my property if there was anything remaining. They later advised us to forget the issue all together saying we should try to acquire more wealth as nothing was going to be found.

The police could not help us find our property. The nearest police station was Changamwe where we reported but it was sad that they didn't help us. Everything was taken by people in our estates. For instance, I had four bicycles, a TV, refrigerators and clothes. Everything was stolen. Up to this day, no substantial help has come our way. Not even the government has come to us and asked us what we lost. We have been neglected by our government. It is like we came from Somalia. We have suffered enough. There were threats in Changamwe where we lived. They used to say Kikuyus had stolen their wealth. They told me, "You are a very young man, your business has expanded. There must be a place where you get all this money, and we have also heard that Equity Bank gives you all this money." They said they would make sure they destroyed Equity Bank. They also said, "you must go and leave all this wealth to us." Because I am a businessman, I am used to taking risks and infact I was not very keen on the threats because I was used to hearing such phrases.

All the shops belonging to Kikuyus and Merus were marked with X. When they started breaking them, they left out the ones belonging to Luhyas, Luos or Kisiis and burnt those belonging to Kikuyus and Merus. This was carefully planned and executed simply because they chose what to destroy and what to leave behind. My neighbor is a Luhya, another one a Taita and on the opposite a Luo and a Meru. Funny enough, the shops belonging to other members of other communities were not touched but mine and the other Meru were destroyed. Don't you see this as something planned?

Q: Can you forgive those who caused you pain?

A: Presently, I can forgive them because we stay with most of them. I have opened another business near my house. Most of those who participated do claim that they were misled and so I feel like forgiving them anyway. They are suffering because we are the ones who used to feed them before they invaded our businesses. We are now equal and I can see they have realized their mistakes. They were cheated that if they chased us they would be rewarded but upto now no one has paid them anything. They regret. I have thus forgiven them fully. We live with them in the estate. I can't punish any of them simply because there is nothing I will gain if I did that. Most of them did not know the repercussions of their actions.

I will urge them to reflect on their lives. Politicians after every five years promise to create jobs; they also make us fight for their selfish interests. For example, they tell you to chase Kikuyus, where will they go? Kenya is ours whether one is Meru, Kikuyu, Mijikenda and so on. Even those who were given politicians' phone numbers, right now they cannot get them on phone or even in those offices they used to go. It is absurd that once a politician gets a ministerial or MP's post the salary is beneficial to him and his family alone and no outsider will gain anything from him/her. It is only a fool and a common citizen who suffer after all. The common citizen shapes the way for him but after that, this person does not gain anything.

Q: Who should be blamed for what happened?

A: When the police and journalists came the first house was already burning. The second house was mine and the police had a perfect chance to stop them but they didn't do anything. This really saddened me. I really blame the government for this because they did not take any measures to stop the menace. Shops and houses were burnt in full view of the police. I was shocked that something of this magnitude could happen in Mombasa without the NSIS knowing and other government organs.

Q: What should the government do to prevent a repeat of the violence?

A: To stop a repeat of the same the government should organize workshops to enlighten people on the pros and cons of doing such things. Secondly, the government should compensate or make sure people get their property from those who stole them.

Q: Were you involved in any way during the campaigns?

A: I did not participate in the campaigns in any way. I continued with my businesses full time.

Q: Do you know why you were attacked?

A: I believe I was attacked because of my ethnicity. From their songs, I know those who attacked me, they are our neighbours, we live with them and surely they did not come from afar!

Frightened IDPs disembark from a lorry. Photo by Antony Gitonga

THEY HAD ARROWS...

My name is Pauline Wambui from Kimangu. Originally we came from Kipkambus forest but I have grown up in Rongai. In Rongai I had a small business and was in some groups where we took loans for business. Kimangu is near a place called Kiandutura. This is where the violence started in Rongai area and after the burning we had no option but to flee. To get there, one has to go to Rongai ride a *boda boda* to a place called Line well known for illicit brews and a few meters from there is our home Kimangu.

We were living in our farm that is in the upper part of Rongai where there are many farms. The farms belong to us legally and that is why we are so pained and want to go back to our places and start lives afresh. There are many activities like farming and we get firewood from the forest and other business like selling vegetables all the way to Rongai town. I used to sell vegetables. There are many ethnic communities but the Kikuyus and Kalenjins are the majority. There are also Kisiis and the Luhyas.

During the 1992 clashes we ran to Naivasha for one month after it was reported that there would be attacks. We were not affected though there were those rumors but this time round in 2007 we were affected by the chaos.

In the 2005 referendum things were bad with abuses and threats from the Luhyas and the Kalenjins as they had joined hands against the Kikuyus and they were the ones abusing us. We just kept quiet and didn't say whether we supported Banana or Orange until we voted.

Prior to the 2007 elections there was tension, tribal splits and the locals didn't want to see Kibaki's portrait instead they wanted that one of Raila. We thought it was normal but it wasn't. During the campaigns it was very bad as there are some areas you could not go to as a PNU supporter. Like my husband was involved in the campaigns and they were nearly beaten by some Kalenjins and Luhyas in some areas after they went to campaign. They were attacked using stones though none was injured but we were later attacked on the night that the election results were announced.

On the voting day it was tense and all we did was just vote and go back home to wait for the results. After the elections ended on the 27th of December we waited though we received all kind of threats and when Kibaki won problems started and even on the eve of 24th of December we had spent the night in the church. When Kibaki was announced as the winner on Sunday 30th December 2007 at 6.00 pm we were at the centre and we celebrated apart from the Kalenjins. By 7.00 pm the chief came and told people to go home as things were not good. At 11pm, the Kalenjins started screaming and burning houses belonging to the Kikuyus. Police were called and the attackers stopped. After two hours we thought all was well but by 5.00 am, they started screaming again which is their sign to attack and the violence went a notch higher and the Kikuyus had to escape. Police came and shot one of the attackers and the Kalenjins got mad and wanted the police to bring him back alive. Things went out of hand as an elderly man called Mgongo Chuma was killed in our area. We left the body there and he stayed there for two days before he was buried one week later.

On Tuesday, the violence got intense and it was being fought during day time and one youth was killed by the Kalenjins. When police came, they accused the Kikuyus of burning their own houses and told us to collect our things and move out. However, there was a policeman at the police-post who was passing the message to the Kalenjins on when more reinforcement would come in. But I hear he was sacked after it emerged that he was behind the attacks. When the army came in, there was peace and we are getting calls telling us to go back. The attackers were beaten up so that they could stop the violence and at the moment there were Administration Police still on the ground. We were attacked twice and we first ran to the church for three days and later we went back home. After two days we were attacked again and we escaped to a nearby church before escaping to Naivasha. The attackers first looted and later burnt everything in the house. They burnt my husband's home and all the property. I only carried some clothes though I have received some assistance while here in Naivasha.

The people attacking were people we know well because they called each other by name and when we argued they called us by our names. They had arrows and they used them to injure a lot of people unlike the Kikuyus who had clubs only. I knew some of those killed i.e. a youth who was killed by an arrow and an elderly man who was killed by an axe. One of my family members was injured by the arrows during the second attack. They came through the farms and met the youth and attacked him and he was injured as he tried to escape.

The chief assisted us a lot but he was overpowered at the last minute after the police defied his orders and am told he has left the area because his life was threatened. We came to Naivasha from Rongai after I had called one of my cousins who stays here. We boarded a vehicle and since we had no money it was paid when we got here. We came with several of my relatives who had also fled the chaos and needed shelter. We were received well in Naivasha although the place was very cold. In the church where we were camping there were so many problems because there were no beddings and we slept on the floor and by the time we left I was already sick. Later people started dying of hunger and though we adjusted we are still hungry as we don't get food. In Kinungi where we stay, things are worse. We rely on casual jobs to earn a living.

We think it was organized because the attacks were well planned. Even before, we would get threats from the locals. The first chaos was orchestrated just by the locals but the second one youths were hired to beat us and that is when we ran. There were rumors of the attackers being paid for every person killed or house burnt and that youths were getting between Kshs. 1,000 and Kshs. 2,000. Among the attackers who were killed the money was found in their pockets. We are not sure if politicians were involved because the man we elected as MP was new to us though the locals were for him. In addition, they did not support the Kikuyu councilor who we were supporting as they preferred a Kalenjin councilor.

Q: Do you think you can forgive those who attacked you?

A: We can forgive them but they have to first return all that they took from us. Indeed it would be painful to see your neighbor with the things he took from your home.

Q: Would you go back to your home?

A: I can go back because we are dying of hunger here and we are made to understand that security has been intensified. The reason I haven't gone back is that we have no food and the little money we get we use it for the very reason. We don't have fare to go back and that is why we are asking the government to come to our aid.

Q: What would you do if you meet your attackers?

A: If I were to meet with those who attacked us, I wouldn't speak to them and first they should return what they took from us before I even think of talking to them. They should return our goods and later repent and act by action rather than blaming Satan as they always do for what they did to us.

Q: Has your life changed much?

A: My life has really changed. I have lost so much weight. I am psychologically tortured, traumatized and for the last three weeks I have not slept well. The children are demanding to know why they have not gone back to school or to our home. One is in class one and he refuses to go to school as he wants to go back to his home.

There are many problems because we think a lot and even if I want to go back I need a donkey to restart my job which is money. We need food to survive and even if I go back where do I start? The government should therefore give us a small token and I will go back immediately. Though little, this can help one settle and restart our lives afresh. The government has abandoned us because where we stay we never get any assistance despite handing our names to the chief. We do not get any food or money from the government and we are many IDPs who are suffering.

We stay at a centre together with other IDPs from various parts of the country. They too escaped because of the violence and by looking at it you can see that there are problems. To make matters worse, my husband is not working, he stays at home.

Q: In 2012 there will be elections. What can the government do to stop such violence?

A: They should talk to people and offer security. Police should be mixed up and mainly hold dialogue among the youths who were involved in the chaos.

Q: Politicians have been accused of abandoning you for politics. Is it true?

A: It is true because the two big leaders were together and never fought but the local people were split and things will never be the same for them again.

Q: If you were to meet President Kibaki, what would you like him to do?

A: He should help us and give us security because we are always in fear and thus one cannot invest in anything lest it's burnt.

Q: Did the police give you ample security during the chaos?

A: Yes they assisted us but later changed. During the second round of clashes they accused the Kikuyus of burning their own houses. The police moved to the attackers' side instead of protecting us.

Q: *Tell me about all the problems that you are currently facing?*

A: It's mainly food, diseases and schooling for my children. Like in third term (2008) the headmaster sent away our children saying that we had money and had refused to pay. Even my daughter has skin infections on the head and has yet to receive any treatment. The area DC has never visited us to establish if we have any problems at all. The only person who has assisted us is the local councilor who even gives us food and money.

Q: *What is your message to Kenyans on the need to stay peacefully?*

A: They should fear God and by doing so they wouldn't dare to kill one another and people will live peacefully.

A Mid 40's Old Man who lived in Turbo for 23 Years

My name is Paul Mbogo Wainana and I came from Eldoret North constituency in Turbo. I was a trader who bought maize and took it to the National Cereals Board. The chaos started on the 29th of December 2007 when a prominent politician from the Rift Valley was at the KICC arguing. The youth got agitated and started destroying fridges in town. That is the time my pastor called to tell me that things were bad.

Turbo is in Eldoret North constituency and 32km from Eldoret town and along the road to Uganda. Most Kikuyus living there are in business. I went there in 1984 to visit my sister and later went back to Kipkambus in Uasin Gishu and then went to Onfa. In 1992 my brother escaped from the area when he got a job in Oserian Flower Farm. I started staying in Turbo in 1988, married and settled there for all those years. There are many ethnic groups like Kalenjins, Luhyas, Kisii and basically all other communities. I used to sell maize to the cereal board and also beans where I would deliver to united millers store. We would buy the produce from the farmers, dry it up and sell it to the millers. The business was able to feed my family and educate my children. My son is in form four and he went to school with no problems. Plus the younger one and I even fed them well with no problems at all.

During the 2005 referendum there was tension though there was no violence but the Kalenjins were supporting Orange and believed all Kikuyus were for Banana. At the time there was word that if Orange won, they would take over the government and they started to threaten us. A petrol station in Turbo and some stores were nearly burnt. There came a man who threatened us and a Kamba man who came there was so happy and nearly beat us up. But no problem came up.

During the 2007 campaigns there were problems mainly for those people in the interior. As in any election there is always violence and people are killed and houses burnt, but the 2008 chaos was serious as even Turbo town was affected. It was peaceful during the campaign time though I feared getting involved. Market days were very quiet and we did not discuss our votes. We told them we were to vote for Raila though they never believed us. They openly told us that if Kibaki won there would be violence no matter what. On 26th December 2007 I went to Sugoi primary which is owned by a Mr Muchemi and one of my nieces was there and there was so much tension. On our way back, our bike got spoilt and the Kalenjins were asking us why we had not left.

The Voting Day was quite okay and there was a high turn out and even the weak and the old ones were there. I voted in Western Kenya for fear and that is where many of us who lived in Turbo voted. Just before the results were announced, Raila first led then Kibaki overturned things and that is the time violence erupted on the 29th of December 2007. At that time I was in Kilimani in Lugari buying maize as I never thought things would be serious. Then I received a call and was told that my wife was out and the kids were alone but a neighbor picked them and took them to the police station where we met.

There was a lot of destruction as they spoilt many things. They burnt houses, businesses and petrol stations belonging to Kikuyus. They also burnt maize in stores but their target were things belonging to Kikuyus. In Turbo, not many people were killed as we ran away but there is one man who had been left at home as he had had an accident. They killed and burnt him as he could not escape. I lived in town near a place called Roadblock. They broke into my house, stole some things and left others. They also burnt the maize in the stores. They spoilt a lot of things like fridges and stole from hotels. They also destroyed a lot of property, burnt houses and hotels. They came in big numbers and it was something that they seemed to have arranged.

My stay at the police station was a painful reminder as we had a hard time though we had a lot of food in our stores. The millers were closed over the December holidays and it all went to waste. We had no money and at the police station things like sugar and food were very expensive. It was hard to know if those who beat us were ferried in as the Kalenjins were so many and ruthless and even the Luhyas joined them to beat us. They broke into our houses and looted before burning them. We could not thus face them. The officer in charge of the police station even said that the junior officers were not obeying him. When the election results were announced, there was tension with reports of an attack and a melee ensued. And in the process my wife and child went missing. I could not trace her and the neighbors didn't know where she was. One officer even threatened me as I searched for my wife and he told me that it was our own making and should therefore suffer.

We stayed there until the roads were opened as they had been closed down using poles and stones by youths. We left when the GSU came in and later the army used their trucks to transport most of us out of that place. I had managed to save some properties and the GSU assisted us to recover the rest including a phone that had been stolen and we used a pick-up to transport them to the police station. I later used the trailer after the driver assisted us for free and carried our properties while being escorted by the army. We would consult if the roads were okay and that is how I arrived in Naivasha on the 17th of January 2008 after so much suffering. We went to the police station Red Cross came later. They gave us open tents but they were not enough. It was also cold as a result of rain and I developed chest problems which I am still nursing up to now.

Things were very hard and we stayed in Vineyard Church before getting a house or even a job. I got a job at Wild Fire Flower Farm and the wages were low at Kshs. 120 per day and we could not survive on this. I had to feed myself and also my family and most of the time we went hungry. I received assistance from my pastor who gave me some money and I added some more and bought some second hand clothes and started hawking them. Like now things are hard as the market is bad and we are no longer getting food from the churches yet my children want to eat. My first born has been sent home over school fees and some teachers won't understand. They say that we have been given Kshs. 10,000. But the Integrated IDPs are not getting any help and I even went to hospital over the chest problem and the Red Cross refused to assist us. There are so many problems and we are really suffering. Right now we are asking the government to give us the Kshs. 10,000 that they have been giving other IDPs. The government has abandoned us because those IDPs in the camps are given food and shelter plus the Kshs. 10,000 but we are not getting the same.

In my view, I think we were attacked because we are hard working people. We were involved in many income generating activities like buying maize as I used to. Even as visiting communities we over-did them and I think that these people were jealous of our diligence.

Q: Do you know the people who attacked you?

A: Those who beat us we knew some of them while others were strangers. But after results were announced, so many people were ferried in and they attacked from different sides. The reports that some politicians were involved are true because the attackers would bow whenever they saw a promiment politician's portrait.

Q: Are you ready to forgive?

A: I can forgive but even the Lord's Prayer says that people are forgiven if they repent. I am ready to forgive because I am a Christian but I cannot go back because of the fear. The problem is that though they say that things are over they still have bad feelings. They treat us with suspicion and even people in Turbo have taken over our plots and we cannot take them back. We cannot therefore live together as they have even refused to return what they took from us. I can forgive if they can return the looted things.

Previously, in 1992 we were in a place called Onfa and we heard what happened in other areas. We talked with my brother over the phone and he told me what was happening and warned me from coming to the area as strangers were being killed. In 1992, 1997 and now in 2008, there has always been chaos in these areas and especially during the elections.

Q: Can you return back to Turbo?

A: I don't think I can go back to Turbo from what I saw and my grandmother was also evicted from the area some years ago. Though I have lived there all my life, what I saw was bad and I will never forget it and cannot therefore go back.

Q: *How has your life changed since the violence started?*

A: My life has changed since the violence as we were used to looking for food and now we are getting aid, we can't work and minors want to eat no matter what. I have so many problems as we can't feed, dress and do other things as getting a job is even a problem. The government should come in and assist us as we are undergoing untold suffering.

Q: *What can the government do so that we do not experience such chaos again?*

A: The government should have a new constitution so that we shall no longer have any more violence again.

Q: *What should be done to those people who beat you and the organizers?*

A: They should return what they took and repent. I am saved and the word of God says that we should forgive and they should repent while they mean it.

Q: *And how can the government assist?*

A: The government should assist us with resettlement, and give us money to restart so that we can start businesses because as of now we are staying with relatives. They should maybe build us houses and give us cattle and later we can repay them in future.

Q: *Is it true that the provincial administration has failed to assist you?*

A: The only person who assists us is the D.O (1) as others ignore us and we have so many problems.

Q: *Lastly what is your message to Kenyans at large?*

A: My message is that if the attackers have surrendered we can forgive them. The Government should also show by action that it is ready to assist us by coming to our assistance and alleviate the suffering.

MY HEART IS NOT AT PEACE

My name is Jane Wambui Njuguna from Kaptagat Eldoret and I am fifty years old. I was born and brought up in a place called Kaptagat forest before I later moved to the town centre. I bought a plot and resided there and was comfortable and loved the place. I was a trader who dealt in maize, beans and gunny bags. I sold my produce in different parts of the country.

When multiparty politics started and Kibaki and others started DP, we Kikuyus from Rift Valley went to see Kibaki in Jacaranda Hotel. We talked to him and he told us to promote the party as Matiba was then abroad and he told us that they were brothers. I was elected as a women chairlady in Uasin Gishu a position I have held for ten years. When Kibaki joined NARC, I followed him and campaigned and later moved to PNU where I was more active by distributing T-shirts. I was known all over as Mama TV and that is how the Kalenjins came to hate me. I left Eldoret in January 14th 2008 as people were asking me what I was doing there. I said that I would be the last to leave. I passed the message to various ministers and warned them that we would die but they failed to act. However, I was saved by the Kalenjins who told me that my life was in danger as there was a plan to kill me.

Eldoret is a town with a mixture of all ethnic groups but the biggest traders are the Kikuyus, Kisii and Luhyas. It has been a good town until the last clashes where violence broke out displacing us. Earlier there were clashes but they were mainly in the farms, away from the town.

During the 1992/97 clashes, violence was in the farms but it was peaceful in the town. But my parents were affected in the 1997 violence and their house burnt by the Kalenjins. They are always talking about land and this has been a burning issue. We bought land from a white man but this was later taken by the Kalenjins yet it was legally ours.

In the 2005 referendum, things were bad and that is why we felt left out as the government seemed to have forgotten us. We campaigned for Banana which was defeated. Each community leaned on certain sides and this led to other communities avoiding the Kikuyus but we are hard working people who are ready to invest anywhere.

In 2007 the campaign was hard and in Rift Valley it was even harder. We never got campaign money and all we did was to assist as the money was given to other people. Before the elections, I talked to the youths and told them to register as voters as this was the only way of exercising their rights. I told them that without voters' card they could not change anything and I gave them examples. This changed them and many decided to register as voters. I moved from place to place although nobody recognized my efforts and my love for Kibaki. I even told him once when he was campaigning that he would lead us and he told me to continue praying for him.

On the voting day I went to the polling stations late because I am old and the queues were long and the largest number of voters were Kikuyus. I finally voted and this was the best election that I have ever seen due to the high turn out. All the Kikuyus came out to vote and we voted for a Mr. Jonathan Bii who was opposing Hon. William Ruto. I now believe that elections were rigged as we fully supported Bii but he lost in an unclear manner.

After the voting we went home and heard that Raila was leading with over one million votes. We were very uncomfortable as we saw signs of attack since during campaign time, some leaders used hate songs that were openly sung. They were threatening songs, like a Luhya song always sung in burial. They always sung the songs which said that Kibaki should go back to Othaya. During the launch of PNU, we were attacked by Luos using stones. We saw all signs that we would be beaten. When finally Kibaki was announced as the winner we did not celebrate as things got bad and fear was all over as houses were burnt. It's a very painful memory.

In town, all businesses were closed down and people stayed indoors. There was no celebration and things were bad. I received reports that the house of the area Democratic Party (DP) chairman had been burnt. I stayed in Langas estate and at one time some youths came asking for my place but they were misled. They left after being told that I had sold the plot. My son who was there said that the faces were new and he told me that I should leave as I was an unpopular figure. I didn't sleep in my house for the following days and after the threatening messages I decided to leave the place. I have since gone back to Eldoret but my heart is not at peace.

In Eldoret all leaders were marked and later all the Kikuyus. We were once told that a prominent politician from the Rift Valley said that all the Kikuyus would go home in one pick up meaning in 'ashes'. Roads were closed after that and it was impossible to even leave the place. From where I live, houses belonging to Kikuyus were burnt and I could see smoke all over. I called a powerful politician in the current government, though getting credit was impossible, and we started seeing helicopters.

I even called another legislature who said that women and children could go to churches. The army came in and since then there was a little bit of peace but people had taken refuge at the Eldoret showground and at the police station. The burnt church at Kiambaa was in the farm and we just heard what happened as I didn't go there.

Kenya Assemblies of God Church in Kiambaa destroyed. Photo by Kimani Njogu

In the camps like the show ground, things were bad. Everyone was really moved. We saw some people who had acquired a lot of wealth saying their houses had been reduced to ashes. It was a terrible place. People had many problems. For instance, living in a single tent with all their families. They were living very hard lives with no privacy and since it rained it became even harder to get sleep on the ground. Those wounds are too fresh to heal. Maybe it's only God who can heal them.

I escaped from there and by the time I came, roads were now open though we left in groups. We left with some of my relatives and headed to Githunguri to other relatives. Later I came to Naivasha but didn't go back to the IDP camp. Life was difficult for us, as we have not received any assistance from the government apart from the churches which have given us food and clothes. We are renting our houses something I have not done for over thirty years.

My life has really changed. It is hard. I am still worried though we have peace here. I have gone to Eldoret twice but I am not settled and I am always fearful. I always leave the place in a hurry for Naivasha. We have learnt so much about the Kalenjins. They always carry each other in vehicles with twigs and we know that they are going to attack and also they are very secretive. The attackers were people well known to us and even after some were arrested, they were easily identified.

Q: Do you think politicians were involved?

A: I believe that the politicians participated because the youths could not start such violence without money for fuel and for food. This was something that was well planned and funded.

Q: Can you forgive those who destroyed your property?

A: You forgive if someone repents but how can you forgive someone who has not repented? Again you can forgive someone but the picture that you saw will always remain in your mind. I still fear when I think about Eldoret. All the attacks were organized and the organizers should be arrested for killing and burning and the law should take its course and punish those responsible.

The government should assist us because we were beaten for supporting it. It should do something to encourage us so that come another election we can vote. As at the moment we are traumatized and we seem to have been forgotten. We assisted Kibaki whenever he came to Uasin Gishu but he has forgotten us. Let him think of the people who do not want to go back. The government should buy us land and resettle us.

The integrated IDPs in Naivasha are from all areas of Kenya. We have filled some forms and handed them to the provincial administration. Let the government buy us land and resettle us. We bought our land in Rift Valley with our own finances and we were never given by Kenyatta as many say. The same Kalenjins sold us their land and later complained that we had taken away their land.

Q: Can you go back to Eldoret?

A: Oh! My God, I cannot. The government should come to us so that they can know what we want instead of forcing us to go back to that area. I have done enough of running and I cannot therefore go back there again.

Q: What can the government do for people to stay in peace?

A: In my opinion, the government should check and confirm that we bought the land. The Kalenjins should also be reminded that we bought that land and there are no free things. All communities should live as friends and brothers as we coexisted during the colonial times. However it is us the parents who are to blame for inciting our kids who have lived with each other peacefully.

Q: In 2012, there will be another election, what can the government do to stop any violence?

A: ECK should be overhauled. All vote counting should be done at the polling station whenever one votes. Because if one feels that he will lose he will start fighting and thus some people will fear to vote.

Q: What about a new constitution?

A: The new constitution should be dealt with by the learned. It should unite all Kenyans and discard tribalism.

I Cannot Forgive

My name is Judith Atieno from Karachuonyo and I came to Naivasha looking for a job. I am currently working at Sher Agencies flower farm. At the Sher farm I work as a flower harvester. I used to live in Oserian and later moved to Karagita where I have lived for seven years. The place is on your way from Naivasha town and near the flower farms. Many communities live there including the Luos, the Luhyas among others. Most of those who live there are the flower farm workers because many companies don't have housing and thus the workers stay there as it's cheap. I came here in 1999 and got a job at Oserian farm and worked for one year before going to Sher Agencies. I lived with my family members at the time.

Before the post election violence, things were okay in Naivasha and we lived peacefully with other communities like the Kikuyus. I could even discipline a Kikuyu child and things would be okay. During the 2005 constitutional referendum I had gone back to my rural home. The campaigns were however not violent though people argued between the Orange and the Banana groups and we kept from each other.

The 2007 election campaigns were okay but our Kikuyu neighbours turned against us when it came to Raila and Kibaki. They warned us that we would leave as the Luos had boasted that they would not pay house rent if Raila won. The Kikuyus told us that we would leave the town whether Kibaki won or lost. Before elections there were no chaos but afterwards, the chaos started. I was involved in the campaigns as I was a chief campaigner for ODM. We campaigned using pick-ups and we always sung Luo songs in support for Raila. We insulted each other. Raila was insulted that he was an uncircumcised man. There were however no chaos until after the elections. Nobody was beaten; only that people abused each other. I voted in Karagita at around 6.00 pm and returned back home. There was however a problem at the polling station as there was an ODM and PNU line and the police never intervened as the Luos could not stand behind a Kikuyu.

That night after voting we waited to know what was going on and we waited for three days as they counted the votes. We were at work when the violence started and one Luo man who was a chief campaigner for ODM was beaten up in Karagita and died. Later on it was said that Raila was leading with I think 4,000 or 40,000 votes and that is when violence started. They threw stones into our business and mainly where my husband had a tailoring shop.

When the results were announced there was violence and we left from work. We were called from our work places and told that violence had broken in Karagita and we should therefore go and pick all our things. On the way the driver warned us that things were bad as the Luos and the Kalenjins were being killed and we should therefore alight from the vehicle and avoid the area. We insisted and on the way we found Kikuyus armed with all kind of weapons and they attacked the Luos, killing them. What happened next was that we did not sleep as one Luo was killed after being thrown out of the car. He was beaten up, slashed on the head and vomited before passing away.

The following day we slept at Sher Agencies and as I was preparing to go to work I thought about my shop and house in Karagita. At the stage I found two men who asked me whether I knew where my brother was. He had relocated from the rural home to come and live in Naivasha. He even got married here. I told them he had run away as he knew of the clashes. They told me that he had been killed and I took a car to where my brother was killed. I was dropped midway and walked to where I lived. They had slashed his hand and stuffed his private parts in his mouth. It was a terrible site and I don't know how I walked back before a flower truck gave me a lift to Sher and told my husband. I couldn't take him to the mortuary as I had no transport. At 6.00 pm, two other people came and told me that since my brother died at 10.00 am he was still at the spot covered in blood and flies.

The following day he was still there and some dogs were eating his private parts. One police officer told me that my brother had already died and he had taken the body to the mortuary in Naivasha. The body stayed there for one week before we took him home for burial, as we are orphans. My slain brother's three year old son saw everything. Up to now he is still in trauma and the best I can do is just pray for him. The wife watched as her husband was killed as he came to check on me at around 8.00 am. The wife was almost raped but they stopped because she was pregnant. She told them that she was ailing and she was taken to where the other IDPs were.

We sought refuge where we worked, as Luos were being killed. Life was hard as we had no food and people went to live with their relatives and since I didn't have any relatives I hang around the security gates. Later on we left for the school where we camped and then the government sent more buses that took us to Kedong camp. Life in "Darfur" was okay as there was food and other things. Some people who worked in other farms also came there and got food. All of our property was looted and others burnt. I think we were beaten because we voted for Raila. I don't know the attackers as they were different people and new in Naivasha.

I witnessed an incident where one person was thrown out of a car and killed near the road side. Some people were brought in to beat the Luos and then those who came from Kisumu and other areas incited the locals to beat us as they had also been beaten where they had come from. It is true politicians were involved because there were claims that a certain politician was the one who sponsored the violence as we had voted for the current MP though he was not in ODM.

I can't forgive as I haven't gotten someone to counsel me from what I saw. If I can get someone to counsel me I would consider forgiving them. If possible, the government should call us together and reconcile us so that we can forgive each other. We should talk about the problems we are having and the government should bring us together to solve this problem. For those who killed and stole from us, the government should make sure that we get those things back as the people who took them are here in Karagita. The law should also take its course.

I cannot go back to Karagita for all my life. I cannot forget what I saw and whenever I pass there I still have the painful memories of what happened to me and my brother. Since that day, my life changed and if I can get counseling maybe I can change. There is a big responsibility on my part in terms of my brother's son who is mentally disturbed and I don't have parents. My brothers' wife gave birth to a deformed baby and they all rely on me and from what I earn; we are barely surviving. My husband stays in the house and just relies on me. We are around nine people in the house and they all rely on me for support.

The government has forgotten us since they gave us Kshs. 10,000 only. They have never met us and don't know how we are living, whether we died or how our lives are. They should assist us further as they said that the Kshs. 10,000 was for transport. They should talk to donors and think of how they can assist us restart our businesses.

Our main problem as a family is survival, things are difficult and even sometimes neighbours come to our aid as the economy has changed for the worst. The house rent is Kshs. 1,500, flour is around Kshs. 35 per kilo and we use 3 kgs per day so that people can get enough.

In my view, to avoid a repeat of the violence before the 2012 elections, the government should be keen and offer security and make sure that they deal with those trying to cause violence. The police did not assist us because when my brother was killed, they were there and said that they could not take him to hospital as he had not died. One of them warned me that the same thing would befall me if I continued to argue with him.

The provincial administration never assisted as people were butchered as they watched.

Q: In your opinion, what can the government do in future to avoid such killings?

A: In my view, the government has crooks, especially here in Naivasha. In 2012, there should be tight security as the police laxed during the past elections. Next time they should be ready and strict.

Q: What is in your mind now?

A: My life will change when we live comfortably with my relatives. If I can get assistance, I would appreciate as I still have a loan and all the salary goes towards servicing it. I am also asking for assistance in counseling my nephew and more assistance in general so that we can live well.

Q: How do you feel when you meet the Kikuyus?

A: I feel bad and pained from what they did to my brother and if I can get a counselor I would appreciate, because even when I go to church I forget the teachings and the images of dogs feeding on my brother always come back to my mind.

Q: What would you like to tell Kenyans about peace?

A: It is good to see the peace campaigns going on and all of us should be called and have discussions rather than road shows.

Q: How is life in Kamere and are you still in fear?

A: I still live in fear as I have received letters warning me of death and after 6.00 pm, I am always afraid of being attacked. At Kedong camp I received a warning that they wanted my head and that of my husband. The letter also said that they were waiting for the Kshs. 10,000. Even after going to the police I did not get any assistance as they told me to wait. The policeman in Kongoni was a Kikuyus and he told me that such investigations took long before completion.

Q: As we wind up, what is your parting shot?

A: We should forgive each other but first we should be put together so that we can have dialogue. In many times it's the Kikuyu who sell food and it is time the government brought us together so that we can coexist like we used to before the violence.

WE WERE CALLED MADOADOA

My names are Julius Mwangi Njuguna and I come from Ainamoi in Kericho. At the moment I am in Naivasha town. I was born in Kericho, went to school there, married and later started business. Kericho is my home. I used to live in Kericho Township doing business on Moi Road. I was also a shoemaker. I came to Naivasha when violence erupted in Kericho after the area MP was killed. That was when I decided to leave the place and come here. I was welcomed by good Samaritans with whom I still live.

Ainamoi is mostly inhabited by the Kipsigis. They are the ones we used to live and work together with for a long time. We did not have problems. We only experienced problems after the referendum: women were killed and found without breasts. The DC stationed there at that time was transferred and another one took over. When he came we had a meeting with him and they said that they did not want the Kikuyu DC to address them. He said that he would investigate the murders and establish the root cause. After the DC addressed us they started singing in their mother tongue in the presence of some local politicians. After some days we went back for another meeting and that is when they said that there was a businessman who had bought those women's breasts. In the meeting it was passed that the businessman leaves the town. Residents searched for him at his business premises but he was nowhere to be found. The police guarded his property and as a result he sold some of his businesses and went to Nairobi. Later it was alleged that the Kisiis (since the businessman was a Kisii) were bringing in Chang'aa and they were also accused of witchcraft so that the Kipsigis' cows would not produce milk. Therefore, they decided to force the Kisiis out of the town. They were removed from every estate in Kericho.

We felt that this was just a cover up for the things they were planning in order to avoid a leakage. Later on we had several parties that came up. The ODM were looking for their contestant and the PNU too. I was the chief campaigner for Noah Too in ODM since we had agreed as Kericho residents that we would vote someone who would cater for our interests and among all the other contestants we felt that Noah Too was the one who would cater for us. Therefore we united and voted for Noah Too but when we voted him in, the residents there said that Too could not lead them. They said they wanted someone of their own who would remove the *madoadoa* (stains) and therefore they decided that we would leave Kericho, so most of them voted for the late David Kimutai Too. We also needed a councilor for Biashara Ward and there was one we wanted but the Kipsigis voted for someone else. During the election we did not vote for David Kimutai Too as our MP and Raila as our president; instead we voted for PNU. All along we had been told that whether we win or not we would leave. After campaigns we voted and waited. David Too was voted as the MP for Ainamoi. At that time we were not conducting our businesses; instead we were all awaiting the presidential poll results. At the time we stayed at a place called Kwa Councilor Ngugi.

On the day that the election results were announced at around 3.00 pm a certain politician *(now deceased)*, came with ten vehicles carrying youths and they went past where we were. At around 5.00 pm it was announced that Kibaki had won. We started celebrating and even walked for more than 1km as we celebrated for more than half an hour. At around 6.00 pm, violence erupted and houses were burnt. The whole night was filled with violence. At around 8.00 pm we heard that Kericho town was a no-go-zone. There were gunshots at Kericho Cooperative Bank, Equity Bank and near the supermarket. The youths wanted to loot these places. Several people were killed by the police and this continued till dawn. I personally witnessed over ten people dead and four being gunned down. Some were my friends but at that time we were divided. We were either in ODM or PNU and the attackers were ODM supporters. These people had arrows and by bad luck they met with the police who shot three of them and another one was shot later. After some days violence stopped and calm returned. We thought of staying for some days and assess the situation while we camped at the DC's place: men, women, children and people with disabilities. But I still used to sleep in my house. I noticed that things were changing for the better and I told my wife that we ought to take all our property to the DC and bring it back when the violence stopped. If the violence continued we would keep the property there since I could not believe that I would leave Kericho.

On 3rd February 2008, the area MP David Kimutai Too was killed in Eldoret. I had gone to town to continue with my business when violence erupted. I put all my items in the store and ran to the police station. When we got there we were a group of people. We stayed there for more than two hours so that the police could differentiate those who were attacking others and those who were there seeking security. Some people went to the OCPD's house at night and killed the policeman who was guarding the Ainamoi DO and ran away with four guns. The situation became worse and they declared that no Kikuyu would be left in the town. The DC availed vehicles. The African Highland and Unilever also gave out their vehicles. The vehicles were to be used to transport us from Kericho. The Kisiis were taken to their rural home while the Kikuyus were taken to Nakuru. These people had declared that the MP who had died would not be buried when the Kikuyus were still in Kericho. If there would be any Kikuyu, he would be killed. When the MP was killed, they hacked one man to death and shot another with an arrow. He is currently at Nakuru Show Ground.

Three days after the announcement of the election results, my brother who stays at Likia Farm was shot with an arrow. As he was being taken to the hospital the roads had been blocked and therefore no car was able to go to Nakuru. They took him to Mau Narok where he died. When he died his wife called me and told me about it. I told her that we would go there but we were not able to do so since the road had been blocked. She called me again at around 6.00 pm and asked us not to go there because it was dangerous. They said that they would carry on with the funeral without us so most of our family members did not attend the funeral. He was buried by his wife and their neighbours. I do not know those who killed my brother but they must have been Kipsigis since Likia Farm belongs to Kikuyus and neighbouring Mauche belongs to the Kipsigis. After the election they left Mauche and went to fight the Kikuyus. He was killed at his home.

On the fourth day after the MP was killed I realized that the situation was not changing so I got a lorry and carried all my property to Nakuru Show Ground. That is when I looked for the means to go to Gilgil where I have a piece of land at Mbaruk.

In Ainamoi, I removed half of my property and took it to the DC's place. The rest was still in the house because I thought that we would go back. In the house I left our clothes and three beds. I did not carry any of the items I used at my business. I have never gone back to Ainamoi to know what happened to this property. I had three machines at the business and other materials for shoe making but I did not carry any of these items.

A friend of mine, a Kisii, was killed by the police in Ainamoi and also a son of one of my friends was also killed. There is one friend of mine by the name Kuria who was shot with an arrow. He is at the Nakuru Show Ground. Another man who was a very close friend of mine since we were young, was attacked and seriously injured when it was announced that the MP had been killed. We left him at Kericho Nursing Home still undergoing treatment and at the moment I don't know his state. I have a wife and five children. I have a son who sat for KCPE in 2007 and has not been able to get his results. He was not able to join secondary school. At the moment he is still at home and I hope he will join secondary school next year. I have not been able to get the results due to the challenges we faced since we became IDPs.

Since the start of multi-party politics, I have always been in the opposition. I like fighting for democracy and our rights. In the 2002 elections in Ainamoi I supported NARC. We worked together and ensured that the current president won. During the referendum I supported the Banana Group and when we came to the election time I supported PNU but the Kipsigis and the ones we worked together with in 2002 supported ODM. In Ainamoi the Kikuyus and the Kisiis were supporting PNU. Even if the ODMwould have won, they still had plans to take our land.

Previously in 1992 we had a lot of problems as these people saw that the then president would be voted out by the citizens, through Ford Asili and Ford Kenya. They started violence so that the then president would remain in power. I remember some friends were involved in this violence as leaders. In the year 1997 these same people were involved in the violence as they believed Moi would never leave the seat. However, in 2002 Moi relinquished power. They now wanted Uhuru to take over because they said that they wanted the person Moi had appointed. Therefore these clashes are not triggered by either land or tribes but by politics. I don't understand how we live peacefully with these people only to realize that I am a Kikuyu and that he is a Kalenjin during the elections. Politics starts with our leaders. I have noted that the people who incite Kenyans are never convicted but those who were incited are the ones who get convicted. I therefore suggest that if one incites another to cause violence, the inciter should be convicted and sentenced to death. Politicians should talk of how they will help to develop the country but not incite citizens against fellow citizens.

In my opinion, the reason why we were attacked was because after the referendum, people from Nyanza wanted leadership and the Kipsigis wanted the land. They had been promised land. We would ask them why they were doing it now as they say that they do not work together with those who are uncircumcised. They told us they wanted the person from Nyanza because he would be the one who would remove us from there and ensure that we go to Nyeri. Therefore, we had to leave that place as it had been planned way before the election.

A day after the announcement of the results, people came in to burn our house. I pleaded with them not to and I had a good look at them. This violence was planned since the first person I saw was carrying an arrow to scare us away, another one was carrying a lit lamp and another one was carrying a black book recording those who were participating and the houses they were to burn. They also have plots and had to ensure that they did not burn houses of the people from theircommunity. I looked at them but did not recognize anyone. They were networked. There were those who were telling them where the police were and directing them where to go. In fact there were rumours that some people *(names withheld)* were coordinating the attacks. These people had a base at Kipkelion and Matobo.

Forgiveness is difficult on one side but it is easy on the other. If someone accepts his mistakes and asks for forgiveness, then it becomes easier to forgive. But those who attacked us have not accepted their mistakes. How then can we forgive them? I don't think we can forgive them since one cannot force them to accept forgiveness while they have not accepted their mistakes. So forgiveness has to be two sided. Two people have to come together and the offenders say that they did this and that, the reason they did it and ask for forgiveness. We can easily forgive them because we are human beings and have to forget but these people have not come out and accepted what they did. Yet some other people are asking us to forgive them. I don't think that is right.

In Naivasha, living as integrated IDPs, we are facing a lot of challenges which are not caused by the government but by the civil servants. The first office that should deal with problems is the office of the chief, the office of the DO 1 who is involved with internal issues and the office of DO 2 who is involved with special programmes. What has really annoyed me is that since we came here the government has been issuing donations to the IDPs but they do not get to the needy. As the Chairman of the integrated IDPs, I know we have people with different problems. We have the aged, the widowed and orphans amongst us. In general, people have different problems. They lost everything and came here empty handed but when they go to the hospital, they are asked for twenty shillings for the card whereas some may have slept on empty stomachs. One day we went to look for food at the DO 1's place and he told us that food had been brought and we went to the chief but before we got there the DO asked me for the list of the people who wanted food. The list I had given him at first had 195 people but when we got to the Kabati Chief's office we were over 400.

We had nine *debes* (buckets) of food. When I saw the nine debes I was astounded because I did not know who to give and who to leave out. We stayed there with my panel and I told them it was not right. I didn't understand how the government could issue nine debes to be distributed to over 400 people. I asked the panel that we go back to the DO to ask for advice. We started having differences amongst ourselves. An officer from the special programmes came and I asked him for assistance in issuing the food. He advised us to take back the food so that the government would be pushed to bring more food that would assist the people. That was my suggestion too but my panel had a problem with that. We took back three debes which were in a sack. When we took it back, I heard that those who were left behind shared the food amongst themselves. My wish was to take back the food to the DO so that we could have enough evidence to ascertain whether that was the food they had issued us. The food was divided so that we would not have enough evidence.

Q: How many integrated IDPs are here and what kind of assistance would you want to get from the government?

A: We are over 400 integrated IDPs. Some have not been registered. I would request the government to add the amount they are giving. People have different problems and one cannot start a business with only ten thousand shillings. There are people I have mentioned who are over 70 years old, they of course cannot start businesses. We have widows who were only expecting to get something from their husbands who were killed.

The integrated IDPs come from different parts; Eldoret, Ainamoi, Turbo and other affected parts of Rift Valley. I was involved in business and if am to be assisted in business then I will gladly go on well. Some cannot get into business and the government should assist those who lost their bread winners and are aged to get the necessary assistance. The widows and orphans should also be assisted according to their status. These people are a burden to the churches and the residents here. Since life has to go on, the government needs to establish a proper plan to assist such people.

Q: What can the government do to avoid such kind of violence in future?

A: As I said earlier, in the constitution that the government wants to institute, there should be a clause that states that politicians who go to ask for votes and incite people together with those who carry out the attacks should be sentenced to death. This is because if these people were not incited, they could not have carried out the attacks. They get motivation from those who incite them. Those who were killing come from poor families. They were being given ten thousand shillings and a vehicle to go and fight. So this is something that was arranged by these leaders.

Q: Do you have anything else to add?

A: The integrated IDPs have had problems with the chief's office and the DO 2 office who deal with special programmes. We don't understand what is happening yet we have suffered enough and we want to follow the right procedure. Therefore, we would like to request you to report in the newspaper so that the whole world can know that the integrated IDPs in Naivasha have suffered enough and the government is not assisting us; only the church and the Naivasha residents are assisting us. It seems like we have been forgotten.

MY CHILDREN SCREAM AT NIGHT

My name is Agnes Wangui Maina and I come from Eldoret but at the moment I am living in Naivasha as one of those who were affected by the violence. As we voted we did not know that this would happen to us. We are even surprised today that we are now going hungry, our children are not going to school and we have lost a lot of things due to the violence. We are thankful to God for the gift of life. We encountered problems that one could not expect in one's own country.

There was violence in Eldoret even as we were voting since violence started on 26th December 2007 at Langas. There was an estate that had a Luo name and people wanted to rename the place. Therefore the violence was not due to the elections. Enmity started developing yet they were people we used to live with as neighbours. I am astounded to see that I am no longer there and I am only facing problems here in Naivasha. On the night before the voting day violence spread even to our estate. We went to the hospital and found people who had been badly injured. They told us that it was due to the estate that had a Luo name and that Nandi were fighting with Luos. There was enmity amongst all the ethnic communities yet we had coexisted peacefully. I was a businessperson and used to sell second hand clothes. We used to go to markets in different places and we were well known and had joined several groups. We used to engage in business with the Nandis even at their estates. Before the violence, they took items on credit and promised to pay on 24th December 2007. One person asked us not to go there on the said date because we would be the first ones to be attacked. We could not understand why since we had been working with those people.

We felt that was our home but they kept this secret and did not even pay us what they owed us. They said that we had gotten enough from them and it was now their turn to get from us. We thought that we were teaching them how to conduct business and in return they would teach us something else. So at the moment in Eldoret, no one is at peace and able to conduct business. As we are here in Naivasha, we have no capital to start businesses. The Nandis joined hands with the Luos and beat us. We did not know where to run to. I ran away without my children to the police station. My children were in another village known as Munyaka which was worse. That was the place where churches and schools were burnt.

Even where we took refuge, the Nandis still tried to attack us. We were thousands of people; some women screaming and others praying. We would try to light fire and prepare tea using cans. Most of us ran away and left our properties, this made us paupers. That showed that they had planned this since the referendum on the new constitution. It was confirmed by one of the Nandis - a Kipsigis lady who told us that we should watch and see if the Nandis were carrying out their circumcision ceremony because if they were not, then violence would erupt. She requested us not to go back for the money since they were saying that we had conducted business for a long time and had now become rich. We became confused as this led to the downfall of our businesses because they owed us a lot of money.

On 26th December 2007 violence erupted in Langas and when we voted it was said that there was rigging in the election but where I was the exercise was conducted well and there was no problem. We had prayed for the election because their plan was to stop us, Kikuyus, from voting. The votes were then counted well although there was tension.

On 30th December 2007 some of the Luos started questioning where the one million votes had come from yet president Kibaki was behind Raila with one million votes. They started saying that the votes had been stolen and hence started swearing that they would not stay with us in the same area. We, Kikuyu, had a lot of problems since the Luo and the Luhya joined hands with the Nandis to attack us. But the whole exercise was conducted by the Nandis. The Luos and the Luhyas would tell them where we were hiding. Therefore we, the Kikuyus, were the target. My two children were at the estate looking after our property and as they were there, they did not have any weapons yet the ones who were attacking us had arrows. When the violence continued, one person said that he had contacts of a personal doctor of a prominent politician. We called him and asked him to give us the politician's number. The doctor assisted us and we told him our problems and he asked us to give him just a few minutes. The police in the area were offering the Nandis security so that they would be able to fight. We did not have anybody to assist us. Houses had been burnt and people killed. We then realized that they were not people from within because they were being transported with lorries and they would attack in turns. We did not have anybody to assist us at the police station as they were following us even to the police station.

Later some vehicles were sent in order to transport us and we were told that anybody who had money could leave but that was before the army came because when they came, the place was a little bit calmer. These people started fighting the army and that was the time the army shot them. When we checked five of them who had been shot dead, they had money in their pockets and one of them before he died, confessed that they had been paid by a prominent politician to attack the Kikuyus. Some had Kshs. 30,000 in their pockets. They were being paid according to how they carried out the attacks. For example, if one burnt a house made of grass, there was a certain amount for that and if it was made of stones, it also attracted a higher pay.

The most astonishing thing is that we (who were affected by this violence) have never been assisted by the government. We have suffered a lot and our children have dropped out of school since we are unable to work and earn a living. We are also unable to get whatever we wanted from that town not knowing that one day we would be sent packing from our own homes. When we came here we did not know this place. I came in a lorry that carries bread and as you know, these vehicles do not have windows and when I got here, it was late at night. I did not even know where I was but the residents here welcomed us and assisted us. On our way here, I saw my children who had been led by the older one to the police station and I was very happy.

At the moment we are not getting any assistance from the government because we have no one to talk on our behalf. It seems like no one knows of our existence. The other day we went to ask for the DO but he asked us to go back where we came from yet we left that place a long time ago and we do not know what is going on in that place. We have suffered a lot. We are hungry. The ten thousand shillings the government is giving to the IDPs has never come our way. When we asked about it we were told that the government does not know of our existence. Our question is: Who knows about our existence if at all the one in charge of this area doesn't know anything about us? We are requesting to be given the ten thousand shillings so that we can go back to where we came from and assess the situation there and continue with our livelihood. All of us have reached the point of losing hope. For example some of us did not get tents and therefore we were told to look for houses around. Area residents assisted us because they thought it would be just for a few days but they are now tired because the cost of living here is very high.

This is why we are requesting for government's assistance, as the integrated IDPs. The other day when they were giving the ten thousand shillings to those who were in the camps, the DO told us that they don't know about integrated IDPs. Yet, we had informed him of our existence earlier but he is saying that our names have not yet been taken to Nairobi.

I have lived in Eldoret since 1991 and have been there for all those years because my husband was employed there. I was selling second hand clothes which we used to get from Nairobi. We liked the place since it is conducive for business. When we went there in 1991, there was violence in 1992 and we did not know anything. The violence started at night and was caused by the Nandis. We fail to understand the Nandis since they say that the land we have there is theirs. When the violence erupted, I remember I had a very young child who was just a few days old. We ran away in the morning looking for a safe place to stay. In 1992 I was living in Langas but I vacated and went to Kamukunji and I was there when the violence erupted. I was conducting business there and used to go to Western region and to other markets to sell clothes. Equally in 1997 there was violence in Molo which did not reach Eldoret. Since then, we have been experiencing such problems but this time it was very bad. We would be very happy if something was done to ensure that no such violence ever occurs again. We are sad to see that we no longer have the relationship we had with these people. Yet we know that incitement started from the top. MPs are the cause of this.

During the 2007 election campaigns things were bad because in one instance there was a Kikuyu woman who wanted to contest for a civic seat. But some men did not want her to win so there were a lot of problems. When the votes were counted, it was announced that the woman had won but it seems like the votes were stolen since it was later announced that someone else had won. I was not involved in the campaigns. I was very committed to my business, hence could not leave it to go campaigning.

Then came the 2007 voting exercise and it was conducted well since we had prayed for that day. Though violence had started on 26th December 2007 on that day it was a little bit calm. After we finished voting the violence continued. On the day the results were announced, we were sad since we had already been told that they would send us back to Central Kenya. Therefore, we knew whether Kibaki won or lost, we would be attacked. However, I did not lose any household items but they spoilt my business. One of the Luos went to the store where our stock was and sent some street children to burn our stalls and the store. Some goods were burnt and others looted by the Nandis. I did not identify the attackers since they used to come after every two hours in lorries to relieve the ones who were there who would then leave.

I can forgive them since according to the Bible, we are told that we should forgive seventy times seven times (70x7). I can therefore easily forgive them but they have not yet said anything. They should first own up to what they did and accept their mistakes. When they do this and confess, then we can forgive them since they no longer hold grudges. As a family we were so much affected. My children stayed away from me and went hungry as they were running away and were not able to go back to school. They have nightmares and scream at night saying that the Nandis are coming after them because they witnessed houses, schools and churches being burnt. They are scared that they might experience the same thing again. My husband lost his job and is not able to earn a living having lived there for over twenty years. He first worked with a blankets firm but it was closed down. He also worked with Faulu Bakery but it was closed down due to threats that it would be burnt down. He was affected in that way. Politicians were involved because if it weren't for politics then there would have been no violence. We had been warned that whether we vote or not or whether Kibaki wins or not violence had to erupt. There was an indication that the leaders were involved. The chiefs were in it too.

We experienced a lot of problems here in Naivasha since we didn't know anyone here. We have suffered a lot and do not have money to start businesses. We have even come to the point of giving up since the people who are assisting us with a place to stay are now getting tired. They have given us notice to vacate and most of us don't know where to go, where to get food or even where to sleep. I still don't know why I was attacked since the hatred started during the referendum on the new constitution.

Q: The government has given other IDPs ten thousand shillings. In your opinion, what kind of assistance would you want from the government?

A: Our request is that they also give us the ten thousand shillings. I earlier said that we have been forgotten by the leaders here. The DO told us that the government does not recognize us. Hence our prayer is that we be remembered and be given the ten thousand shillings because we have no shelter and no food to eat and have not got any assistance from the government.

Q: *If you were to be given another chance, would you go back to Eldoret and conduct business again?*

A: Yes, but I would live in fear since those people have not yet calmed down. They are still saying that they are not satisfied with the outcome.

Q: *What is their problem?*

A: Their problem is land.

Q: *What would you say to those who attacked you?*

A: I cannot talk to them first because they are still angry. They should first ask for forgiveness so that we can bring back the relationship we once had. If am not welcomed in that place then I cannot be able to stay in that town.

Q: *What can the government do to ensure that we do not experience such violence in future?*

A: The government should jointly work together and remember that the citizens are the ones who voted them in because a leader with no followers is not a leader. Therefore the government should learn the best way to live with Kenyans in order to eliminate this violence once and for all.

Q: *What action would you want to be taken against those who attacked you or the leaders who incited them?*

A: The leaders who incited the attackers should be arrested and the right action taken against them because there is still that enmity in the people they used. They should also be given life imprisonment since they affected human beings.

Q: *What about the youths who were used to cause these attacks? What action should be taken against them?*

A: These people were paid and that is why they attacked us. Maybe if they had not been paid then they would not have done it. Therefore these children should be forgiven.

Q: *Do you have anything else to add?*

A: I have nothing else to add but we would like the government to remember integrated IDPs because we have been forgotten.

IMPUNITY BREEDS IMPUNITY

My name is David Kilo. I was born here in Naivasha in 1973 and went to school here. I am a fisherman and a tour guide. I take tourists round the lake using boats. Naivasha is in the Rift Valley. Economic activities include flower farms, tourist attraction sites and small businesses that have come up due to the flower farms. It is also a cosmopolitan town since we have different ethnic communities.

During the 2005 constitutional referendum, there were those who were supporting and those who were opposing the draft constitution. I was among those who were opposing the constitution since this was not the constitution many Kenyans wanted. The referendum divided people along tribal lines. Some joined the opposition and others supported the government but there was no violence at the time.

The year 2007 started well and the campaigns were conducted well. We as the ODM continued with campaigns because the referendum had positioned us according to political parties. In Naivasha there was a good political atmosphere during the campaigns though we did not know what the rest were planning. When we met our friends from the other parties, we had a good time since we used to conduct business with them and we even went to school with some of them. So there was no violence during that time. I was the Chief Agent of the ODM presidential candidate in this area. We continued with our campaigns well and had a good relationship with the opposition. In other parts of the country for example, Kuresoi it was reported that there was violence, but that did not incite anything here.

However, there were instances when I experienced hostility. For instance, there was a time when we were going to Suswa and met youths who were supporters of PNU. We were told that they had been sent by a politician to attack us. We were going to a meeting with Maasais which is held once in a year. They attacked us and some of our youth were injured. One of them died later due to the injuries he sustained.

On the voting day we had no problems. As the ODM Chief Agent, I was able to go round the whole constituency to ensure that everything was okay. After the voting was over, there arose problems during the tallying of the votes which did not affect the opposition or the ODM. It involved PNU alone especially the parliamentary where two opponents were not in agreement. We as the ODM were satisfied with the results. However, the announcement of the results was delayed. As we waited for the announcement here, the media had already announced the results. This astounded us since we could not understand how the results had already been communicated to Nairobi yet at the constituency level the exercise was not yet over.

Later on due to the problems we had during the announcement of the results in Naivasha, I was asked to go to Nairobi at night to explain what had happened as the Lead Agent. When the presidential results were announced I was in Nairobi at the KICC. I called to know how Naivasha was since we had seen the reaction in Nairobi and the surrounding towns like Limuru. There were some celebrations which were also marked with violence. When I asked, I was told that the situation was the same in Naivasha and there were demonstrations too. There were celebrations in some parts of the country and in some there were protests. Some people were not satisfied with the results.

During these celebrations, some people vandalized our ODM office, burnt it and looted property. Some of our supporters' businesses were also vandalized and there was a lot of tension in Naivasha. After the presidential results were announced, Naivasha was no longer safe since we started getting threats. They made a list of those who would be killed. We no longer had peace since we did not know who was after us.

Personally, I received more than 50 sms; some were from our opponents telling us that they had won which is normal and I would tell them there must be a winner and a loser. Some were threats to my life telling me that I should vacate this place and that they were looking for my head. Some even threatened my family. It took me some time to feel safe in town. I had to look for a safe place to stay at the South Lake estate until when we thought things had settled. That was after a week and a half and then I came back to Naivasha.

The situation continued for sometime. Those who were opposing us thought that our community had voted in the current MP so they started planning ways of punishing us. Those who were campaigning for the former MP did not accept that she had lost the seat. They felt that our party had voted in the current MP.

Violence in Naivasha erupted on the 27th January 2008. On the previous day, I went home from work where I sell fish. It is directly opposite one of the famous hotels in Naivasha. Once there, I noticed different cars that belonged to businessmen in Naivasha. They had parked them there as they were having a meeting in the hotel. They started streaming into the hotel at around 5.00 pm and the meeting went on till after 8.00 pm when I closed down my business. We were worried because most of them were supporters were our opponents and were in the frontline during her campaigns. This was due to the position I held during the campaigns and since this had a bad record, I became more worried. We realized that they had a hidden agenda and there were also claims that some people were being ferried in that night from Nairobi. Therefore, it was evident that the business owners in Naivasha were aware of what was going to happen.

On the material day, I had to take some goods to Nairobi. I woke up very early and went to look for matatus so that I travel. I went to the bus stop and immediately I noticed that there were no matatus in town. This was an indication that things were not right. I decided that since the load was not too heavy and Nairobi is not too far, I could drive. I went and took the load of fish. When I arrived at Kangemi I started receiving messages some asking me where I was and I told them that I was at home. They then asked me to leave the house since some youth were coming in to attack me. Things were worsening. I went to the Gikomba market where I delivered the load of fish and I started heading back though many people warned me not to come back because the youth were carrying pangas and were saying that they were looking for me. I was not at peace since I had left my family in Naivasha. Therefore, I drove back to Naivasha even after being warned. I used the Maai Mahiu road to Naivasha. When I arrived at Longonot and called one policeman to inquire about the situation and he told me that if I was not in Naivasha

I should not come back. But since my family was there, I found it difficult not to go back. So I drove to South Lake where it was a bit calm, hid my vehicle, took one of my boats and sailed. I was not able to get to town but I stayed at the shores.

While there, I communicated with my family and told them to seek help from the neighbours. But since it looked as if a certain community had taken an oath, it was difficult for neighbours to assist. They also had fear of being attacked. I was looking for a way to vacate my family but I had no one to assist them since no one was willing. At around 10.00 pm I was still at the shores of the lake. I called one of the railway policemen and told him where I was. He looked for a taxi and came for me. We crossed the lake and went home to rescue my family. Therefore, I did not witness what was happening in town.

I remember spending the whole of Sunday, Monday and Tuesday at the lake. Then I called a friend in Nairobi who sent us a plane that airlifted us from where we were to Nairobi and another one to Kisumu. When I was there, I tried to find out how the people who had been affected could be transported from Naivasha. I succeeded to communicate with MPs and the Prime Minister though he had not been appointed at that time. They set aside a committee of MPs to assist the people who had been affected and we were able to assist them. The affected were transported to their rural homes. In our community, one must have a house at the rural home and so most of them had a place to go to.

In the days that followed, the attackers looted people's houses and burnt their properties and the things that were not valuable but they carried the valuable ones. They also tried to break down my shop where I sell fish but the police were able to stop them. Then they went to the shores where I keep my boats and burnt one of them. But there is an American who was my partner and had enough security so they were not able to get in and burn the other boats.

After the violence, I stayed in Kisumu for the whole of February 2008 but life became difficult because I am not used to that place and therefore I went to Nairobi in March till July where I used to commute to Naivasha. I came back but the place is no longer the same since I have not been able to get back to the position I was before. I have been attacked once by thugs at my house and have been confronted twice on my way home so the place is no longer safe. At times, some of our customers at the shop tell us that they are being threatened; especially the hotels that buy fish from us. Therefore, you find that we have to look for someone else to take the fish to them since there is a lot of tribalism which we were not used to.

Some of the people from my ethnic community are employed in the flower farms and in offices around. Therefore, most of them do not conduct businesses but are employed. I was not the only one who was targeted, but most businessmen from our community were also targeted. This showed that there was some enmity from some of our fellow businessmen. You will also find that they were targeting our property. Before the violence erupted, there were rumors that a curfew and prison wardens had caused the violence. But in my opinion, I don't think the prison wardens were the cause of the violence because I don't think that two wrongs make a right. There were ways of stopping what they were doing and they should not have attacked a certain community. There was a way of dealing with the prison wardens if at all they were not working as they were supposed to. Since this violence was directed at my community, I wouldn't say that all the prison wardens were from my ethnic community and therefore I don't think they were the cause of the violence.

There were also rumors that the attackers were ferried into Naivasha but I don't think there was anybody who was ferried in. Naivasha was used as a safe haven for the displaced and therefore you will find that there are those who had come from places like Molo and Narok. As they were coming in there was tension in the town due to the stories they were telling the residents. This contributed to the violence here. For the attackers who were from Naivasha they had wigs that had dread locks. Some had applied Kiwi polish on their face. Therefore they were people from the town who used a lot of ways to disguise themselves. If they were people who had been ferried in, then they would not have been able to identify people's houses and property. Therefore, I still don't believe that people were ferried in. They were people from around who were able to identify our business premises, property and houses. I think they are the well known businessmen in Naivasha we went to school with; our friends whom we live with and even eat together; the people we work hand in hand with and even people we go to church with. For example, we Catholics go for prayers in people's houses and if these people know where their colleagues live, I think this really exposed us.

It is true some politicians were involved because when I was at the shop on the 26th December 2007 I noticed several people at the hotel. I also saw a local politician there leaving very late in the night. As the attackers went round houses they would ask for IDs and voters cards to destroy them. This was established when some people went to the IDP camps and offered money to the victims so that they could burn their voters cards and ID cards. I know those who attacked me. Most of them are guilty and cannot even face me. This has taught me the best way to live in this town.

The issue of forgiveness is sensitive. I was the first person to come back to Naivasha, that is, from the list of the people who were to be killed. Since I came there has never been any form of reconciliation or any attempt to have Naivasha residents who were involved come out to confess that they were responsible. Therefore the question is: Who are you to forgive? For there to be forgiveness people have to accept their mistakes and say how they contributed. But up to now no one has done this. Therefore, we cannot forgive before we know the ones who were involved and in what ways. When we came back we thought we would find committees in place established from the communities within so that they would look for modalities in which people can live the way they used to but nothing has happened. Therefore, people are still living in tension not knowing whether they will be attacked once again. The community that attacked us is also living in fear because they don't know whether those who are coming back are planning to revenge.

My life has really changed because since I started living in Naivasha, I never thought about tribalism since most of my friends came from the community that attacked us. We have visited one another's rural home. I have visited them in Nyeri and Murang'a and I know almost the whole of Central Province due to my friends. I did not know that my friends would one day come to me with pangas or write to me threatening messages or even burn my property. But I have been able to know the weight of friendship or a better relationship. This has led to a situation where it has become difficult to love them again. Like the friends I had, it has become difficult for them to face me and even console me. I have more than seven months since I came back and these friends have even distanced themselves from me. This shows that they contributed in these skirmishes because they thought that we would never come back. My children do not even know their mother tongue. As we went back home they were forced to learn a new language. They would often ask me why they were not going to school and I would not be able to answer them. They would also ask why they could not get some of their items and I was not be able to tell them where theyt were. Therefore at first, it was really painful for us to explain to them. It will take us a long time for us to heal and to forgive.

Q: What should the government do to avoid a repeat of such kind of violence in future?

A: From my understanding there was a group during the Moi regime that was known as Special Branch. Such things could not happen with the existence of an effective Special Branch that was later turned to National Security Intelligence Services (NSIS). These groups were able to get such plans may it be in Naivasha, Nakuru, Eldoret. The intelligence must have had this information before it was executed. When we get a regime that does not see the need of such groups like Special Branch, then such things will recur. I see the way the government is handling this matter especially the provincial administration. I think they are making people get used to it. Therefore, in 2012 it may even be worse. People will have been used to staying in camps, to experiencing problems and could do anything since there will be no changes. The government should change its attitude towards the IDPs.

Q: In your own opinion what should the government do for those who were affected by this violence?

A: The first thing I would want the government to do is to ensure that those people who were working were taken back to their work stations. By doing this, they will be ensuring that there is security. But when you find that in a particular bank, people working there are from one community, I think this will lead to tribalism and differences because people will only be working in their areas.

People fled from their homes during the skirmishes. If one worked in a bank they were sent to work near his rural home. I think the government is dividing people instead of bringing them together. This is different from the way people would want to live knowing that they can live in any part of the country. We no longer uphold that brotherhood or sisterhood. About compensation, I think this has opened up people's wounds because of the way the government and the provincial administration are handling it. It is even more painful as the victims are discriminated against and even made to remember the skirmishes. I think the people who are supposed to handle the IDP issues should be people who have sympathy and those who have done courses in counseling. They know how to handle the kind of problems the IDPs have. People from the Provincial Administration enforce whatever they want and are not sympathetic. Therefore, they should use different people; not the administration officers.

Q: In your opinion, what action should be taken against those who planned the attacks and even those who attacked others?

A: Whatever they did was against the law of this country. Planning attacks and carrying them out is an offence. Therefore, whoever was involved in anyway or was mentioned should be prosecuted according to the law. They should be arrested and arraigned in court and if found guilty, let the law take its course.

Q: What is your message to fellow Kenyans?

A: My message is especially to those who live here in Naivasha. Your neighbor is more of your brother than the one you expect. People were complaining about Kibaki, others Raila, but when problems started you find that you look for help from the people you have always been meeting and living with. Therefore, my message is that no one chose to come from a particular community. No one chose to be poor. No one chose where to live. But our various problems made us find ourselves where we are now. The fact that we are all from different communities, we should stop discriminating people due to their origin. If we do, then we are taking God's work into our hands.

Q: Do you have anything else to add?

A: I would like the truth to be established. For all those who were mentioned in the violence, be it in Naivasha, Nakuru, Eldoret or even Kisumu action must be taken against them. If we do not, our children may think of doing something of the sought. Impunity breeds impunity so even in forty years to come the same can happen. If action is taken we can avoid a repeat of the same in future. These people should be arrested and arraigned in court. It will be a lesson to all those who may plan to do such a thing again. But if nothing is done, those who did it will still feel proud of what they did yet they are known. They are people we live with and are even mentioned in one way or another. This should not be handled like the way previous reports have been handled by being kept away in their cabinets. Action must be taken on them be; it the ministers or anybody else for that matter. They should face the law like any other Kenyan since there is no big nor small offence.

MY HEAD WAS HACKED SEVERAL TIMES

My name is Kenneth Kamau, an IDP at Naivasha Stadium Camp. I was born in Gatanga, Thika, but when I was in class three my father sold our land. Life became unbearable and I could not go on with my education after class four. I got assistance from well-wishers and was able to complete my primary education. From there I started looking for odd jobs in towns and later went to live in Narok town where I lived between the year 2000 and 2007. To earn a living, I used to fetch water for three shillings a jerrican and sell it at ten shillings, carrying on a bicycle. The bicycle was however stolen together with the jerricans I used. I also lost my phone and the shoes I was wearing.

There are different ethnic communities living in Narok. Some are businessmen and women and some are farmers but we used to coexist well until after the election when the violence erupted. I was attacked and left for dead. I bled till morning. Some people found me lying there and took me to hospital. I did not recognize them since I was unconscious. Later on I went to the police station where I camped till March 2008 when we were brought to Naivasha.

During the 2005 referendum I was still living in Narok but I was not involved in politics at that time. During the 2007 elections, voting went on well and we cast our votes without fear. But when the results were announced, people started screaming at the market near where I lived. When I went there, I found that the market was on fire. Indeed that was the time violence erupted and some other people were killed. The attackers vowed to hold demonstrations on 16th January 2008, but people locked themselves up. But I decided to continue with my day to day activities, and on 12th January 2008 they held the demonstration instead of 16th January 2008. That was when I came face to face with those who attacked me. I did not know why they were demonstrating though there were some ODM supporters who said that they would demonstrate because they heard that Kibaki had won. I didn't understand what they meant because every time they said they would hold a demonstration, they ended up fighting.

What I cannot tell is exactly who was leading the attacks because since 1998 we have had violence in Narok. This time round ODM supporters were fighting the PNU supporters since they did not accept that Kibaki had won the presidential elections.

On 12th January 2008 I was attacked by people I did not recognize. They cut me on the head and hand and since then I have not recovered. I am still here with nowhere to go. I am asking for assistance to foot my medical bills as I am unable to do anything on my own to earn a living. On that day I woke up and started fetching and selling water as usual. But in the evening as I went back home from town, I came across some Maasai youths who had clubs and machetes. They first hit me on the head using a club and I started bleeding. Then they came near me and asked me to surrender everything I had and go home. I gave them my bicycle and phone and they even took my shoes. When I started walking, they ran after me. When they caught up with me they took me to a nearby forest where they started hacking me on the head. They even cut one of my fingers on my right hand, while the left one was badly cut and I had to be stitched. The hand was not well treated and I have had problems since January 2008 until recently. A Good Samaritan, an American, took me to hospital where I was operated on but it has not yet healed. The people who attacked me left me to die. I was found by some passersby who took me to hospital. When I came out of the hospital, I went to the police station because there was a camp there. I stayed there for sometime till I came to Naivasha.

I have been here at the camp for the last eight months. The Red Cross has really assisted me but since they left, I have no one to assist me. I have never gone back to Narok but I suspect everything in my house was stolen and I have no hopes of going back. In fact, if I can get assistance to get to another place to stay I wouldn't want to go back to Narok. Though I didn't know the attackers, I believe they were Maasais from

Narok. Actually I was not able to recognize anyone because when they started beating me I could not see them because I was in pain and bleeding profusely. I forgave the attackers since I did not even recognize them. God assists those who forgive those that offend them. God will forgive them since this violence erupted in most parts of the country. I still don't know why they attacked me for I never took anybody's property. I was doing my own work and we were living in peace before this violence.

I would like the government to assist me because due to the injuries I sustained I cannot be able to go back to the life I once had. Before the post election violence I had problems too but not as much as now. Before I was able to work and earn a living. If it is possible I would like the government to give me a plot and help me build a house to live in. Alternatively, they can assist me get a way to earn a living because I have gotten better though I cannot handle difficult tasks with the hand that was badly hurt. I didn't get proper education so I cannot get a better job. I need the government's assistance.

At the camp we have a lot of problems. When it rains the camp gets flooded. Some of us have disabilities and are unable to take shelter and it really gets cold. Since the Red Cross left, it takes time before we get food. At times we have to wait for a month or two to get food. At the moment we have no water around so we are experiencing a lot of hardships. I also have problems with my hand. I even thought that it would be amputated but that person came and assisted me. At times I go hungry since I have no one to assist me in cooking. Worse still, the drugs I am taking require me to eat a lot of food before I take them. Sometimes I do not take the drugs as I don't have food to eat.

The government has only given us this place where we have camped and nothing else. Equally, the amount of money the government promised to give us is too little. When the person who took me to hospital was asked to pay the bill it amounted to twenty one thousand shillings. After I was admitted and discharged, he was once again called and asked to pay some more money. Now am wondering if the deposit was twenty one thousand shillings and here we are being given ten thousand shillings would the amount have helped me in treatment, rent a house or feed and clothe myself? I just fail to understand. That amount is just too little. Yet the problems we encountered were caused by politicians; the same ones we had voted for.

First and foremost, the government should look for land and build houses for us. By doing this they will have assisted us because we will be able to begin a new life away from the camp. Secondly, they should also look at those whose lives were badly affected through injuries and offer them medical assistance. Thirdly, the amount they are giving us is just too little. They should give us a place to stay to begin our lives again and be able to support ourselves. Everything changed because at the moment I cannot do anything to earn a living. I depend on other people's donations. This is something I am not happy about and I am afraid that this might continue for a long time since I don't have any kind of assistance. Only the government or other residents can assist me. Secondly, I feel that I am a refugee in my own country.

As for the attackers, there are those that were arrested and though they were just incited, I think the law should be followed. The government was supposed to solve the problem and citizens should not have taken the law into their hands. To avoid a repeat of such kind of violence in future the government should investigate how the election was conducted and those who caused the violence be prosecuted. The government should also establish a way to ensure that there is security for all Kenyans as people were killed even when law enforcers were there.

In my opinion the police did not do their best since there was violence for many days and those who were arrested were just a few. Most culprits escaped arrest.

Q: What should the government do in 2012 during the election to avoid a repeat of such kind of violence?

A: Since the committees have done their investigations and asked us to go back home, the government should have proper plans to ensure that violence does not recur.

Q: Who can you blame for this violence?

A: I think these are government issues. We voted but when the announcement was made, we the citizens that had voted experienced problems. Therefore, I would blame the leaders in government since they are the ones who caused this violence and we are still in the IDP camps. They have not established a way to assist us and we are still waiting for their assistance.

Q: What can fellow citizens do to live in peace?

A: First, the leaders should talk to their people to show love between neighbours so that such problems do not recur again. Secondly, what has been found after the investigation as the root cause of the problem should also be solved so that people can live in peace.

Q: Some people say that this was caused by unemployment of the youths. What would you say?

A: If that was the case, they should be assisted to get jobs so that in future they are not incited by leaders who give them a small fee to cause violence.

Q: What can you tell Kenyans to avoid violence and ensure that there is peace?

A: I would like to say that nobody chose to be born in a particular ethnic group. It was just God's wish. Therefore, we should live in peace and avoid taking the law into our own hands; killing and attacking other people for no reason.

Burning Started Before the Elections

My name is Milka Kiarie from Molo. I went to Molo in 1994 and have been there for more than ten years. I started a business and was able to buy a plot and build. The plot was not burnt but my business was burnt and that is the reason I left Molo.

I bought the plot in 1999 and built immediately. I used to sell new shoes which I would get from Uganda since I had a passport. I used to get the shoes and sell them in wholesale and retail. Molo originally was in Nakuru district but it has now become a district on its own. It is on the highway. You branch at a place called Kibunja around 4 km to Molo town. It was a good town but it has since changed and one cannot live there peacefully. I was living in an estate called Total, which is a trading centre. I am a single mother since my husband died in 1988 and I was alone in my business. I have five children; two have completed their secondary education but have not yet gone to college – they are still with me – two are married and I am left with one who was in Form Three.

In 1992 I lived in Likia Farm where we were beaten by the Maasai who damaged a lot of our property and we lost so much. In 1997 I was in Molo and I also lost a lot of things but not as I have lost during the current violence. So I was still affected by those other clashes. In 1992 it was the first time to experience the fights in which so many people were killed, others seriously injured and houses burnt. We witnessed all of these. One of my neighbours was killed during that time yet he had just got married and did not have any children. In 1997 they only burnt houses.

During the 1992 and 1997 clashes we were beaten because we were not voting for the then sitting president but for Kenneth Matiba the Ford Asili's candidate. Though Matiba won, the then president did not let him take the seat and we accepted the defeat. In 1997 during the time for Democratic Party (DP) we voted for Kibaki who won but the sitting president did not relinquish the seat. So we also accepted the defeat. At that time the government was fighting us and they wanted us to leave the Rift Valley.

During the 2005 referendum on the new constitution, we voted. We prayed and God heard our prayers because we knew that we would be beaten. When we voted and were defeated, we accepted but still there was no peace. We were being threatened by our neighbours, the Nandis.

In 2007 fighting started in November. That was when they started burning Kamwaura and people came to Molo town. When voting in December 2007, we had already been beaten and only wanted to have some place to stay till the voting day so that we could vote for Kibaki. We voted and on 30th December 2007 when Kibaki was sworn in, we thanked God but since then we have never slept in our houses.

In January 2008, we never had shelter; houses were being burnt; we witnessed people being killed; children being killed and we thought it was wise to leave Molo and look for a better place to stay. They burnt the village I was living in on 22nd February 2008. We still stayed there on 22nd and 23rd February when the violence was still high and on 26th February as we went to the police station. We saw it was wise to leave the place and that was when we came here.

The people who were attacking us had shorts, arrows and machetes and they were Nandis. We know that the Nandis are the only ones who fight us in Molo. They came and told us that we had to leave since it was their land which they were given at independence and the Rift Valley belonged to them. A lot of my property was destroyed. For instance, I didn't carry anything from my shop. Everything was burnt to ashes. I had tailoring machines and the clothes I was sewing for my customers were all burnt down. Nothing was salvaged. We ran away when they started burning houses. We threatened them too and they ran away but when we left, they came and burnt everything at around three o'clock in the evening. They would attack any man they found around. So we gave up and left them to burn what they could burn.

We reported to the police who tried to help but some of them were not assisting because they were favoring their side as most of them were Nandis. We ran to Total Police Station at Mau Summit where we were given a place to stay for a few days. At the police station we had a lot of problems because we did not have shelter and food and we had children who were crying for food. The place was also cold. In fact some of the children got pneumonia. We stayed at the police station for four days looking for means to get out of that place. That was when we hiked lifts in lorries and came to Naivasha.

We have so many problems here especially for people like me who had never been to a camp. We were welcomed by a person named "Faite" and stayed at KANU grounds for three days. I met with my brothers who took me to their house. We encountered many challenges at that time but the residents assisted us. We have no clothes, no food to give to our children and no rent to pay for our houses. To make the matter worse the government has not assisted us in any way especially those of us renting houses.

We have not yet received any kind of assistance from them. They only gave us food for two days and have never gotten anything else. We get assistance from good Samaritans and when we don't, we go hungry. We also don't have money to buy full school uniforms so our children are always sent home. My daughter is no longer going to school. She became pregnant and got married but was later brought back to me. Apart from food and money we have other problems. For example, business people like me had loans at Equity bank and we were not able to repay them in time and even the debts we had with other people.

Displaced children at Muiri-ini Farm Camp in Kibunja, Molo. Photo by Kimani Njogu

I would like the government to assist me with a premise to continue conducting my business because some people who were in town were doing businesses and others were in the farms and dealing with farms. Everybody should be assisted with what they lost. For example, they can assist me with capital to restart my business. It is difficult for me to forgive because according to the kind of life I am leading now, it is totally different from what I had. I owned a house, my own business and did not depend on anyone. I lived with the Nandis and they never even warned me on what they wanted to do. So I still find it difficult to forgive them. I would want them to be disciplined first so that they can also know that I am a Kenyan too. No Kenyan is supposed to abandon property. They should know that the land we bought there was ours rightfully and it belongs to us. Since they gave us title deeds, they should be satisfied with what he/she was left with.

During the previous regime they were convinced by the then president that we would leave Rift Valley and they would be given our land and the houses we had built. So violence started with the then government and fanned by some of them who are still in government today.

The politicians caused this violence because there were claims that the ODM leaders had told the Nandi youth to kick us (Kikuyus) out so that they could be left with our land. If they hadn't told them that, they could not have evicted us. They would tell them during the campaigns that they should not let us stay there, whether they won or lost. And since we are neighbours we got to know.

What I would like to see happen is for these people to first accept that they did wrong and ask for forgiveness from the people whose lives they destroyed. They cannot repay us but they should be punished to avoid a repeat of the same. We knew most of them as some were from our area although others were ferried in. Since then, my life has changed. I had money and my own house. I was not used to renting a house but now I am forced to. I used to run my own business and was able to feed and clothe my children. But now I am not able to do that. In fact I have really lost weight due to the hardships I am going through.

I would want the government to send representatives here to go round this place find out what we do to earn a living and assist us accordingly so that we can resume our normal lives. For those who have not yet started any economic activity, they should be assisted too in the best way possible. I heard the government was giving ten thousand shillings but I have not received anything. I would urge them to give us what they had promised so that we can be able to start a new life. If it is the ten thousand shillings, then they should give it to us.

Q: What do you think about the 2012 elections?

A: About the year 2012 I would request that we have proper planning during the election to avoid such kind of violence. Had the politicians not incited people, then there would have been no violence. People should also accept defeat because if they had accepted it, violence would not have erupted.

Q: Are you ready to return home?

A: I don't think I can go back to Total if there is no proper planning. I still fear that violence can erupt once more. But if the government has a proper plan to prevent violence, then I can go back.

Q: What else would you like to tell Kenyans?

A: I would like to pass a message to those who attacked others to stop attacking their fellow Kenyans. We integrated IDPs do not get any assistance because all the food is taken to the camps. We also have psychological problems due to what we experienced during the violence.

I would like to buy a plot in Naivasha, build a house and start a new life here. I believe that we are lucky that we walked away from that place especially with our sons. They were the main target and age didn't matter. I knew two men who were killed. I witnessed one of them being beaten and then burnt by our attackers as he was going back to get his title deed. We only buried his bones because he was burnt beyond recognition. The other one was hacked into pieces. They also killed another man on the day we voted as he was going to help his neighbor who was screaming. Violence had started on the night we voted.

They burnt houses using petrol and kerosene which they would pour on the house and light it. The attackers were accompanied by their wives who collected the looted items. They would then come the following day to collect the roofing materials. So we were not able to salvage anything. The attackers were men of between 20 to 25 years.

Q: *Do you think politicians were involved?*

A: I don't know if politicians were involved but if one of the Nandis was killed, he would be found with money in his pockets which meant that one was paid five hundred shillings for every house burnt. If he killed someone, he was given two thousand shillings.

Q: *Did the police assist you?*

A: The police would assist us at times. But the police from the Nandi community would do nothing and would even watch as the youths burnt down our houses. Police from other ethnic groups would assist us. At the police station we were a bit secure.

Q: *What about your relatives?*

A: I have relatives who assist me but as you know they cannot afford to assist with everything. In fact my relatives gave me capital to start a small business near Kafico so as to pay my rent and get food for my children. However, I still have problems as I still don't have many customers. I still get shoes from Uganda and sell them here. We travel to Uganda during the day though we are always afraid when we get between Kericho and Molo. We are usually at peace when we get to Kisumu. We are afraid that we might be attacked once again.

Q: What about the Chief?

A: The area Chief witnessed a man being killed and did not do anything to stop it. Yet he was his neighbour. Actually, he was the one who had sold him land. The place at the moment is calm but we are not comfortable there anymore.

Q: Did they occupy your houses?

A: The Nandis did not occupy our houses and though they had allocated themselves the big houses the Kikuyus owned incase ODM won. The only thing they did was to vandalize them and spoil completely as ODM did not win the elections. My house was one of the ones they wanted to take so they didn't burn it. My plot and house are still there but they stole windows, doors and roofing materials on one side of the house. I would like to sell the plot and the house since I am not confident of going back there, especially after experiencing the violence three times. The house I had rented for business was also not completely burnt since it belonged to one of the Nandis. They only stole the windows and looted everything that was inside. They burnt part of it, and left the house without burning it.

Q: If you had a chance to talk to Kibaki, what would you tell him?

A: I would ask him to assist his community since he is the only one we are looking up to. We are experiencing all these problems because we voted him in as the president of this country. So I would ask him to assist Kikuyus and all the other tribes that were affected by the clashes.

Q: What would you tell the politicians who have started campaigning for 2012?

A: I would request them to first go back to Kenyans and talk to them to help foster peace especially in the Rift Valley. The leaders should support those who are still living in the tents so that they can vote them in once again. When they start campaigning now we will feel that they have abandoned us.

Q: What can be done for the Nandis and the Kikuyus to coexist peacefully?

A: The Nandis should be advised to respect the fact that we legally own land since we have title deeds. We are all suffering due to this violence, and both our children and theirs are out of school since they burnt schools also. They should also stop listening to the politicians since they are the cause of all this. They should know that we are their neighbours and can assist one another in times of need. We should stop looking at each other along tribal lines. We should also stop those people who come from other villages to cause enmity among us. Some Nandis would come all the way from Bomet and Kericho to fight us in Molo. So if they are convinced about this, they will not let these people come and cause violence here because we are the ones left behind with problems.

Q: It is said that Kibaki did not assist during the violence. What is your take on that?

A: I would say it was good he did not because if he did, it could have been worse. So, it is good that he did not speak up during the violence. This shows that he is patient and may God bless him for that.

Q: Do you still have that fear?

A: I am still afraid and do not think we can be able to sit together with the Nandis. I always remember what they did to us when I meet them.

IDPs protest over inaccessibility of health care services at the camp. Photo by Antony Gitonga

SECTION II

NARRATIVES OF MERCY

Raising Voices for Peace[1]

"When the spider webs unite, they can tie a lion" *African Proverb*

My mobile rang incessantly the morning after Mwai Kibaki was sworn in. One caller was persistent. Three times I was asked, "Irungu, we need to meet, when are we meeting?" With images of anger and mayhem from the entire country flooding my television, it seemed futile. However, we did meet that afternoon on the 31st December 2007 at the offices of the Peace and Development Network in Kilimani, Nairobi.

Thankfully, during the post election crisis, there were very few moments over the next sixty days that I allowed a sense of powerlessness to paralyse me again. Throughout, I kept the words of South Africa's Oliver Tambo to a young Winnie Mandela close. When she shared how worried she was, he told her, "When at a loss, history provides. Do not do anything. History will provide a situation for you to react. Remember that always, in life. Just wait there. History will rescue you. You will get guidance from within, from yourself".

With barely three hours notice, forty of us met that afternoon and reviewed the rising tide of hatred and violence. Luos being forcefully circumcised in Gachie and Nakuru, the burning of Kisii, Gikuyu and Indian homes in Kakamega, looting and police shootings in Kisumu, rising number of deaths in Burnt Forest, Kapenguria and Narok, the ban on live reporting and the silence from our leaders. An inescapable set of thoughts ran through my mind in those early days. As political affiliations and ethnicity fused, we were facing the greatest onslaught on our national identity. Our only hope as a country lay in non-violent ways of resolving the election crisis. ODM, PNU and ODM-K political leaders needed to find a pathway to resolving the highly contentious elections and the violence had to be stopped.

On the eve of the elections, Kenya had a functional Government, Judiciary, no less than 6,000 non-governmental organisations, 100,000s of community based organisations, one of the most sophisticated mass media sector in the region, 1000s of international organisations and corporations including the headquarters of various United Nations

Agencies. Their collective silence that first week of January suggested that they had all left Kenya. We were about to be reminded of an important lesson. Organisations are as effective as the individuals who work within them. In a time of profound upheaval, it is to individuals that we must look to catalyse and bring people and organisations together.

Raising Voices for Peace

At least five new initiatives sprouted over the first three days in Nairobi. Around the Peace and Development Network, the People for Peace Network, Maendeleo ya Wanawake, ActionAid, Oxfam and World Vision created the Election Violence Response Initiative (EVRI-1) to call for peace and re-establish the national network of community peace-workers (http://www.peaceinkenya.net). Under the auspices of the Inter-religious Leaders Forum, a social intervention taskforce of humanitarian agencies began to assess and plan for the emerging humanitarian need. Governance, legal and human rights organisations began to call for a rejection of the results of the General Elections. Convened by the Kenyan National Commission of Human Rights, this lobby became known as the Kenya Peace, Truth and Justice network. Elsewhere, Kenyan artists formed Musicians for Peace and Concerned Kenyan Writers. Recognised peace-workers and professional mediators within the Horn formed Concerned Citizens for Peace, a lobby that operated from Serena hotel.

The Concerned Citizens for Peace pre-occupied itself with three priorities namely; publicly calling for an end to violence, mediated dialogue at the highest level of the two large parties PNU and ODM and creating a space for concerned citizens to act. It was clear to me that the ODM policy of mass action and the PNU policy of mass denial were recipe for further chaos. Unleashed by a flawed political election, the character of the violence found its shape in social and economic identities. Kenyans were being attacked for being the "wrong tribe", for being women and girls, for having property or wealth or for being old.

In those days, our radios, televisions, mobile phones and the Internet were flooded with stories and graphic images of this violence. That this was also fuelling the violence was one thing I could agree with the Minister of Information. However, in context of suspicion that the newly elected Executive had rigged itself to power and national uncertainty, the attempt to ban live broadcasting would prove unpopular and futile.

The task was to create a third voice, one that called for an end to the violence and a mediated conversation on a political solution.

The role of the Media Owners Council was crucial. The media had to look beyond the sensationalism of youth carrying pangas at roadblocks along the major highways of the Rift Valley, the crowds in our informal urban settlements and the numerous press conferences calling for Kenya to be made ungovernable. CCP had to find and promote the peacemakers, those Kenyans who were trying to hold inter-ethnic communities together, to build dialogue and alternative ways of expressing their frustration with the political process or even the gross inequities they experienced. A diverse list of fifty men and women from different communities, professions, regions and political affiliations was prepared and sent to media houses for them to interview on the way forward.

Later, media activists working in both CCP and EVRI-1 composed several peace messages that were later sent round by the major mobile phone companies. One of the most powerful calls for peace was performed by several of Kenya's finest gospel musicians. It was at one of the early press conferences by CCP that the song Umoja Pamoja was given substantive and free airplay. Members of CCP, the Concerned Writers for Kenya would produce over 100 articles for international and national newspapers and magazines by February 6 2008 (http://www.kwani.org/blog). This proved very successful and soon dominated the airwaves and front-pages by January 7 2008. A key important message at this time was "we can fix this".

The international media on the other hand, found itself stuck in the pornography of mayhem and genocide long after the national media had shifted to more balanced reporting. The Media Council issued a statement to these agencies counselling against the "mention of particular tribes involved in the violence by name" as it was fuelling already heightened emotions. They called for the international press to "apply the same international principles ... while faced with similar circumstances in western countries where the dignity of the human person is respected and observed". Lastly, they declared "The local media has taken a stand to unite and use resources available to them to help contain the violence in Kenya and not to exacerbate it. Do join us in these efforts."

CALLING ON OUR POLITICAL LEADERS TO STOP THE VIOLENCE

Placing direct pressure on the top leadership of ODM and PNU to agree on a way forward on the flawed and disputed elections was the other major focus at the time. This was a pre-occupation not only of the peace groups at the time but the international community whose capitals were seized with influencing the two Presidential candidates or Principles as they became known to come to the table. Throughout the crisis, we attempted this is different ways. The first early attempt was an evening vigil march to the offices of ODM, ODM-K and PNU led by the religious leaders. A diverse range of musicians, spiritual and development leaders were supported to convene a well-attended press conference. After that fifty of us climbed into buses and presented a single open letter to the offices calling for immediate dialogue.

Later, we would write and widely circulate with the political leaders an options paper "A Citizens Agenda", several press statements and another open letter to the main Principles calling on them to personally lead the process of finding a solution. All opportunities were used to offer guidance. The Serena hotel corridors proved very spacious for sharing materials with the various mediators, political leaders and even those like us who were trying to influence the process. The ODM Presidential candidate even found himself being offered alternative reading material when he stopped to have his haircut at the Serena Hotel salon. Over February, consistent briefing meetings were held with the AU Mediation Team led by H.E. Kofi Annan. A reader on wealth and inequity was prepared for the largely non-Kenyan technical staff working on the draft Agreements. During the AU Summit at the end of January, a daily newsletter prepared in Nairobi was circulated to national delegates and the AU Commission conflict-monitoring unit.

It was these actions that established trust with the formal mediation process and allowed us to access and circulate widely the Agreements as soon as they were concluded. Indeed, we found ourselves a source of information for the media and other interest groups on the progress of the talks before the Mediation Team established its own system of consistent reporting back.

EXPANDING THE COMMUNITY OF PEACEMAKERS

While many of the efforts of the first month were centred in Nairobi, they were accompanied by important initiatives to support the establishment of peace corridors and safety spaces for ordinary people seeking refuge. Visits were made to camps for the internally displaced and inter-ethnic football matches were organised for youth in Kibera, Korogocho, Dandora and Baba Ndogo. Community newsletters like the *Kibera Journal* published calls for the communities not to burn down their houses and destroy shops and schools. Counsellors and social workers in the Rift Valley accepted to offer free counselling services in Eldoret and Nakuru and university students were financially supported to convene meetings when campuses finally re-opened. Peace monitors were sent phone credit to maintain their surveillance. The Kenya Veterans for Peace would discourage its members from supporting the militia with their military skills. An e-newsletter *Amani Sasa* ran as a daily page for the first month and then became a weekly of several pages providing analysis of planned events and profiles of peace actions and peacemakers.

At their height, seventy men and women would meet daily each morning in the Karna room of the Serena hotel. The meetings ranged from 1-3 hours and were designed around the principle of harvesting ideas. Many of the actions mentioned above and the successful Valentines day flower memorial in Uhuru Park were hatched in this room. While all these actions were taking place, the virus of suspicion and division was always present in the highly diverse space this enabled. Supporters from antagonistic parties including former Ministers and Ambassadors, youth and the elderly, the careered and the unemployed, Kenyan staff of Embassies met daily to share information and agree on actions. This diversity became uncomfortably apparent one morning when three men stood up and introduced themselves as members of Mungiki sect and that they too, were trying to bring an end to the violence. The Convenors were careful to moderate language and the space given to different viewpoints. The sessions always started and closed with first three stanzas of the national anthem. The best moments for me were when we reflected and decided on a course of action in the morning, acted by the end of the day and reported the next. The worst were when we spent too much time analysing the context or discussing how we should be organised and not agreeing on a practical action to take.

By the end of February, it was clear the tide had turned. The skilful mediation of H.E. Kofi Annan and his team, the national outcry backed internationally for a political solution and a return to the rule of law had wrested the mindset of mass denial and mass action from PNU and ODM. The sense of urgency began to be replaced by a sense of relief. This victory came not without cost to the various initiatives.

The voluntarism that had fuelled the ideas, actions and resources began to wane. This voluntarism had seen guards offer to protect peacemakers going into the Rift Valley and designers, journalists, singers, writers and Kiswahili translators produce and publicly distribute peace materials. University graduates daily recorded and circulated minutes, photocopied documents and lobbied our leaders. Social workers, mediators and drivers had voluntarily gone into heal communities, temper and channel their anger constructively. Former campaign party activists had cut thousands of peace ribbons, spoke to their party leaders, held peace rallies and night vigils and mobilised young men and women to protect persecuted communities.

Without sustained funding and firm organisational structures, this voluntarism could not be sustained. Focus and momentum disappeared. Perhaps this was inevitable in these circumstances. Many of us could now return to our normal lives, our jobs and families. Yet, this was not without the lingering feeling that we had come very close to losing our nation. We had held together and if Kenya was threatened, we could find each other and do the same again.

NOTE

[1] Irungu Houghton is Pan Africa Director for Oxfam <irunguh@oxfam.org.uk> based in Nairobi. This is a personal testimony only in one sense. The views contained are that of the writer. The events described in the testimony were the collective efforts of many Kenyans who over the two months of post election violence voluntarily gave their time, money and relationships to the pursuit of one Kenya and a political and non-violent solution to the crisis. The writer is proud to have stood among them.

WE HAD GOOD LIVES

My name is Emily Wambui Kosgei, I live in Wainaina Estate and I am married to a Kalenjin. Last year, I was living here on my plot. In this area there are Kikuyus, Luhyas and Luos and we lived peacefully together. At the far end of the estate there is a place called Kurio where we now have the Kalenjins. There are also Luos who have rented houses from the Kikuyus and those who have built their own houses. Before the violence this year, life was so sweet. We lived peacefully with each other and even had farms elsewhere where we went farming, as far as 10 kilometers away. We had good lives and all our business transactions with other ethnic groups were excellent.

On the voting day we went to Arrasen Primary School at around 4.00 am and found our neighbors, the Kalenjins. We also went with other communities to the polling station. After voting, the situation remained calm until Saturday 29th December 2007 when the young men from the Kalenjin community started singing unusual songs saying that if Raila Odinga didn't win the presidency they would chase Kikuyus to Othaya, and the first stage would be Kinungi. We were frightened and we now suspected that all was not well. In fact, we didn't sleep on that particular day as we saw that Kiptega village was already on fire. When the results were finally announced, in less than an hour, Kitingia was on fire. Later, Ng'arua was in smoke and now the general mood had changed. We felt so bad that our bodies literally shook.

That night I asked my niece Shiro who had visited me during the holidays to cook for the children and at around 6.50 pm we had eaten. Suddenly, we saw fire at the lower side of our estate. My sister and I took the children and hurried to the church where other people were running for refuge. We left my house and on enquiring in the morning, I found out that my house had not been burnt. I removed property like clothes, utensils among others and took them to the police station. When we reached the road, we found people from Rukwiri carrying trees and branches saying that 'si kuzuri' (it is not safe). They didn't have anything as all they had was destroyed. I realized that they were very hungry. There was a friend of mine called Kimani from this village who told me that "Mama Faith kile tumetendewa hata siwezi kusema. Nyumba yetu imechomwa, ng'ombe zimeenda, bratha yangu ameuliwa" (Faith's mother, I can't explain what has happened to us. Our house has been razed to the ground, our cows stolen and my brother killed). I didn't have words. Instead I started crying uncontrollably. I had to help those people with food and clothes. I gave them both physical and moral support since they needed counseling. Being a mother, I found myself helping so many people especially those with children and the elderly. I gave clothes to the children, food and whatever else that was at my disposal. I also gave out utensils. I could not afford to see mothers and their children suffering yet my house was spared and I had things that could be used to help those in need.

Q: Would you help if violence erupted again?

A: Yes, I can help them again though my prayer is that this does not happen again. It was a very sad experience. I know God blessed me because of giving.

Q: By helping did you subject yourself to any danger?

A: Definitely, since I am married to a Kalenjin I risked my life through helping others. I hid myself whenever I heard the Kalenjins because they didn't want to hear about that. Also some of the Kikuyus hated me for marrying a Kalenjin but I stood firm.

Q: Can you forgive those who attacked people?

A: I forgave those who attacked others because I am a Christian. Even if I don't forgive them, I won't help in any way. Secondly, I would like the Kalenjins to ask for forgiveness if they like peace. I would also like them to return all the property they looted. The Kikuyus are bitter because of the property they lost.

Q: Were the attacks planned for?

A: I didn't know that these war/clashes would erupt. In fact, after visiting I just went home and since I had a small child I spent most of my time indoors. I didn't go to the town center to know what people were saying. So the clashes were a total shock to me. In 1992, I was still living at home so I didn't know about clashes. By 1997, I had gotten married and lived in Kisumu so I didn't help anyone.

Q: What can the government do to help the IDPs?

A: I would like the government to continue helping the victims of post election violence. It's good that they are giving them Kshs. 10,000 and Kshs. 25,000. I wish every person would get this money though, it's not enough but it's good for a start. I would also like the government to give food and build houses for these people. You know, there is a lot of hunger here. Children are not getting enough food. They are exposed to tough conditions like cold and diseases in these tiny tents. The government should move them from the tents to their farms and ensure maximum security forever.

In my view, the government and the NGOs should come up with a lasting solution to these clashes. Prevention is better than cure.

THE BOYS WHO CAME TO BURN OUR HOUSE WERE PUPILS FROM MY SCHOOL...

My name is Beatrice Kimani and I was living in Burnt forest centre at Wainaina estate. We lived together with the Kikuyus, the Kalenjins, the Kisiis and the Luos. All of them used to rent houses and even the Kalenjins who brewed illicit drinks were our neighbours. They were very friendly and there was no tribalism. We cared for each other and helped each other in times of need.

Before the elections we were okay. The situation changed during the referendum and campaigns. During the referendum in 2005, people divided themselves in terms of "Oranges"- Orange Democratic Movement (ODM) and "Bananas"- Party of National Unity (PNU). That is when all we see today started. There were rumours that if the Banana side won there would be clashes. It was also said that land would not be given to daughters. The issue of Majimbo was also put into sharp focus. They said that if anyone could not live the way they wanted, he/she would be forced to vacate those areas. Then followed the campaigns. ODM was formed during the referendum and the hatred which was there was now brought to the open. Everybody could see it and tell that everything was not okay.

Eeeh, politics changed our livelihood. I know that all these things were planned many years ago. I know this and I am sure of it because during the referendum we were told openly that we would vacate this area. It was only that ODM won the referendum results otherwise if the PNU had won, then I am sure we would have been told to vacate this place then.

I helped those who were affected by the clashes. I remember there was a man who was diabetic, as well as a boy and a girl who were Kisiis. We were hesitant to give them any help because we didn't know which side the Kisiis were in. Later we realized that they were also being chased away by the Kalenjins.

At around 3.00 pm the attackers came to burn our house and I told my people to go and take refuge at the Catholic Church. An hour later, we were informed by a good Samaritan that houses belonging to the Kisii communities were also being torched. This is when we became sure that they were in the PNU. During the skirmishes one person was shot with an arrow, but the others were allowed to go safely. So, I helped the people and children and led them to the Catholic Church. Later, I received a call from the Rural Women Peace Link (RWPL) and the women informed me that there were some old women who were nearly raped in a certain village. They also informed me that there was another woman who had sought refuge in one of their homes. I made efforts to bring her to the camp. I also went for a mentally disturbed man with the help of the police. Those Kalenjin women from the RWPL helped me so much.

I remember there was a man in a certain village who had been beaten thoroughly. Those women called to inform me that he was being eaten by ants. They thought he was already dead but to our surprise he was not. I talked to the family and we sent our boys to collect him. Although they went with some police officers, those women from the RWPL stood there until the body was collected. The man was taken to Burnt Forest health centre and later to Nakuru hospital where he died. There were also old people who were left in the houses or in the shambas. I wasn't able to help those who were left but RWPL took charge.

There were also bodies in Rurigi. Fourteen (14) bodies were lying in this village so I talked to the police in Arrensens Primary School where the RDU had camped and asked them to go for those bodies at Rurigi, Kaisleen and Olare. I also saved lives of some people who were writhing in pain. The attackers thought they were dead only for us to realize they were still alive.

Q: Why did you help?

A: Aaah! I helped those people because I didn't want to engage myself in bitterness. Secondly, I knew that we cannot live without peace. Thirdly,

I understood that though we were all from different ethnic groups, we still needed each other. When I talked to those Kalenjin boys I felt so strong. They also tried to attack a woman who had just given birth and I talked to them calling them by names. They listened and stopped. This is when I felt that through talking I could help people and I could get recognized.

Q: *By helping did you put yourself in danger?*

A: I risked my life through helping those people. People hated me especially when I wanted to re-start my school. I am the deputy head teacher in my school and when those NGOs i.e. the UNICEF, Red Cross, Human Rights etc. came I was the contact person. I told the parents and pupils that our school would accommodate pupils from all the communities. This is when I went through a very bitter experience. I told the Kikuyus "get ready to welcome the Kalenjins". After saying those words, one of the volunteer teachers in the school got hold of me and slapped me. He also wanted to strangle me. The Kikuyus didn't want to mix with the rest of the children from ODM supporters. There was a policeman who came to help me after realizing everyone was against me. I used to receive short messages (sms) which were threatening and I felt insecure.

I was also given conditions on how to admit pupils. When I failed to go by their orders I would receive a short message saying that I would die soon and that I should not be seen in the center by 7.00 pm. I had also made another mistake. The Red Cross people had given me 56 pieces of *sufurias* (cooking pots) to give to the teachers. I gave those *sufurias* to all teachers regardless of ethnic affiliation. So I was again threatened by almost everybody in Burnt Forest and even the village elders. Everybody was saying that I was the one who was helping those who had attacked 'us' and destroyed our property. I was told to vacate this place as they regarded me as a total stranger. If such a case happens again I would surely help again.

Q: *Given a chance can you identify the attackers?*

A: The boys who came to burn our house were pupils from my school aged 12-15 years. In fact, I knew them all and called them by names and told them to stop it.

I Feared my Children Would Betray Me

My name is Mama Kiplagat and I have lived in Koilet, Burnt Forest for 29 years. In Burnt Forest and its environs we live as a community from different ethnic groups. Majority are the Kikuyu and the Kalenjins. Others include the Luo, the Kisii and the Luhyas who came as laborers and traders. Being one of the smallest towns in Kenya, we have lived together with the people from diverse communities for a long time. We have done everything together; for example business and farming. We also schooled together and even intermarried. We have attended church together and this has always been the case since we were young children. But since 2007 and thereafter, things have not been normal.

In the year 2007, our lifestyle changed for the worse especially during the campaign period. When we were heading towards the general election, hatred based on ethnic affiliation emerged. Though it had always been a culture that politics cuts across ethnicity based on parties, the 2007 campaigns were marred with violence that can be traced back to the referendum and politicians. The people of Kenya were divided along ethnic lines i.e. majority of the Orange Democratic Movement (ODM) wing were from Nyanza and Rift valley, while PNU who supported the defeated proposed constitution were the Mt. Kenya (Central Province) communities. So when the 2007 elections campaign came, the same picture emerged that most Kikuyus were in PNU and most non-Kikuyus were in ODM.

These two political parties struggled to solicit votes to have their candidate be the flag bearer. This situation worsened during the campaigns because politicians preached hatred to the leaders, the parents and even to the children. The strategies used during campaign were not good because of propaganda. In school where I teach for example, you could hear pupils say ODM stands for '*Ondoa Damu Mbaya*' and PNU means '*Pitia Nyeri Uone,*' when translated it meant 'Remove Bad Blood' and 'Go via Nyeri at Your Risk' respectively. This propaganda elicited reactions in 2007 elections. Other propaganda used included the Majimbo debate championed by ODM but misinterpreted by their rivals that it meant everybody should go back to their ancestral land. When the violence broke out in 2007 things were never the same again.

When violence erupted I did my best to help a family (a mother and her three children). Since majority of the Kikuyus lived in town and majority of the Kalenjin in rural areas, when the disputed presidential election results were announced, the Kikuyus were attacked in my area and were forced out of Burnt Forest town (urban) where majority of them lived. During this period when mayhem had rocked the area, I happened to save my immediate neighbor, who was a Kikuyu from being attacked by the Kalenjins. This was one of the risks I put myself through because I took the woman (widow) and her three children and hid them in my house for two days. In fact, it was only me who knew and I made sure that nobody else knew about it. If Kalenjins realized I had helped a Kikuyu, they would have even killed me. It was very risky and I was in danger because of suspicion and even feared that my children would betray me if they knew about it. However, I cared for them, fed them, and provided for their needs.

Q: Why did you help?

A: I helped as a Christian because we have lived as good neighbors even before her husband died. We had lived like brothers and sisters. We could borrow everything from each other like flour when I am late to go to the posho mill. I risked by locking them in my house and I knew I was in trouble if they found out. I was in so much danger that if violence ever occurred again I do not think I can help. I was not comfortable and there was suspicion that I had betrayed my community. I cannot help again because the widow I helped did not thank me after resettlement but accused me of driving them out of their home.

Q: In your view, can you forgive those who attacked others?

A: On my side, I can forgive those who wronged and attacked others. But before forgiveness, I urge them to accept what happened and forgive as the Bible wants us to.

Q: What would you recommend to the government?

The government should in the first place give Kenyans a new constitution that caters for all so that we can live in harmony. The executive powers of the president should be reduced and thorough electoral commission reforms undertaken. There's need to serialize form 16A and other electoral documents. Election supervisors like presiding officers and their deputies should be from different areas.

All in all, I feel everybody should preach peace, togetherness, development and educate people on the impact of violence. The government and other organizations should also preach peace and educate people on the effects of violence as well as importance of living together in peace.

THE ATTACKERS ARE STILL LIVING IN ABJECT POVERTY...

My name is Grace Cheruiyot and I live in Lingway. We used to live peacefully with the Kikuyus, the Luhyas and the Luos. We cooperated in everything that we did. We sold our commodities to them and they also sold theirs to us. We also helped each other whenever a problem arose and there was no fear or suspicion among us. When the campaigns begun all was well. However, after the elections that is when we heard people saying that if the incumbent president won, the Kikuyus would have to go. Otherwise even when we were going to the polling stations we were very happy together.

When the presidential results were announced, I realized that the Kalenjins were so bitter that they attacked the Kikuyus. They burnt their houses and fighting started seriously. Even though the Kikuyus burnt our houses in retaliation, we were not as affected as they were. I was surprised because we were with Kikuyus all through yet I didn't know what was being plotted against them. I liked the Kikuyus so much and I used to interact with them more than I did with my own community. The hatred between the Kalenjins and the Kikuyus emerged when Kalenjins said that Kibaki was not fit to be the president and that since he was a Kikuyu it must be Kikuyus who had elected him. That is why they fought the Kikuyus. Equally, they destroyed their homes and seriously injured others.

In 1992 and 1997 I was still living here. I think fighting erupted because of the elections. It's just like ball game. Sometimes whenever certain teams win, the losers may even start fighting because of the bitterness of losing that game.

I didn't take part in the campaigns, I only helped victims especially those from Lingway as I pitied them so much. Most of them were my friends and I could not afford to see them suffering. I gave them milk and clothes because their animals had been stolen and their clothes burnt. We also hid some Kikuyus during that night of clashes until the following morning. In fact, at some point I risked my life. Some Kalenjin men saw the Kikuyus coming from my compound and so they seriously wanted to burn my house. They said that I voted for PNU which they opposed saying that it was a Kikuyu party.

Personally, I swear I didn't know that war would erupt that evening. Earlier, the Kikuyus had come and I gave them food and we wished each other a happy new year. That night, they were attacked and they came to question why I had not alerted them. I was so bitter and I was in tears since that day it was announced that Kikuyus and Kalenjins were enemies. I didn't know or understand how things changed so fast. So we started running and Kikuyus also ran for their lives. Kikuyus were in great problems because they were caught unawares by so many Kalenjin men. Oh! I wish God would forgive us.

I think the reason why we didn't know about this war was because the Kalenjin men are not open to their wives. Whenever they talk, no woman is involved in their talks and there is no interaction. I think they organized the war whenever they met in drinking places or in political meetings. There was also that issue of stolen votes. During the month of December the youth indulge in alcohol, as it is a festive season. These youths shouted that the ODM votes were stolen whereas the Kikuyu youths celebrated that Kibaki had won. I think this argument sparked off the fighting. Although different communities owned houses in Lingway, the Kalenjins didn't lose as much as the Kikuyus did.

Q: Would you forgive those who attacked others?

A: Yes, as far as I am concerned I can forgive my fellow Kalenjins who out of the blues started hating the Kikuyus. I blame the last general elections that brought about bitterness in the lives we live today.

Q: What is your message to Kenyans?

A: I would like the government to intervene and help people live in peace in this area forever. I would also advice the elders from both communities to talk to the youth because all that dirty work was done by the youth. Through dialogue we can arrive at a lasting solution in Lingway. The Kikuyus have already started coming back to their farms and are very peaceful. They greet us with good hearts whenever we meet. I ask them for forgiveness on behalf of Kalenjins. Sometimes they speak to me and ask me the reason why it happened. But whenever I ask for forgiveness they tend to heal faster.

My advice to fellow Kalenjins is that; forgiveness and repentance is very powerful. I know most Kalenjins are still living in poverty. Despite the fact that they stole and even burnt stores full of maize, wheat and beans, they didn't benefit in any way. In fact they are living under a curse. I think there was an evil spirit or a demon of destruction. But I see my people have learnt a lesson; a good lesson in life. They wonder why they chased away the Kikuyus yet they still live in great poverty whereas the Kikuyus are happy and willing to help them. May God bless our Kalenjins.

THEY CUT OFF THEIR TALK

My name is Fanice Akivambo and I live in Kahuho estate. Last year, I was living in the town centre of Burnt Forest. Before the clashes, we used to live in unity with the Kalenjins, the Kisiis, the Luhyas and the Luos. There were also Turkanas. We used to help each other in many ways like when I lacked stock for my business, I borrowed money from my neighbours who were Kalenjins. I also run a clinic. Indeed life was quite good.

During the campaign season, the Kalenjins had started to threaten people. They started saying that Kikuyus must go to Othaya whether PNU or ODM won. Some even came to my shop and beseeched me not to stock my shop so much since everything would not work out well. We also had a group for women but at some point the Kalenjins advised that members should not be given loans as usual. They said that loans will only be given after the elections. Also they started to isolate themselves from us. Many are the times when they avoided our company and we suspected that there was something bad cooking. Whenever we found them talking, they cut off their talk and I suspected something was afoot.

Before the presidential results were announced, I saw people standing in groups all over. When I asked them what was happening they told me that tension was rising because Kalenjins had isolated themselves from Kikuyus. They had grouped themselves into three groups: One at the far end of Chomazone, another one at Turudi area and another strong group of teenage men at the shopping centre. Immediately the results were announced the Kalenjins started blocking the roads, others burnt houses, others looted the shops before burning them, and injured thousands and killed hundreds of people. My child and I didn't go anywhere, I was so scared. In fact, I didn't have strength to carry anything from the house. I took my child and ran to the church where everybody else was running to.

In the morning, I went back to the house and carried away my property to the church. But that didn't help because some people stole them. Finally, all that remained is what I used to help the other victims with. Even if my things were stolen at the church compound, I found myself far much better than those who came empty handed from the villages. So I helped them with food and clothes especially women and small children. Life in the camps was terrible. Children slept all over, diseases erupted, as confusion and psychological torture lingered in the minds of many. Most people could not locate their family members and their cries filled the air.

Q: Why did you help?

A: I helped the clash victims not because they were my friends but mainly because I felt compassion for them. I gave them clothes, blankets, utensils and everything I had. I didn't care risking my life in doing so. I helped them because I also knew that I would need assistance at some point.

Q: If this problem recurred would you help them again?

A: Helping people is a must because we need each other. Problems don't only come during clashes but every day for we live in problems. You cannot just sit and watch people suffering. At least out of humane heart, you lend a hand. We must continue to help people.

Q: Can you forgive those who attacked others?

A: I must forgive them though it's hard. I might end up dying with bitterness which won't help. It's better to force ourselves to forgive them because even if we fail to do so, we won't gain anything. I also would like to advice the Kalenjins to ask for forgiveness and return all the property they looted.

Q: What should the government do to avoid a repeat?

A: The government should also try to bring people together at the grass roots through chiefs, DOs and MPs. They should also give people hope. It is good for the government to organize *barazas* to meet people because people have different views. It is these people who fought each other and peace won't be forced on to them. It has to come naturally from them. As for me, I love them because my career doesn't favor anyone more than the other. They come to the clinic and I assist them equally. I work wholeheartedly for everyone.

Q: Where were you during the 1992 and 1997 clashes? Did you help?

A: In 1992 and 1997 I was still here. I helped the clash victims a lot. I also had a clinic by then and I treated the victims free of charge. This year I didn't treat people because everything was stolen from the clinic. Later, after we had bought some medicine and clinical equipments I started treating victims although this time I charged them some little money.

Q: What can the government do to help those who were affected?

A: The government together with NGOs should establish guiding and counseling seminars. People do have psychological problems and they really need counseling, especially the youth and women. The government should also continue supplying food to everybody. Right now they are only giving food to those in the villages whereas we in the shopping centre get nothing yet we also need food. When those people came from the village we were the ones who gave them all we had. We gave them food and clothes. This year there was no farming nor did we carry out any business so we are all the same and we need equal assistance from the government. They should also give the business people some funds for upkeep in their daily lives. The operation *'Rudi Nyumbani'* has failed. People are being told to go back home yet there are no houses and no security. People have just been taken from one camp to another. The government should have given them time to heal first and counseling should have been done. Also children were highly affected. Initially, there were no schools in the villages and children suffered from the memories of what they saw. The future of this country depends on children, yet there is no hope for them. When they were returned to their farms they suffered a lot. There were no schools and no teachers. Parents had to volunteer for the sake of their children's education yet they had no teaching qualifications. The government should have taken time before acting this way.

I Rescued Them

My name is John Maina and I live in Burnt Forest. In 2007 I was living here. Though Burnt forest is a small town, there are different communities who live here. The Kikuyus and Kalenjins are the majority. Before 2007, these communities were living here happily and even intermarried. We also schooled and worked together.

During the election, things changed because the campaigns were very competitive. The Kalenjins were supporting ODM while the Kikuyus supported PNU. Both parties were so strong so no one could tell which party would win the elections. Both communities were so confident that their respective parties would win. This brought about a lot of expectations among the Kalenjin and the Kikuyus. Indeed this election was hotter than that of 1992 and 1997.

I helped my neighbours the Kalenjin who were attacked in the town centre. Those Kikuyus who lived in the villages were attacked by Kalenjins and they ran to Burnt Forest shopping centre. The Kalenjins who lived in the town centre were also attacked by Kikuyus because they were outnumbered. I can remember an instance where I went to save my best friend who happened to be my neighbor. I did all I could to rescue him and his family. The Kikuyus wanted to kill me when they realized that I had hidden them in my shop but they didn't succeed. When I was travelling to Central province, I hid that Kalenjin in my lorry together with my stock, covered the lorry with a tight tarpaulin and rescued them. I also carried their clothes and to date they keep thanking me.

Q: Why did you help them?

A: I helped them because they were my friends. We worked together and even shared a borehole. I didn't like it when they were suffering.

Q: If such a thing ever happened can you assist again?

A: If this war comes again I can still help those in need. I would like the government to try and help people who are under attack. The government delayed in rescuing victims from the hands of the attackers. I would like the government to unite people and to stop using divisive language during campaigns. The new constitution should be well revised to cater for the needs of every Kenyan.

Q: In 1992 and 1997 there were similar clashes. Did you assist?

A: In 1992 the clashes were not so hot so I didn't help people. In 1997 the clashes were in the village and didn't affect the centre where I lived. I didn't know that war would erupt but there reached a time when the Kalenjins complained about the election results but we didn't know the destruction would be to that extent.

Q: When you were assisting, did you jeopardize your life?

A: When I helped the Kalenjin, I feared that the Kikuyus would attack me for hiding their perceived enemies.

Q: Your final message?

A: Finally, I would like the government and NGO's to preach peace and to address the issues of land. The government should also assist the victims and urge the communities to stop tribalism and focus on development.

THEY SAID I WAS BRIBED TO DISCLOSE SECRETS

My name is Samuel Chirchir. I was born in Londiani and went to school there. All my life I have lived in Londiani near the town. I work in the forest near town and I live there. I operate a saw-mill. This area has a high population, the majority being the Kalenjins and Kikuyus. We also have a few from other tribes like the Luo, Kisii, Maasai and Turkana.

Here in Londiani we did not have problems in the past until after the inception of multipartism. This was in 1992. People started falling out and disagreed along their political party lines which were based on their ethnic affiliations. Every group turned to its leader of choice. There were supporters of many parties like Democratic Party (DP), Kenya African National Union (KANU) and Forum for Restoration of Democracy-Asili (FORD Asili) etc. and people disagreed along tribal lines because they supported leaders from their communities.

Subsequently, there was conflict among these communities, because if you were a Kikuyu, you had to stick to the leading party that your community was supporting. Leaders in that party also had to be from the Kikuyu community. In 1992, the most significant parties were DP, KANU and FORD-Asili. The Kalenjins supported KANU led by Moi, while the Kikuyus supported DP led by Mwai Kibaki. On the other hand the Luos and the Luhyas supported Ford-Kenya.

It was all about parties in 1992 and that is how the conflict broke out and also in 1997. After that, enmity set in and tribalism was evident. If I am a Kalenjin, I had to follow a Kalenjin leader. That was when the seed of hatred was propagated and people started fighting and burning houses. Mostly, it was the Kalenjins burning the Kikuyu houses. Even the most recent violence, majority of the victims were the Kikuyus. I also helped the Kikuyu children who had been left behind. I had to give them food because some of them were with my siblings, about seven of them. During that time I was perturbed and could not understand why people who had lived as friends for so long were fighting.

From that time, we started leading normal lives and people forgot about the conflict until November in 2007. There was confusion caused by political parties again. The Kalenjins joined ODM and the Kikuyus joined PNU. There was tension and hatred was spread. By the end of year 2007, after the results were announced, war started and houses were burnt. I saw what happened to my neighbours in Londiani Farmers where I live. After the results were announced, it did not take 30 minutes before war started. There were screams and houses went up in flames. It was where the Kikuyus lived. Their houses were burnt by the Kalenjin youth who were armed with arrows, pangas and petrol.

The following day it was chaotic and more houses were burnt. I tried to communicate with my friends from the Kikuyu populated areas. I was not able to communicate with any of them because I was not in a position to access their place. I only spoke with Kimani a friend who lived in Kahurura because I heard that the attackers were on their way there and therefore warned him. He lived in Kahurura, about two and a half kilometres from where I lived. Later on, he asked me to go and pick him. I borrowed a car from the Forestry Department and went for him. Many people wanted my help but I did not get another car. After that, we found some Kalenjin youth with stolen livestock and we did our best to return the livestock.

I also remember we found some stolen cows hidden somewhere and we identified them because we used to graze them together with ours in the forest. They belonged to someone called Gachiri Mwangi of Londiani Farmers. I did my best to see that the cattle were returned. They were saying that the cattle belonged to the enemy. It was about 4.00 pm and after we quarrelled with the youth there were some among the armed group who were scared, that after the chaos they would be followed up so they left the cattle and with the help of security officers, the livestock was returned to Londiani Farmers.

After about 2-3 days, I found a stranded woman with kids. I took her to my house where she stayed for 3 days and then I escorted her to St. Kizito Church where she camped. Later on, I found another woman who still lives at my neighbours' house because she did not have anywhere to go. I helped them with food, clothing and blankets for the young ones.

As I assisted those who were displaced from their homes, I got a lot of trouble because the Kalenjins were saying they did not want to hear of any other ethnic group especially, the Kikuyus. Some came asking why I was helping and some even suspected that I was bribed to disclose their secrets when they were going to attack a certain place. I was even threatened. I was scared because they said I was a traitor as I associated myself with the enemy. I presented my case to the elders because they were not involved with the violence. The youth were warned not to touch or destroy their property.

Q: *Would you help if such violence occurs again?*

A: Yes, I would because I love helping. I don't understand why a person should be mistreated and yet we have lived with them as friends for so long and they don't have anywhere else to go.

Q: *Would you forgive those who attacked others?*

A: Forgiving someone who hurt a fellow human being is hard. Forgiveness would be to teach them that they should respect other people's rights to life. I also disagree with forgiveness to those who burnt houses because there was no need of destroying people's investments or tormenting them so much.

Q: *Before all these happened, did you know there would be war?*

A: As I said before, back in November hatred had already set in and people started getting suspicious of each other. Even friends fell out and these were just signs.

Q: *What do you think the government should do to prevent this from happening again?*

A: The government should educate Kenyans that the leaders we elect won't just be for the communities they come from alone. They are Kenyan leaders to ensure development, hospitals and education it's all for Kenyans.

Q: *How do you think the government would abolish tribalism?*

A: The government should employ different tribes in administration offices e.g. a Kikuyu chief and a Kalenjin elder and that would bring harmony in communities and also allow intermarriages. The citizens should cooperate in activities like in churches just like they did before.

Q: *What would you like the government to do for people like you who helped during the violence?*

A: That would be hard to answer because no one knows that we helped. My appeal is that we continue living in peace as we did because it would take a very long time for them to understand if it's true or false.

I Warned Them They Would Bring a Curse

I am an administrator at Kapkatet Location in Bureti. The famous Kapkatet stadium, which hosts all important Kipsigis political meetings is within my location. In fact it is situated about three hundred meters from my office. Kapkatet location, including Kapkatet trading centre, has about thirty thousand people, most of them being the youth.

In the run-up to the 2007 general elections, three big meetings were held here by the Party of National Unity (PNU) and the last was held by Orange Democratic Movement (ODM). The PNU meeting was led by Hon. Njenga Karume and the first lady, Mrs. Lucy Kibaki. The PNU meetings saw a lot of mobilization of people from all the districts of this area – Kipkelion, Bureti, Bomet, Sotik and to some extent Transmara. This mobilization was done by provincial administration mainly Chiefs, Assistant Chiefs, District Officers and District Commissioners. It is this involvement that was to put us into trouble with supporters of ODM. All the three meetings went on without any threats being issued, except for one local politician who threatened the provincial administration for taking sides.

Let me now describe to you how events unfolded. On the voting day of 27th December, I came to my office very early – at about 4.00 am. I then proceeded to the polling station at Itoik primary school and was surprised at the orderliness at the polling station. In fact, I was told that I was late in arriving at the station. The voting then proceeded smoothly like other parts of Kenya. The challenging part was during the last moments before the presidential polls results were announced.

It was on 30th December 2007 that I sensed that tension was going to erupt into violence in my location. I therefore decided to take some precautionary steps. We had fifteen administration police officers at Kapkatet. It was clear to me that we could easily be overwhelmed by the youth who had begun to group menacingly. I advised the *askaris* (police officers) not to use any force and instead to be friendly to the youth. I also told them not to harass anybody who sought refuge in our offices. By this time (30th December 2007) there were about five hundred people in my camp – Kikuyu, Kisiis and a few others. I believe that this approach worked since nobody was shot by the askaris in Kapkatet.

By 31st December 2007, the youth had started targeting chiefs on grounds that they had ferried people to Kapkatet in an attempt to make them vote for PNU. It was in January 2008 when some youth called me – at about 2.00 pm and told me that they were going to be my guests. I guessed that they either wanted to burn my house or demand to be given a bull or an ox, as it had happened to my colleagues.

The District Commissioner of Bureti got wind of what the youth wanted to do to me, and asked if he could send some askaris to guard my place. I politely declined the offer. I told the youth that they were welcome to my home and that I was waiting for them.

It was at around 5.00 pm that I met a crowd of about five hundred youth at the entrance of my compound. I then proceeded to address them and reprimanded them for being late. I told them that they had indicated that they had other business to attend to, i. e. going to "visit" other chiefs and therefore their lateness reflected poorly on their time management. My address – delivered calmly – touched them. Infact one of the leaders wanted to tell his colleagues to leave me alone but I invited them to come into my compound.

It is to be noted that all this time I was alone, since members of my family had left at around 4.00 pm. When the youth sat around I asked them what their agenda was. One youth who appeared to be their leader stated that they had come with the intention of burning my house but they had not expected to find me. He then excused himself saying as a leader I had done them no wrong. As their leader he was against them harassing me. He only requested that I get them something to eat. When the youth leader finished speaking I said that was grateful to be visited by such friends on 1st January 2008.

Indeed I had been waiting for my guests with members of my family, only that the guests were late. As for something to eat I told them that their priority was to burn my house and not getting a cow to slaughter. I asked them to begin their work by burning me and then my house. I then told them that the Kipsigis community had already recognized them as brave, but they had overdone some things and therefore committed an abomination. They needed to be cleansed. I gave them the comparison of the seclusion hut after boys are circumcised that has to be cleansed if it is accidentally burnt. I gave them this example because they were all circumcised people.

I further warned them that they should not continue with their activities beyond that day – of 1st January 2008. If they did, they would bring curses upon themselves and their children and their wives would get children with defects. I then prayed to God to help them. Concerning their requests for the cow, I considered that to be a small problem. Traditionally men are given a bull or an ox to slaughter when they return victorious from a raid. I told them that I did not have either a bull or an ox. Instead I gave them a fat cow and a small bull. I told them I would have slaughtered the cow if my son was getting married. I told them the cow was a gift to them and not a curse. I then strongly warned them against stepping into any chief's house. The youths were so touched by what I had done and they pleaded with me to go and talk to them at the Kapkatet centre the following day. Infact one of them wanted the small bull returned to me, saying that one cow was enough for them but I told them to take both the cow and the bull.

We parted with the youth on agreement that I will address them at Kapkatet stadium the following day. On the material day, I found the youth grouped near a soda depot at the shopping centre. I requested them to move the meeting to the stadium and they agreed. I had joked with them that they should open the ODM office in Kapkatet stadium. I had carried a special stick *'nogirwet'* – given to me by the Maasai. The stick is used in Maasai land to restrain youths in times of raids. Once an elder raises the stick, the youths are not allowed to go for a raid. Those who defy do so at their own peril. Thus the Kipsigis saying *'mogisire nogirwo'* – do not defy the *nogirwo* stick. (Do not defy elders' edicts). I went on to give them the list of people they should not attack again. Chiefs, former MPs and other politicians. I specifically told them not to target the immediate former MP, Paul Sang. I reminded them that at some point, they liked him so much that they re-elected him.

Surely he could not have become very bad all of sudden. I also forbade the youth from asking for cows from PNU supporters. All the cows that had been taken from PNU supporters should be sold and money shared. No youth should take any cow gotten through the post-election violence to his home. I am proud to state that as a result of my intervention, no chief's house was burnt. The only chiefs' houses burnt were on the Sotik division side. I only regret that former Permanent Secretary Mr. Josiah Sang' was attacked, embarrassed and forced to donate three cows to the youths. Mr. Sang' was said to have been on the Banana side during the Referendum (2005) and was sympathetic to PNU in the general election.

WE HID THEM

My name is Ayub Mwale. In 2007, I was living in Majengo a small town in Vihiga district. This is a very busy town consisting of people from various backgrounds doing business. Most of the residents are the Luhyas and the Kikuyus, followed closely by the Luos, the Nandis and other small communities.

All along, these people have been coexisting peacefully, partnering in business. Vihiga is a big place with rental premises. People who live in those houses are a mixture of communities; one door is a Luhya, the other a Kikuyu, a Nandi and so on. They have lived together in a brotherly way. Life was good in 2007 and before then.

It was during the elections that trouble started. It emerged that people expected a certain community to take over the leadership of the country. Others alleged there was a certain community that has been in leadership for a very long time. People continued with their daily lives knowing that this was a year of change. When they voted, the results went against their expectations; something which brought along the post poll chaos.

During that period, people watched TVs from their houses boasting how their favourite candidates would win. The first and second day passed well until the date for announcing the presidential results was due. I remember it was about 3.00-4.00 pm on 30th December 2007 when Hon. Mwai Kibaki was announced winner. It was like people had waited for that in order to loot Kikuyus' shops. Everything we saw with our eyes was unbelievable during that spell of looting. Actually the Kikuyus were the target of their attack. All the Kikuyus who lived in Majengo were forced to flee for safety at the Vihiga police station. There was lawlessness, property was stolen and more so Kikuyus' property. There were attempts by the police to stop them but they were overpowered by the huge crowd. Whenever the police emerged from one side, the other one would be broken into. There were a lot of casualties and even deaths but in Majengo people were mainly injured.

I was with my Kikuyu neighbour and since we had stayed together for a very long time we were like a family. When chaos erupted, they were forced to shift to our house where we hid them the whole day. The following day, they were left with no option but to leave before people saw them. We took some of our family members to take care of their houses to prevent cases of burglary at night. However, we used to cook food and take it secretly to the police station where they were being sheltered. We made this a habit such that by around 8.00 pm we would cook and walk stealthily with the food to the police station. After they had eaten one would take a different route to avoid being spotted. If you were to be spotted, that could have been more trouble for you. It was dangerous to take food there because if spotted you were perceived to be an enemy of your people and they could attack you even if you belonged to the same community. We did this until they got a police vehicle to collect their belongings from their houses to the police station.

We helped them because the whole issue was not amusing at all. First, we have been living with our neighbours for more than ten years and secondly, we saw no logic in chasing them away. We used to help one another and most of the time we bought commodities from their shops. We boarded their vehicles and so there was no cause of harming them.

If such chaos arose again, I would still help. We need to learn that despite people voting, it is hard to know who voted for whom simply because voting is one's secret. Why then should one hurt another for something he/she is not sure of? Furthermore, Kenya is a free and independent country where everyone has democratic rights to do as he or she wishes. Denying someone the right to decide is outdated. Therefore, if we want to be Kenyans, everyone should enjoy his/her citizenship and live like brothers. Kenya has no residential boundaries. Anybody can live anywhere one wishes so long as there is space.

Q: Can you forgive those who attacked others?

A: I can forgive those who attacked others because the Bible says if your brother wrongs you seven times, you should forgive him seventy times seven times. Moreover, doing a mistake once is not a mistake; it is when the mistake is repeated that it becomes one. It is better to find out the cause of that problem then solve it once and for all. If I met those who attacked others, I would ask them why they did so. What they were thinking and lastly what pushed them to act that way. If you observe keenly, it is the youth who did that and they are the ones who use drugs. I will urge the youths to stop using drugs and shun those who mislead them. This is dangerous for us and our economy. If you look back you will notice that the Kenya which was built in 40 years, was at the brink of total destruction in just one day. In the end, the one who suffers is you and your family.

Q: *Did you know that violence would erupt?*

A: Surely, I didn't know if such a thing would happen.

Q: *Did you help those who were affected by the 1992 and 1997 poll violence?*

A: During that period I was still young. I only hear about the violence.

Q: *What do you think the government should do to help poll violence victims in future?*

A: I would like the government to emulate Red Cross and also partner with them. If possible it should give Red Cross support where they are stuck. To help citizens live in peace, the government should listen to the voice of the people by catering for their needs and then encourage cohesion among people. Church leaders should unite and speak with one voice. Each leader should preach peace before sermons. The youth in schools and colleges should learn about peace building.

Q: *Is there anything you would like to add?*

A: There is only one Kenya with 42 ethnic groups. Let us unite and be one, valuing each other. We need to be like brothers and sisters, shun tribalism in order to build a free Kenya where everyone can live and do business anywhere. In the end Kenya will be a good country to live in.

I AM A RED CROSS VOLUNTEER

My name is Julius Lumadede and I am a businessman. I also work as a Red Cross volunteer. I am a resident of Vihiga Central Maragoli location, Imanda sub-location, Kidudu village.

In 2007, I was in Vihiga because I was one of the contestants for the post of councillorship under the KENDA ticket. I vividly remember the campaigning and voting but when it came to the results, violence erupted. I was at Vihiga market near the police station watching the poll results from my neighbour's TV set. Then I heard a police Land Rover from Majengo with the police shooting in the air. That was when I sensed danger at around 6.00 pm in the evening. I tried to look at the police station to know what was happening. All I saw were vehicles carrying displaced people. I also saw businessmen. That was when I knew that all was not well and that it was not safe.

We live here with different ethnic groups who do business. There are also some civil servants who work in government offices. Many business people here are Kisiis and Kikuyus; most of them were born here and so work here too. All these people live a normal life because they have small farms where they carry out subsistence farming. If I look keenly, our problem here is hunger because most people earn meager income.

Life was good until 2007. There was a lot of cooperation and interaction in business. People lived well, they greeted each other and actually there were no problems. But during the election differences emerged among people. One group rose against another because of ideological differences. It was not the Kikuyus only who had problems but also people from our ethnic group (Luhya) belonging to the "wrong" party. These differences depicted a weakness in us because there was mistrust and jealousy between people.

I helped people who were attacked here at Vihiga. I had sat at a friend's shop in the shopping center when I received a call from the CID at Majengo. He told me that he knew I was a Red Cross Volunteer and that he wanted to know where I was. I told him I was at the Vihiga shopping center. He told me that there were dead bodies at Majengo which he needed me to go and collect. He also wanted me to help in ferrying people to the hospital. I told him there were no vehicles on the road but he pleaded with me to find a way there. I had no choice but to go to the police station and collect a stretcher and look for two boys to help me. When we got there, I found two children; one of them had been shot in the leg and it was broken. The child was not speaking. As I went on I found a neighbour's child there who was dead. There was also another boy who was dead. I decided to start with the child who was shot but was breathing. I had to rush him to Vihiga Dispensary. I got the clinical officer to attend to him as he had lost a lot of blood. Thereafter, I attended to the dead bodies bringing them to the mortuary. It was unfortunate that the boy I took to the clinical officer later on died.

It was a big burden to me because those who I was working with at the Red Cross were afraid. So I worked single handedly in the field. It was difficult because gun shots filled the air and the police shot carelessly in all directions. The only thing that saved me was the Red Cross uniform which is known universally and also most people knew me before as a volunteer.

Religious leaders and Red Cross members consult each other at Kedong Camp in Naivasha.
Photo by Antony Gitonga

When cases of gunshots started, many children ran over there to check out what was happening. The police shot carelessly especially at those looting shops. Those who bribed their way were not shot by police. So these children had gone to witness what was happening, the chaos went on and on. If one wanted to go looting, he had to repeat the whole process of bribing the police to be allowed to loot. Those who wanted to use force in order to loot met their untimely death by being gunned down.

As I was carrying out my duties, looting of shops was going on as usual. We could see everything because it was happening in broad day light. Looting had become the norm. For instance the police also looted from one of the Indian shops and later set it ablaze when they had finished looting it. I even have a video clip of that particular incident. They carried property worth about 20 million shillings and then set the shop on fire. I always visit that Indian and he occasionally asks me what the government was doing to compensate them. Up to date, he has not rebuilt the premise because he incurred huge losses and so now he has built a small store where he sells a few items. If you watch that footage you will surely see how the police watched without doing anything to help. They even carried some of the things in their Land Rover to their houses. That is what I witnessed.

I helped those children because I have a kind heart and also in the Red Cross we have been taught principles of helping selflessly without discriminating. When I remember that, I cannot sit back and watch someone suffering. I must try to find a solution to any problem I encounter. So, being a Red Cross guy and well known by people in Vihiga, I could have failed in my responsibilities if I didn't do what I did at that particular time. I helped fully without considering that I was a contestant in a certain party. I participated in that until when all the affected received help. When rescuing, I was in great danger because there were gunshots all over the place and it was hard to tell what could happen at any one time. But I did that with my Red Cross uniform. When I was collecting information I was not worried at all, I could have been in great danger if I was wearing civilian clothes. I could not carry out that operation if I was not in Red Cross uniform because I know there are many enemies who might use that chance to attack me because the party ticket I used to contest was not popular in this area.

If such a problem arises again, I will help because I am a kind-hearted person who has the will to help people. If I look back where I have come from and where we are, I think I have helped many people here in Vihiga. This is because many IDPs have not gotten any help upto this minute. Had I not used my personal initiative, they could still be in camps, but I thought of ways to help and in the end I came up with an idea of Jamii Bora Micro Finance- Vihiga. That has really helped them especially by enabling them to move out of the tents and IDP camps to run their own businesses again. Had we waited for the government, we could not have realized anything and instead people could still be in camps suffering. My friend Mr. Oganda and I together with Jamii Bora did our best to move them from the camp.

Jamii Bora is an organization that gives out small amounts of loans, and also fund other projects. So for the IDP's, I saw it suitable for them to get disaster loans. There are very many people in Vihiga who are poor. When they borrow funds, they are charged an interest as high as 0.5% as compared to the banks which charge an interest of 25%. Jamii Bora also takes care of those who fall sick. I sincerely believe in helping people and the people are responding well to it. My partnership with Jamii Bora started after the post election violence. Had it not been the post election violence I couldn't have known about Jamii Bora. When I discovered that it was a good organization, I decided to form a partnership with them. People are very happy and this has led to the opening of Jamii Bora offices here.

Q: Would you forgive those who attacked others?

A: I can forgive those who attacked their neighbours. I have a kind heart. I can forgive them because they didn't know what they were doing. For instance, those who looted have not changed their lives in anyway. In fact they are poorer than before and have not even bought a car. They have more problems than before. When I meet such people, I don't wish to remind them about the post election violence. Instead I just greet them and urge them to join projects that can help them improve the community. When I look at most of the attackers, they have gone insane. They are mad because they killed people.

Q: What can the government do to help people live in peace?

A: The government should organize peace and reconciliation meetings among the communities that were affected by the chaos. The government should use opinion leaders instead of using police or their state machinery.

Q: Did you know that there will be violence?

A: I didn't know that there would be violence, but there were signs that all was not well when I went to do civic registration in Nairobi. That is when I saw a politician mobilizing the police to throw tear gas at people and I developed an instant feeling that there would be violence during the elections.

Q: What precautionary measures did you take when helping people because you were also faced with danger in your duties?

A: As a precaution, I used not to walk alone. Most of the times a friend or two would accompany me wherever I went. I was a contestant of a party which was perceived to have a lot of money. Most people thought that I had benefited but that was not the case. I had no option but to be extra cautious in my movements. By 6.30 pm I was always in my house. In the morning, I had to weigh the situation and plan accordingly before stepping out to read a newspaper.

Q: What do you think the government and other organizations can do to help the victims of post election violence in future?

A: The government should come up with advocacy projects where the community can be enlightened on how to improve their lives and by so doing I think there will be no violence in future.

THEY THREATENED TO BURN MY HOUSE

My name is Margaret Nyokabi Kidiya. I am a resident of Manda sub-location, central Maragoli division of Vihiga District. When violence broke out, I was still living here at Kegendirova. Many people from different communities lived here, some from Embu and others from Kisumu. We had coexisted peacefully for many years, but the violence which was witnessed, brought a negative impact and changed everything in our lives altogether.

Life was fair in 2007 despite some hardships, at least people could help one another. My case was different because I had accommodated a number of people who were affected by violence. My budget had to change to cater for them. It was hard but by the grace of God I managed somehow. Some of the victims I assisted were school children whom I took to school. I also accommodated another lady from Embu who was married here. Their lives were at risk and so they pleaded with me for assistance. They were so scared for their lives because they had received threats that they should leave Kisumu.

By that time, Kisumu was some sort of hell on earth. Chaos had engulfed the entire city of Kisumu. They were chased and their houses destroyed that very night by hostile youth. They were in a dilemma and could not dare seek refuge at Kondele police station as word went round that the youth would next attack there. They had threatened that they would set ablaze any police station that sheltered *"the other"* ethnic communities. That was the reason which made them find their way to where I lived.

I had to accept and welcome them to my house because one never knows what the future holds. My daughter is married in Embu and this reason made me perceive them as one of my close relatives since they were from Embu. I knew I was taking some risks in doing that. It was unfortunate that some of my neighbours continued to talk negatively. Some of them threatened to burn my house claiming that I went to pick unwanted people. I just played it cool and decided that come what may, I would not bow to their pressure. We just helped them in the same way we could have expected them to treat us. I will not get tired of helping if such an incident occurs again. I like helping people because I cannot sit back and watch people suffering from the periphery. I can forgive those who attacked others if they ask for forgiveness. I wouldn't ask them to justify their actions because most of them are more miserable than they were before attacking others. One can only pray for them and hope to see some change.

Q: *What would you like the government to do to help people live in peace?*

A: I will just live it up to the government because even if I suggest an idea, the government often does what it deems right.

Q: *What will you do as an individual to promote peace?*

A: We will just continue talking to people about peace though they are difficult to deal with.

Q: *There were election clashes in 1992 and 1997. Did you help people during that time?*

A: It wasn't that bad during those years and we didn't experience violence here. I urge the leaders in government to fulfill their promises. They should also move people from the camps and resettle them.

MANY CHILDREN LOST TRACK OF THEIR HOMES

My name is Moses Olenya. I live in Ikumba village near Majengo. I was at home near Majengo monitoring how the results were being announced on television. Different ethnic communities live here: Kikuyus, Luos and our neighbours the Kisiis. We have lived together in unity for a very long time and life was good until 2007. It was after the elections that things changed for the worst. All this mess was created by bad politics. We campaigned on ethnic grounds. Luos, Kisiis, Luhyas, Kikuyus and others had their favorite candidates. This was the main cause of violence. People here perceived that the Kikuyus have stayed in power for a very long time and that it was time that they left the seat to other communities.

I helped people who were affected during the violence. I accommodated three children in my house. In the beginning we didn't anticipate the turn of events would be that bad. We were just watching T.V in Majengo when the presidential poll results were announced. It is at this time that hell broke loose. We heard people running up and down outside. On inquiring, we were told that all was not well. The youths took advantage of the confusion to loot shops. The commotion was a pointer that all was not well. The police were moving around ordering people to stay in their houses. Sounds of gunshots filled the air and there was total confusion. It was very dangerous to move around. We decided to run fast through short cuts despite the fact that there was danger. We just convinced ourselves that we were young. In the process we saw houses engulfed in fire and that is when we realized that going closer to the village was safer than the place where we were.

It was during that confusion that many children lost track of their homes. Others literally forgot the names of their villages. This was the circumstance under which I found one child laying on the ground and two others just running. I later on realized that the children had accompanied their parents from Kidudu village to do some trade at the local market. It was everybody for him/herself. I stayed with them for that day only and later on accompanied them to cross the river to try and trace their homes. I ensured the safety of these kids because I am a Christian and I like helping. I risked my life to ensure that the children were safe. I do remember when I went back to Majengo to find out what was going on, a bullet penetrated through the wall of the house I was in, and fell right beside me with its shell. I was really frightened but it did not stop me from assisting. There was need to take care of each other regardless of colour or political affiliation.

It was saddening that one could struggle to rush the injured to hospital using a bicycle, but fail to get a doctor to attend to that person. You could meet the police officers on your way and they would not give you a chance. To be on the safe side, we carried identification marks for instance a Red Cross jacket.

Q: Can you forgive those who attacked others?

A: I can forgive those who attacked others because this was caused by our leaders. Our top political leaders. If I met those people who attacked others I would like to make them understand that they ruined the lives of others.

Q: Were you involved in the 1992 and 1997 clashes?

A: In 1992 and 1997, there was violence but during that time the situation was not to this extreme. That time I participated in elections but they were very peaceful unlike the 2007 which was marred by violence. It was risky during this time but we had to join hands with the police to help people who were attacked.

Q: What can the government do to promote peace?

A: The government should discourage all forms of tribalism first. They should appoint people on the basis of merit. They should also do a balancing act on leadership. One ethnic community should not lead a whole department or ministry. This will bring a great deal of harmony in all the operations.

Q: What about your individual effort in promoting peace?

A: I will strive to live with other people in unity. We should help one another at all times. I will do that as an individual.

Q: Did you know there would be violence?

A: There were no signs of violence at all. We just thought that it was just a small hiccup.

Q: What do you think the government should do in future to help people affected by violence?

A: The government together with NGOs should enlighten the community on the importance of peace. They should equip the Red Cross and St. John's Ambulance with capacity to deal with such cases in times of crisis.

I BECAME A SOCIAL WORKER

"I am not concerned with where people come from, their tribe or race as long as he/she is a human being..." *Rahab Wairuri.*

My name is Rahab Wairuri. I have been a councilor for the last five years, between 2002 and 2007, and I am now a professional counselor and the Executive Director of the Naivasha Disadvantaged Support Group (NADISGO) that deals with children, sexual assault and gender based violence cases here in Naivasha and Kinangop. I have lived in Naivasha since 1978 (that is twenty years) and I have interacted with so many people here. Naivasha is my second home since I come from Mathioya.

I was a councilor for the last five years and previously I had contested for the same seat in 1997 and have also been a business woman in the town. I have been interacting with people from different ethnic groups here in Naivasha and I have been conducting civic education on behalf of Constitution and Reform Education Consortium (CRECO), and also as a human rights activist.

I have met many people and of different abilities and capabilities both the male and female with whom we coexisted well until during the referendum when people were divided into Orange and Banana camps. This alignment later tempered down but came up once again during the 2007 campaigns. I engaged in monitoring the 2007 general elections and was an observer until the voting day. During the campaigns I held several forums in Naivasha district and this was when I noticed that tension had begun which was to explode on 27th December 2007 and result to violence in the North Rift. Before then, Naivasha was a calm town although people have had tension but it soon diminishes and people continue living peacefully.

I have been a member of Release Prisoners Pressure (RPP) group since 1996, the year that I also joined the human rights network. I am also the Chairperson of the Political Committee in National Conventional Executive Council (NCEC). These are the people I have been working with in political activism.

On 30th December 2007, when the poll results were announced, there was a lot of celebration here in Naivasha which I personally witnessed. Later, I received a phone call that there were houses burning at YMCA and the ODM office had been stoned. But the police went there and restored peace. The ODM office was vandalized but it was not burnt.

After that incident, residents of Naivasha lived peacefully though tension was still high. And when the displaced people from North Rift started coming in, that was when situation in Naivasha deteriorated. They started saying that they had to revenge because there were other ethnic groups living here. I have a Luo tenant from whom I sought guidance on the situation at hand and he said that there was nothing to worry about. I also have friends from the targeted community and they never thought anything could happen. Before the violence broke out there was a lot of tension since the leaders always said that they would hold demonstrations that were not materializing. A curfew was imposed from seven o'clock in the evening and no one left his/her house. People said they would demonstrate against this curfew.

The residents were complaining because of the way the curfew was being enforced. It was claimed that the prison wardens who were supposed to ensure people's security would rob people at night. Businessmen too were complaining that their businesses had gone down due to the curfew. Naivasha residents were also unhappy with the state of IDPs from North Rift.

The demonstration materialized on 27th January 2008. On that day, I woke up very early. Usually there is a lot of noise from matatus in the morning but on this particular day, it was very quiet. When I looked out through the window, I saw people in groups from as early as 7.30 am. No business was opened. At around 9.00 am people started blocking the road with stones, as the police who were there removed them. I then received a phone call from a Catholic Church youth leader who wanted the number of the District Commissioner (DC) as Bishop Kairu was in Naivasha and had heard that there were people who had been burnt in

Kabati. So I gave him the DC's number. When we went to the roof top, we saw a large group of people near the Silver Hotel where the DC was. I was still monitoring for CRECO and NCEC head offices about the post election period, so I called them and told them that in Naivasha there was tension and some houses were burning. I also called the OCPD who told me that he was in Nakuru. I then called people from Kenya Human Rights Commission (KHRC) and I told them about Naivasha. When we were still at the rooftop people started clapping and we later learned that the DC had said that the curfew had been removed. We stayed on the rooftop since there was a lot of fear as we saw people running away from the police. Later we saw Elementaita Chemist being vandalized. I called the police and told them about it and they said that they were overwhelmed by what was going on since the situation was worse in Kabati. There was the smell of medicines in Naivasha town because of the medicines that had been looted at Elementaita chemist. Later we noticed that they were moving in groups and some went to Ol Ndonyo chemist.

They divided themselves and went to the shops that belonged to the targeted communities. That was when I called my tenant and asked him how the situation was where he was and he said he hadn't noticed anything. I urged him to take his family to the police station. Later I called him and he told me he was already at the police station. I decided to go to the police station and know their situation. I met some of my neighbours who asked me to call one of my tenants to ask him to come for his family since he was targeted too. So I called him. I went to the police station at around 5.00 pm and found so many people among them a number of my friends. There were no vehicles on the roads. I started consoling them and calling the ones who were not at the police station and we found out that some were still trapped in their houses. I communicated with the OCPD and the DIO who helped in the rescue of some of those who were still in their houses. One of my friends was trapped with his four year old son in a pit latrine where they took refuge and they stayed there for nine hours until we rescued them.

To make matters worse, it started raining. There was no space for all these people who were now trying to take shelter along the corridors and the police were kind enough to even let them stay in their offices. At around 9.00 pm that night, I decided to go back home and on my way back a lady approached me and requested me to take her two young children. We tried to look for a police vehicle since the fighting was still going on. I realized that if I was to go with the children on foot, I would be endangering their lives and mine too so we needed the police for security. Unfortunately all the police vehicles were out. I made the lady understand that I would be endangering their lives by going with them. I was later given two police men to escort me. On my way, I met the area MP who gave me a lift and we went to Kihoto where we found some houses being burnt by a crowd of people. We pleaded with them to stop and they stopped at around 11.00 pm. We also received information that some people had died but on liasing with those who were in prison we realized that they had not died. On the first day we knew that some people had died but we were not able to establish who they were. As we called Bernard Ndege, whose family perished on that day, the people at the prison told us that no one was able to escape from the house but someone else told us that he had seen his wife. We got confused since his neighbours kept insisting that no one was rescued from the house.

NDEGE'S PLIGHT...

Bernard Ndege had lived in Naivasha for more than thirty years, at the Gold Fish area in Kabati. He told us that on that fateful day he was with his family. On that day they heard people beating drums and on going out they saw that the people were like the Akorino religious group and had paint on their faces. They locked themselves in the plot with many other Luos. They started pelting stones at the mob. They were left with no more stones so they started fleeing and Ndege was among those who were able to flee. When he left, the group of people got into the plot and poured petrol all over and they locked the gate and lit it. That is how he lost his eight children and his two wives. One of his wives was pregnant and she was due to deliver. As she lay in the mortuary we could see the child and he was mature. During the post mortem, the doctors had to remove the baby since he was mature. So in total he lost nine children. He was left with one child who was rescued.

On the morning of 28th January 2008 I called my sister who works at Sher where the Kikuyus are a minority and she told me that some people were threatening them. Later on when she called me I was very disturbed and I decided to go to the police station because I had heard no one was able to go past Karagita. I was also afraid of going to South Lake where the Kikuyu are a minority for fear of being attacked. At the police station we tried to look for a police escort as my sister was now calling me with her family and she was crying. Finally I went with one of the pastors and another lady who had her family at South Lake. When we got to Karagita we met with the youths who stopped us and demanded us that we get out of the car. We told them that we were Kikuyus and we were going to rescue our fellow Kikuyus and that was when they allowed us to go.

When we got to Sher we found my sister at the Administration Police (AP) with a group of Kikuyus. The other tribes were not talking to them and when we got there no one talked to us. As you can remember I had said that I was conducting civic education and the last forum was held at Sher. So the people there knew me very well but no one talked to me. The group of Kikuyus got in the car. As everybody got in the car, we realized that a young lady who was a house help of one of the occupants of the car had not gotten some space in the car and we told her that we could not leave her there. The employer walked out crying but there was nothing we could do. We left and at Karagita we met the same youth who had stopped us and once again they stopped us and we told them we had rescued the people we had gone to rescue. They clapped for us and asked us to go and that is when we came back to town. I alighted at my home with three families who worked with my sister at Sher.

At the police station we started going round in order to identify those who were injured and those whose relatives had died so that they could make reports. In order to give them the needed assistance we asked them to appoint leaders. These were the ones we worked with and who helped us in identifying those people who had relatives in hospital and those who had died. They wrote reports using the information gathered. We were liaising with Sister Florence from Upendo village to assist these people. That is when we started identifying the sick and they were taken to hospital. While we camped at the police station, five women delivered babies. One of them delivered at the police station and was helped by other women but the others were taken to hospital.

On identifying those who had died, we found the number of the dead to be twenty five and before that we had confirmed about Ndege's family. We took Ndege to the gender desk where I counseled him. He collapsed and we all broke down as he demanded to go and see them at the mortuary. I felt that I did not have the strength. Since he is a man I could not be able to handle him. I called another counselor (a man) and they were accompanied by the Deputy OCPD to the mortuary to identify the bodies of Ndege's family. I remembered the counselor who went with Ndege. His brother had been killed and he was still at the mortuary. I felt guilty but he understood since he knew that I was also traumatized by the situation.

On Wednesday I called the DC and told him that there were vehicles that were ferrying people out of Naivasha and no one wanted to stay here. I asked him to hold them first so that they could identify their dead relatives at the mortuary. In that way we could help the police when conducting their investigations.

The DC asked me to let them leave since they would go and cry at the mortuary hence raise tension. I went to the DCIO and we both realized that they first had to identify their relatives and post mortem done. We knew how many they were and liaised with the group camping at the prison. We asked them to come with the people from there. We went with the group to the police station and they identified them. They were terrified and had to be escorted by police as they walked on foot. We did not have enough vehicles nor enough police to assist us.

At the mortuary, we found out that some of the bodies were decomposing as they were badly kept. The mortuary had about seventy eight bodies at that time, so it was congested and in a bad state. They identified the bodies and we started planning for the postmortem that Wednesday. On Thursday I called Dr. Okoth who happened to be the hospital superintendent but he had also been displaced and he directed me to the MOH official who was not too willing to assist. We wasted the whole morning but later found someone to carry out the postmortem on those who had been burnt because the cause of death was obvious. After he filled in the forms, I heard that he tore them since he was not being paid. It was difficult to explain to the bereaved families about what had happened because they were traumatized and if they found out that some people were not sympathizing with them, they would be more traumatized. I then called Kenya Human Rights Commission officials and informed them about the predicament we were in and they helped us get a doctor. As we were communicating with the DCIO we agreed that he would look for someone from their headquarters and whichever doctor came first, he would conduct the postmortem. Fortunately we got the doctor from the police and they conducted the postmortem on thirty six bodies. We requested them to carry out the postmortem on all bodies and afterwards we started filling in the burial permits for those who were able to carry their bodies. There was a lady in the group who was unable to identify the body of her husband so we were forced to keep the coffin in the mortuary and we asked her to go and get her parents. The bodies in the mortuary had been badly cut and it needed a lot of courage since some even had their their eyes gouged out. It was a horrible sight and even for those bodies which had started to decompose, you could see maggots coming from the mouths and nose. We all nauseated as we left the mortuary.

The people from our community were at the gate looking at us as if we were traitors. When we went back to the police station we noticed that some children were traumatized, so together with the DCIO we took the children to the police workshop and tried to look for volunteers to teach them but they all demanded for money. So we decided to teach them. I taught children from class one to class three, a social worker became a nursery school teacher, another counselor became a teacher for children from class four to class eight. We realized that teaching was difficult. I came home and took my television and another police officer came with his DVD so that they could watch movies.

The traumatized children received counseling. For example, I noticed one of the kids was very quiet and when I sent the rest outside, I asked him why he was so quiet and he told me "You know what auntie, they cut my father and killed him". I was shocked because I was not prepared for that. I talked to him and later his relatives got transport and they went back to Nyanza. You can imagine if these children have never had any other counseling after that, they are still experiencing the trauma. So many children witnessed their parents being killed and their property destroyed. Whenever I was called and I conversed in Kikuyu, the children would look at me with very strange eyes so I was always forced to converse in Kiswahili whenever I was there. When carrying out the postmortems, we realized that it would be difficult to remove what had been planted in the children's minds, because they saw that this community was full of murderers.

From there we worked together with the other organizations to distribute food. There were times we had a lot of problems since some of the organizations have a lot of bureaucracy. We knew that there were 7,500 people at the police station – men, women and children- as we had done a head count on Thursday night, but when the food came they would insist on first keeping it in the store before they established how many families were there. How do you keep food in a store while people have gone for three days without food? The only thing that helped us was the vegetables we got from the flower farm we used to share the vegetables among them even if they would take it without anything else. But at times we would even feel like breaking those offices. I had so many friends and the food would be cooked at my place and I would take it to them in containers. When we took it there, we would give it to anyone even if we did not know who they were.

Another example of how bureaucracy affected negatively was in the case of this man whose wife was in maternity and had already delivered. He had a vehicle that would take them to Migori. After he identified his brother's body he asked me to take him to the hospital so that he could take her with him. I did not have transport so I called the Red Cross officials and I asked them to assist this man to take his wife since he could not walk by foot because the community was still baying for their blood. The officials refused and they said they don't carry those who are fighting and those who are being beaten. I asked them if they were not the ones who brought the lady to the hospital before she delivered. They said yes but asked me to look for assistance elsewhere. An American journalist who was there assisted him since he had a taxi and he took the lady to the prison and she was able to travel with the rest. There was also a time when the Red Cross officials told us that someone had called them and told them that there was someone trapped in a pit latrine and was communicating through cell phone so the police got into the Red Cross vehicle to go and rescue this man. The Red Cross people opposed this move arguing that they did not carry armed people, so we had to wait for the OCPD to bring his car. By the time they got to Kabati, they noticed that the phone had been switched off. We don't know what happened to this person. These bureaucracies were just too frustrating!

As we were there, we still received calls from those who were still trapped. For example there was a teacher in one of the schools here in town whose child had already gone to the prison and did not know where his mother was. The child said his mother was sick. The child hid and went back home where the neighbours told him that they were giving her food but they asked him to look for means and get her out of the house since people around had started saying that there was a Luo in the house. When he came to the police station with his sister he informed us about his mother and we took the police. On getting to Site to take the lady, the community wanted to attack us. We found the woman had become crazy and did not even recognize her son. She even told her son that we wanted to kill her and we all broke down on realizing that she could not even recognize her own son. When we asked the child to take what he could from the house, he only took his mother's certificate and his books and we left. When we got into the vehicle, we had to tie the lady down because she was very violent, while the community was shouting at us. We took her to the hospital where she was admitted.

Then we heard that there was a man at the Karati forest. He had been there since Sunday and this was on a Friday. While there, his landlady would bring him food. On Thursday night the community went to look for him in the landlady's house but did not get him. That was when the landlady realized that the man's life was in danger and she informed us. So we took the police and went to get him from Karati.

As I said earlier, as a human rights activist, I am not concerned with where people come from, their tribe or race as long as he/she is a human being. So I assisted them because they are human beings who were encountering problems. Also as a counselor, I am supposed to offer my services to anybody who is in need but first of all I do it because I am a human rights activist and I believe in social justice.

Q: While you were assisting them, did you put your life in danger?

A: Yes I did because even as I was going back home in the evening the police would accompany me. For two weeks during this crisis, I used to go there every day from morning until evening. I stopped when they left the police camp to either Kedong' camp or back to their rural homes. All this time the police used to escort me back home because it was not safe. Even our office had been broken into and we lost a computer. I still have that anger in me because people I know did that accusing me of helping the "wrong" people whom they did not want to see assisted. On the night of Monday the 28th January 2008, I went to sleep where my tenant used to stay. When I was there I was very afraid since I did not even know how I would leave the place in the morning. While there some people that I knew came. I pleaded with them and I told them that we had removed all his property and I was the one who wanted to stay in the house. But when I went to the police station, they got into the house and burnt everything that was there. They even spoilt the water cisterns in the toilets.

Q: If such kind of violence were to erupt again, would you still assist?

A: If such violence erupted again, I would run away. I don't think I will have the energy to face it. What I saw is still fresh in my memory because after that, I needed to be ounselled. But these counselors were with me in the field so no one counselled the other well as we still have wounds in our hearts. Even during the Waki Commission hearing, I was supposed to debrief one lady who was testifying. After she testified I just broke down. I don't think I have that energy. We are talking to people to avoid enmity because one is perceived an enemy once he/she declares interest in an electoral seat. People do things because of their leaders while they go and accept one another as friends. The citizens who attacked the others are left guilty and those who were attacked are left with enmity and fear. So we are requesting people to live peacefully because what we saw during those two hot days when people killed one another, was very bad. I cannot stand this again. If it was to happen again I would run away from Naivasha.

Q: Did you know that there would be violence?

A: No, I did not know. It took me by surprise. I only knew that people would demonstrate against the curfew. Leaders did not come out to demonstrate leadership. We even came to a point of thinking that it was just a rumor. The reality that people had been killed struck me when I went to the police station as we had only thought that the attackers were just burning houses. There were so many bad things happening that even some men were forcefully circumcised. For example, I am still counseling a lady who used to stay in Kayole area whose brothers were forcefully circumcised. She had been told that her four year old son too was to be circumcised during the attacks. Fortunately she had dressed him in girl's clothes but they wanted to remove the child's clothes in order to confirm her gender but some mothers in the neighborhood intervened. They ordered her to stay in the house. She was given petrol to pour in the house so that they could be burnt. So they did as they were ordered but when they wanted to set them on fire the police arrived and rescued them. The lady is still traumatized. I requested her to go and testify during the Waki commission but she refused and said that she would be attacked.

Q: For those who attacked others, would you forgive them?

A: No one has asked for forgiveness. They still feel that they were justified in what they did. So if no one has asked for forgiveness then you cannot forgive them. They need to realize that they wronged people. Even those who killed others in North Rift committed crime before God and man. So if they want to be forgiven, they have to ask for it because even now when I meet with those who were active in the violence, I still experience fear. Socializing with them has become difficult because when you go out socializing and you start reprimanding them and telling them that what they did was wrong, one will be risking his/her life. So they must accept their mistakes in order to be forgiven.

Q: If you were to meet with them what would you tell them?

A: I usually meet with them but I don't have anything to tell them because I am still afraid of them. I see them as murderers because of the things they did. Some would even kill and then lick the blood off the panga! So I picture them as animals but I hope that they will one day repent so that we can stay together and be able to say that it was bad politics that made them do what they did.

Q: In 1992 and 1997 there was violence. Did you assist those who were affected?

A: I did not because in 1992 I was not even a registered voter. I voted for the first time in 1997 so I had not even entered political activism. In 1997 I contested. Violence here in Naivasha was in Maella and Enosupukia and as I had just joined the human rights activism. We assisted those who were affected from Enosupukia together with the Catholic Church. Before I was elected in the year 2002 there was violence in Molo and I was the civic education district coordinator Nakuru district. My area of work was Molo, Nakuru municipality and Gilgil. We used to meet those who were affected by tribal clashes and when we were conducting civic education we were encouraging communities to live together. We taught them the reason why people are supposed to live together, i.e. about nationhood and good governance. That was when we were trying to show them the effects of political violence.

Q: In your own view what can the government do so that people can coexist peacefully and avoid such violence in future?

A: First, I would like to say that the government is now handling the underlying issues in the wrong way because at the moment, we the people who were on the ground, are not involved in peace and reconciliation efforts. Like in the Waki Commission hearings, there were recommendations that were made by the internally displaced people. They said that they have not seen the people who attacked them and they have not come face to face to address the problem. When they want to rent houses, they are told to go to the estate to rent houses and it is not the landlords whom they meet but agents. The people they suspect were the leaders of the Naivasha violence are the ones they see in the peace committees so they feel that they are not making any headway. Another thing is that people are deeply traumatized. Nobody has addressed their trauma and if it is not addressed some may think of revenging.

The government is burying its head in the sand because we are supposed to approach this problem in a holistic way. Even if violence will not recur in another five years (which I don't think because the political players are still the same people we have), there are children who saw this and still have enmity in them. When they grow up and are strong enough to take revenge, what do you think they will do? Those children from the aggressor community, we planted a seed in them telling them that the other communities are bad people and we cannot tolerate their cultures, we cannot tolerate their politics. Do you think they will ever agree? This is a ticking time bomb. If not addressed promptly, violence may erupt in the next five years.

Q: What kind of assistance would you want those who were affected to be given by the government or the NGOs?

A: First, I would tell them that the ten thousand shillings they are offering to the IDPs is just too little. These are families who lost everything. Their businesses went up in flames, their property was destroyed and giving them ten thousand shillings is not enough. There is nothing much they can do with it. So people will live in depression for a long time and as we talk to them, they have lost confidence in the current political leadership. As civic educators we have tried to train people on the importance of voting but they now feel that the politicians have neglected them. So the effort that civil society had of training on voter education, I am very sure that come the next election, you will see a quarter of the previous voters turning up to voting.

You find that in some camps husbands were taking the ten thousand shillings and running away with it, spending it on alcohol and finishing everything in two days. Then he would return with nothing only to start a life of frustrations. The government has not done anything much. We would like the organizations to honour their pledges to assist the IDPs in building thirty six thousand houses. The government should help them make the decision to move and not to try to force them out of the camps because they are Kenyans.

The government needs to provide the IDPs with security because that is why we pay taxes and it is a constitutional right. It is the government's obligation. I am sympathizing with those who have refused to leave the camps because they have nowhere to go. Like those who bought land at Maai Mahiu it is just a small piece of land and from there, where do they go? That area is not productive. Many may engage in criminal activities because they have to feed their children. When we left the police station I joined an organization called Centre for Rights Education and Awareness (CREAW) and we went all over the country visiting people in the IDP camps. I was their counselor and wherever I went, for instance the Nakuru show ground, Burnt Forest and Eldoret we found out that women were engaging in prostitution due to the problems they were going through. This might lead to increases in HIV infection since we realized that there were so many in the camps living with HIV and these are the people who were selling their bodies for survival.

Q: What is your message to Kenyans so that they can avoid this kind of violence in future?

A: I would request them to critically look and see that they are fighting because of politicians and when there are no politics we live peacefully. The politicians leading this violence don't belong to our class because in Kenya there are the classes of the haves and the have nots. We the have nots are the ones fighting. If you look at the case of Naivasha, people were not fighting in the posh areas. We were only fighting with those whom we seek assistance from. Now that they left whom shall we ask for assistance? We cannot ask for help from our leaders because we don't belong to their class. I would like to urge the citizens to address the problems that we have. Let us identify who are our real enemies. My real enemy is not that fellow Luo or Kalenjin. Let us address these problems. If it is land, let us identify it as a problem. If it is politics, let us address it and when we are able to identify our enemies we will be able to fight those enemies and the politicians will not be able to take advantage of us again.

I MOVED HOUSE TO HOUSE DISTRIBUTING ARVS

I am Simon Kongodi and I work here at the district hospital in the counseling department. I teach people on how to take ARVs and especially educate them on positive living. I stopped my education in 1989 in Form Three due to lack of school fees and started playing football and that is where I got infected with HIV. I have lived in this status for eleven years and the government saw that I have taken the medicines well. That is when they took me for training on adherence. After acquiring relevant skills I was sent to Naivasha District Hospital to start working in September 2007. I have been here at the Naivasha District Hospital for one year now. I came here last year in June and have been here since then. I started working here as a campaigner of the use of the ARVs; the way they should be taken and how people with HIV should accept themselves.

I am married and I have three children. At first when I got married, I would fall sick without knowing what was wrong with me. At some point my wife ran away and I brought her back with facts on HIV. We are still living together and practice positive living. My family is happy with the way we are living and my wife is not infected with HIV though we know that only God has helped us. At first I was living at Kihoto but I moved to Site and life there is not bad. I meet so many people here at the hospital who come for drugs. There are a lot of challenges as we meet those who are infected since there are many rape cases and also many people who default from taking their drugs especially men here in Naivasha.

In 2007 I was in Nakuru and I came to Naivasha in June when the campaigns were going on I was in Naivasha. During the elections I was here in Kihoto village and that was when we experienced violence that affected our lives negatively. I was actively involved in the election campaign through my vote - something that placed me at loggerheads with my neighbours some of whom torched my house and property. After they burnt it they escorted me to the police station since they knew me. We went there with my wife and child.

On the voting day, there was a very good turn up of voters. Being one of them, I knew that we were voting for the people we wanted. During the referendum on the draft constitution, people were divided into Banana and Orange camps which later sparked off as ethnic divisions. People were divided because there were those who were voting for Banana and others for Orange. Those in the Orange group did not support the constitution amendments while those in the Banana camp were for the amended constitution. The Orange group won. Therefore, the amended constitution was not accepted and that is how division was created.

Politicians had a hand in the referendum thus greatly turning the whole exercise to be political. Before the election, people would talk about who would win or lose. There was a very high turnout of voters. When PNU's Kibaki was announced to have won the presidential election, people celebrated for some few hours, before word went round that votes had been stolen. People got more information by watching television and listening to the radios.

Violence had already been witnessed in other towns but in Naivasha, violence erupted on 27th January 2008 and that was when people were killed, and our houses and property burnt. People sought refuge in police stations and others at the prison premises. Those were some of the problems we encountered. I was in the house on that Sunday night between eleven and twelve at night when the landlord called me. When I opened the house, the landlord told me that people had been sent not to kill me but because they knew that I am a doctor and a Luhya they had come to burn my property since I did not relate well with some of the people. I could not understand and I thought it was a trick. So I asked them why they wanted to burn my property and leave without killing me. They told me that they had been instructed not to kill me or my wife and children but to burn all my property, but if I resisted they would kill me. So I gave in and they started burning my property. I later told them that my drugs were in the house but they could not believe. At first they did not want to allow me to take any drugs but I insisted I had to take them because they are my life. They allowed me to take them and then continued burning my property. They escorted me, my wife and children to the police station. But when we got to a place called Land Panya we met a pedestrian that night, they hacked him even without asking him who he was. They asked me if I understood how they were working, but I kept quiet. As we walked I wanted to be left with one of the watchmen in the light but when we were past the railway line, they told me that they were not going to town and asked me to use the ACK route. We approached ACK and when we got near the police station, I knew that they had no problem with me because they directed me to the police station and asked me to go and look for shelter there until violence stops. Surprisingly, they warned me not to leave Naivasha because I am their doctor.

I camped at the police station for four days with my family until when I got a vehicle that was travelling to upcountry. My wife and children left but I stayed behind. I started assisting my fellow victims especially those who were on ARV drugs. I wanted to ensure that those on medication continued taking them without failure. So I would use the police land rovers and military trucks when they were going to places like Kihoto or Karagita, and on getting there I would try to trace their homes, get the drugs and give them to patients. I was also supplying the ARV drugs to those camping at the police station and at the prison.

There was no proper sanitation, so a couple of children and I fell sick. The World Vision and the Kenya Red Cross came to our rescue and brought water and food respectively. I remember there was a time when one lady screamed at night after dreaming how the attackers killed her husband. People started running away in all directions and trampled on children killing some of them. It was a very difficult time; one that I will never forget.

The camp hosted over three thousand IDPs, among them hundreds of children. Our initial problem was that the police were not cooperative.

But when senior government officials visited the area they became active and started assisting us. The government security agents carried out operations, opening fire at the rowdy youth who then retreated. That was when calm was restored and we were able to go back home. There were some who went to the camps but I did not go to the IDP camps. I went to the house I had left but later vacated to Site where well wishers assisted me to buy some household items. That was where I started life again.

I was badly affected by the violence and even as we speak, my family has not been able to resettle. My wife doesn't want to come back to Naivasha because she is still traumatized as she witnessed the attack on the man we found on our way to the police station. Costs of living changed since basic commodity prices shot up after the violence. Food prices were especially high, at times we even bought bread at Kshs. 100 yet we did not have money. But God helped us through that tough period.

I think I was attacked because I am a Luhya from Busia where some of us are called Onyango. That is why they may have thought I am a Luo. That left me confused since I didn't understand why they had done this to me. I even started thinking that it was during the teaching sessions with them that I made enmity with some of them. When they attacked me and burnt my property, they told me to look at them and see if I knew anyone. In fact I really wanted to identify at least one, because I lost a lot of valuables which I had really worked for but I didn't recognize anyone. The things that were destroyed were my television, DVD, butterfly sofa set, bed, wardrobe and other valuables. In total they were worth over Kshs. 60,000 and I did not salvage anything. I can forgive them but I am still thinking about the property I lost yet I was not given the money that the government was giving to IDPs. I can forgive them but I cannot forget what they did to me.

There were rumors that some people were ferried from elsewhere to Naivasha. I am quite certain about that because when I was at the hospital, someone approached me and used Kikuyu dialect that I have never heard saying 'ngundia mbaki)' (give me tobacco). I could not understand this and when I asked the Kikuyus they told me it is a deep secret, so when he realized that we were tense, he just walked away. Later on he came back and told us that they had come to Naivasha because their people out there had been killed and had come to avenge so everybody should be alert. But we did not take this seriously and thought it was just a rumor and may be this person was drunk.

We have all ethnic groups residing in Naivasha. You find that people from other parts of the country where violence was experienced ran away from those areas and came to Naivasha and Nakuru. Those who came to Naivasha talked about what they had faced and so it seems like the Naivasha violence was to avenge for their fellow brothers and sisters.

Prison wardens tried to save Naivasha residents though there were allegations that they were raping women and robbing motorcycle operators. But I have a feeling that they really helped Naivasha residents. The police were dormant and did not do much to help.

There are so many of us that the government may not be able to assist. I heard the government had given out some money and I think it was a good move because it has assisted the ones who got it to rebuild their lives again. But some of us did not get anything although our property was burnt too. The focus should be on how the government will investigate and establish the root cause of the violence so that we do not have a repeat of the same in 2012. We are all Kenyans and should have the freedom to own land in any part of the country. There are so many people who have declared that they will not vote in 2012 and some of them have burnt their voter's cards because of anger since they voted but are now suffering. I therefore feel that the government should educate Kenyans on their constitutional rights. Without doing this we shall have problems again. Equally, politicians and the government should go back to the ground and find out the root cause of the problem so that in 2012 such violence may not recur.

THE PLIGHT OF THE PEOPLE LIVING WITH HIV DURING VIOLENCE...

I am HIV positive and I deal with those who take ARVs. I try to ensure that they take these drugs in the right way. I remember in the year 1982 to 2000, a lot of people died (700 in a day) and I felt that this should not be happening. I am concerned about the clients because during the clashes so many defaulted on their doses and some HIV +ve mothers started breastfeeding their children since they did not have anything else to feed them on.

HIV infection is very high here because of lack of employment and poverty. So the government should assist in this, as opposed to leaving the burden to the NGOs alone. It should allocate some funds for educating people about HIV and AIDS. Those living with HIV especially, need to be educated on how re-infection happens and how they can lead a better life because the ones living with HIV are the ones who continue spreading it and as a result they get re-infected.

While at the police station, I started thinking about my clients and talked to the OCPD. He said that he would support my work by providing me with a land rover to go get drugs. I took advantage of the police vehicles and would accompany the officers any time they went on patrol so as to reach the patients in need of anti-retrovirals. I tried my level best not to waste the chances I got every time there was a vehicle leaving the police station.

My main challenge was inadequate time to educate patients as I would go with the time schedule of the police officers on patrol. Secondly, we did not have enough drugs. Thirdly, the clients did not have food to take yet these drugs require one to have a proper diet. These were just a few among the multitude of the challenges I faced. I also had a problem of moving around to the required areas because I would use vehicles from NSSF, Medical and Sans Volunteers from Nairobi.

At one time, I went to Kihoto to visit one of the patients who was bedridden. As I alighted from the police vehicle, I came across a group of youth and they asked me where I was going and I told them. They told me that they had to take off my clothes in order to know whether I was circumcised. I gave them a go ahead to prove that I had been. I asked them whether that was the work they had for that day and they told me I was asking too many questions. They also demanded to see the drugs I was carrying. They took the drugs and the little money I had in my pockets but left my phone because they knew that I was using it to look for their people to give them drugs. When I came back I called my brothers in Nairobi and told them I wanted to go back home. My brothers sent me a vehicle but one of the doctors, Mr. Muigai, pleaded with me not to go.

My clients are from Naivasha district while some are from Nyandarua and at that time I was going to Kongoni in Maella because they could not be able to come here for drugs. I used to call them and ask them to meet me at Maella because that place was safe. We would meet and I would give them the drugs then come back. Naivasha has people from various ethnic groups: Turkana, Kalenjins, Kikuyu, Luo, Luhyas and Kamba. The flower farms employ people from various ethnic groups and I was assisting all of them without discrimination.

I put my life at risk because I had been targeted. However, I continued to assist, because I knew that those people that use the ARVs should not skip even one dose. So my aim was to ensure that they continued taking the drugs during that difficult time. There were a number of consequences for not taking the drugs. For instance, I have taken these drugs for eleven years and if I fail to take the dose for two days or one day that is in the morning and in the evening the virus starts gaining a different strength. They then start getting used to the medicine that is in the body and later become resistant. It is just like malaria. Some time back patients used not to complete the malaria dosage and so it would become resistant to drugs. The virus can also become resistant to drugs too. There are some HIV positive people whose lives changed since they left their homes with nothing. Some could not even be accepted back home and most of them were really affected by the violence. All of us did not have a balanced diet. In fact my CD4 count went down from 900 to 400 but I have started to recover. This was due to lack of food. Secondly, they were affected due to sleeping out in the cold because they are vulnerable to such conditions. Thirdly, some had children and were not supposed to breastfeed or breastfeed until they were six months old. So you find that some decided to breastfeed their children again and, thus the children got infected through breastfeeding. Finally, some people have not yet gone back to their jobs hence they started prostitution leading to the spread of the virus.

At the moment I have recorded over 900 defaulters due to the violence. To date I am still tracing some and I am yet to establish the real numbers of those who died. There is one lady I know who was hacked to death. I had a case where one of my patients who was a Luo was beaten, hacked and brought here to the hospital but later died. I saw him before he died, I talked to him and he said he did not hold any grudges. He could not comprehend what had happened.

If such violence erupted again, I would like to be at home. I even hope that I will leave Naivasha before 2012 and go to Busia to avoid going through what I went through and losing what I lost again. It was a very painful period for me because I had just started living a better life. When I was younger and playing football, I wasn't able to complete my education to get a better job but when I got one with APHIA II that was when I was able to improve my financial and living standards. But all that I had worked for so hard was burnt and that has made me live in fear. That is why I feel that I should go back home before 2012.

Q: Did you know that violence would erupt in Naivasha?

A: No, it caught me by surprise. I knew this town had all ethnic groups who have lived together peacefully as neighbors and when it erupted, I imagined it was the work of the devil. I used a lot of money to communicate with my relatives. They would call me from time to time to know whether I was okay and therefore it was a very tough time for me.

Q: Do you think politicians were involved in the Naivasha violence?

A: Yes they were. People say that an MP was involved since people voted for him but those in the flower farms and other parts of Naivasha decided to vote in someone else. In my opinion I think he was not involved in the violence. As the violence was going on, he came to the police station and later went to the prison where he talked to the people who were there telling them that the government would establish the cause of the problem. When he came to Naivasha town, his car was stoned. In fact I witnessed it. It is an indication that he was not involved. He even talked to the youths who attacked him and told them that if any of them was from Naivasha, he would get it rough. But as we talk, he has not been able to get even one of the youth and that means they were not from Naivasha.

Q: In 1992 and 1997 there was violence in some parts of the country, did you assist in any way?

A: In 1992 I was quite young and I did not even vote. In 1997 I was old enough but I was only involved in voting. Many things happen during election time and I would say that politicians contribute a lot to the violence through their talking where they incite people. Every time the politicians are campaigning they talk ill of their opponents instead of telling us of their mission once they get to parliament. So when the voters hear this they also start taking sides. The youth start fighting yet these politicians remain friends. During violence, the ones who suffer are the youth because every time anything comes up it is the youth who are in the front line because they are idle due to unemployment. Politicians are to blame because they are the ones who have money for the campaigns and they use it when inciting. Many youth are idle so when they are given a small amount of money they can do anything; more so if they are not married because they have nothing to leave behind and are fearless.

Q: What can the government and NGOs do to assist those who were affected during the violence?

A: First, they should urgently assist those who were and are still traumatized. My wife cannot come back to Naivasha because of what happened. There are those who lost their property; the government should think of them too. For those who were at the IDP camps, some have nothing and the ten thousand shillings was too little. For example in our house in Busia, we hosted three families (Kikuyus) and they were not given anything by the government so they decided not to go back to Njoro and have started doing businesses there. So the government should put into consideration such people.

Q: Lastly what is your message to fellow Kenyans?

A: I would like Kenyans to think about their lives and see their fellow Kenyans as brothers. We should love one another as we did before. For example, my father lived in Nakuru for forty eight years and never encountered the problems we are now encountering. I would also like us to work together as brothers and sisters.

Q: To avoid the violence that we had what would you tell them?

A: I would like to tell Kenyans that we still need one another so that we can develop our country. We should also stop listening to those who incite us. Maybe no one else can volunteer to teach people about positive living and to accept to come out in the open and declare that they are positive. For that matter we still require one another to develop our country.

LEADERSHIP SHOULD BE HELD ACCOUNTABLE

My name is Sister Florence Muia. I am a member of the Assumption Sisters of Nairobi, the founder and director of Upendo Village based here in Naivasha. It is a home-based care project that reaches out to people living with HIV and AIDS, orphans and vulnerable children. Our services include: health care services, Voluntary Counselling and Testing (VCT) at Karai dispensary, education, nutritional supplements and other basic needs to support care givers within family set ups. I was touched by the plight of the people living with HIV while I was still studying in USA and as I read the statistics I felt it was a turning point for my life. I had to get involved and do whatever I needed to do to help in dealing with the AIDS pandemic in this country as it continued to claim so many lives each day.

Catholic Sisters console displaced persons. Photo by Antony Gitonga

At that time while on study leave I was a Probation Officer in the government, but at the end of my studies, I had made up my mind to resign and get involved in addressing issues related to AIDS. I have been with the Assumption Sisters for more than thirty years and I felt that I received much support when I shared my dream with a congregation about the direction I wanted to take in supporting those who are affected and infected with HIV and AIDS. I am a trained social worker and a professional counselor. Armed with these skills, I felt I could be quite effective in this area and on the other hand I knew that to establish a project like that, I needed to consult with other people who have the expertise in this area. For example I needed people with medical background so that they could compliment my efforts. By combining our efforts we would be able to do something instead of all of us sitting individually and watching as our people were being wiped out by the epidemic.

I discussed the idea with leaders in my community and the Bishop of the Catholic Diocese of Nakuru, the then Bishop Kairu who was very excited about the proposal of establishing this project. He welcomed the idea and that is how we started it in Naivasha. Bishop Kairu decided Naivasha was the ideal place to establish this project in conjunction with the Assumption Sisters. I was excited because it is an area that I was familiar with and very conversant with geographically. I knew the devastation AIDS has caused in the region. So when I started I was very familiar with the needs of the people in this area.

Naivasha is a unique town with interesting and diverse features and it is a town that embraces people from different ethnic communities of Kenya. It is a fast growing town due to the flower growing industry which attracts people from all walks of life who come in search of prospective jobs. Naivasha is located on the highway linking the port of Mombasa to Uganda and also to other parts of the Central Africa like the Republic of Congo, Rwanda, Burundi. All the transits vehicles pass through this town. Many people come here from different parts of the country in search of jobs, and when some fail to get these jobs, sometimes they opt for other means of earning income. You find poor people in town just trying to search for anything to feed themselves and others may turn into sex work. Naivasha is located within Rift Valley which is a tourist attraction because of the geographical features. We also have National Parks around Naivasha, e.g. Hells Gate. It is in Naivasha where the biggest geothermal power station in Africa – the Olkaria - is found. So all these unique features end up bringing in a lot of people from all walks of life. Those who come to get a living and those who come for touring; those with money and those who are looking for money.

Naivasha has been my home town for more than ten years and I know that during the referendum, people went out and voted just like in many other towns. I do not know exactly how residents of Naivasha voted but my guess is that just like other towns that shot down the constitution review, it did at that time. They wanted some amendments to be made before the constitution could be adopted. I am not sure whether they supported the draft constitution or they shot it down because I did not get the statistics and the results of each particular town.

I think Kenyan politics always operate along ethnic lines even before the referendum. You will notice that people have a unique voting pattern and that is evident from the announcement of presidential poll results. For example from Ukambani, it is clear that the Kamba community voted almost autonomously for their own candidate. If it is a presidential candidate, from the central province you find that there was overwhelming voting for that particular candidate from central province and you find the same with western. So the kind of results we have been receiving indicate clearly that we have been voting on ethnic basis. People support their own. We feel, for example, if a Kamba takes the seat, the president will favour the Kamba community. We have not yet changed our mind-set to vote for politicians on the basis of their capabilities and developmental agendas; issues that will affect every Kenyan as opposed to looking at one based on ethnic background. I think we approach politics from a very narrow-minded angle and personally I think we need to outgrow it.

During the campaign period I kept out of public rallies. From past experience we have seen people resorting to violence during the campaign rallies. I opted to keep off because we have not matured in politics and instead of addressing issues we get involved in hate campaigns, attacking individuals and opponents. Candidates at times stoop to sending spies to their opponents' meetings and these goons end up disrupting the meetings violently. This shows how cheap our politics are. I don't know if those utterances may have had led to post election violence. I know that Naivasha was among the towns that were hit by the last wave of the violence. Many other towns started fighting immediately after the announcement of the presidential results. We thought residents of Naivasha were mature enough because it took us almost a whole month without fighting until towards the end of the month when violence broke out. I think people in Naivasha were provoked to revenge because those who were evicted from other areas, e.g., Eldoret, Molo and Kisumu passed through Naivasha and they told the ordeals that they went through. This angered the community in Naivasha and eventually, I believe politics may have also played a role in inciting people to revenge by evicting particularly the Luos and Kalenjins from this area.

On the night of 26th January 2008, some friends in town called me at around 9.00 pm after news bulletin and they told me that I needed to watch out the following morning because there were rumors that there was going to be violence. I took precaution before going out. It was a very scary night. I did not have enough fuel in my vehicle, so I decided to wake up very early the next morning and went to the gas station as I surveyed the town. I had been told that one of the signs I should watch out for as an indicator of trouble was absence of public transport.

We had talked to area residents and asked them not to resort to violence and set an example to other towns by co-existing peacefully. Little did I know that what we had discussed was not going to be long lasting with some people in our circles of work. I drove towards Naivasha town from Caltex gas station along the highway, and I noticed there was no single vehicle on the road. Along the road, I also noticed residents had converged into small groups and there was tension. As I passed the entrance to the district hospital ahead of me, I saw a big crowd beginning to assemble down town and so I decided to pull over by the road side and as I was doing that a man beckoned me showing me to go back. I drove back. I had hardly reached the house when I heard gunshots in town. I knew hell had just broken loose. It was one of the most difficult and painful Sundays because I went to church. The highway was a no go zone.

There was a lot of fighting and I started seeing youth running from the highway chanting 'tutoe Wajaluo, tutoe Wajaluo', (Let's flush out the Luos). My first reaction was to call the police because it was evident that they were going to kill these people and the unsuspecting motorists on the highway who were going to various destinations. When I called the the Officer Commanding the Station (OCS), the mob was in a nearby estate called Kayole. The police responded immediately. On seeing the police, the youth of course dived into the bushes. I was in my house watching the whole scenario. It was like a hide and seek game on the highway. The police were able to run and rescue some of the motorists.

The whole day was marked with running battles between police and other marauding youth who shouted at the Kalenjins and the Luos as they were perceived to have killed Kikuyus from the North Rift and the Luo land. I remember trying to call a certain journalist to find out what was going on because I knew the press was always among the first people to know the unfolding events and when he picked up the phone, he told me, "Sister don't come out, things are so bad". He told me he was on the highway at the junction between the exit to Naivasha town and the highway from Nairobi to Nakuru. So nobody could leave their houses. It was one of the worst Sundays I have ever seen in my life. The following morning I felt I couldn't just sit in the house, and I was tempted to walk around. My employees had been calling me the whole Sunday during the day and night in distress. They were so frightened and scared. They felt like fleeing the town but there were no public service vehicles and as the fighting persisted, I went out and I started evacuating them. I just had to stick my head up high in the midst of the odds and went in the battle zone and evacuate the families of my employees including a few children from some neighbors whom I am not going to name for safety and security. I brought them to the center and put them in the hall.

On that particular day I personally came in contact with two members of the militia. I had just stopped to evacuate the last group when they confronted me. They were in a matatu. One was a driver and the other one was a passenger or a co-driver. They looked very scared from the look at their faces. They stopped and told me they hoped I was not one of those rescuing the Luos lest they kill me and burn my car. They confronted me face to face and I talked back to them in Kikuyu and I told them I was not evacuating them. They looked at me with ugly eyes and just drove off. It was a very frightening experience but that did not deter me from doing what I believed was the right thing. I managed to rescue some families and the following day on Tuesday, again I went to the camps where people had gone camping. I called our pastor in the church, Fr. Kiriti, and I told him that I felt that we could not just sit while people were camping in the police stations.

We needed to go out and find out what was happening and assess the needs of the people who had been evicted and see how we could mobilize well wishers to assist them because as a christian I felt obliged to do something. Whether I was going to risk my life and even lose it, I was determined to do what I felt needed to be done. I felt compelled by my own faith and christian values to go where I was needed. I feel that all human beings are equal regardless of their ethnicity. Nobody has a choice of where he or she is born; whether they are Kikuyus or Luos. Where there is need, I am called to be there so I mobilized the priests and we went to the police station.

On arrival, I was overwhelmed by what I saw. It was a sea of people and children who were so dehydrated; some with wounds which had not been stitched, hungry children as they had not eaten for two days. Remember violence had broken out on Sunday. Some people had fled on Saturday when they got word that there would be violence the following morning. We assessed the situation and I called the District Commissioner to request a meeting with him. We met and he urged whoever was able to mobilize resources to assist. I immediately swung into action and the first thing I did was to mobilize for water because I realized children were so dehydrated. Oserian Flower Farm offered us a water tanker. They gave me a driver and we started collecting water from the Catholic Parish borehole. I talked to the Parish Priest andhe agreed to let us get as much water as was needed. Red Cross officials gave us the statistics because to mobilize resources needed we had to have the numbers of the displaced.

We found out that they didn't even have the forms to collect the data. So the next thing was to try and get the only form available and make some photocopies and remember all the shops in town had been closed. Nothing was functional but eventually we managed to get to one of our schools to photocopy the forms. We were able to collect the data so that even as we mobilized for resources, we could tell potential donors what we were looking for and the quantities. At the same time the DC was negotiating with the flower farms to evacuate some of their employees to safer places within the flower farms. The most pressing issue was lack of sanitation at the police station because there were more than 5,000 people in one compound, excluding those who had fled to the prisons. After that we started looking for those who had been injured and had not received any medical care and sent them to hospital. Once again I found myself using my little car and had to ask for police escort because the situation was still very volatile at the time. We tried to help those who needed medical care. Shock made some expectant women give birth to premature babies. It was a beehive of activities as we also tried to mobilize for medication on the ground. In fact we emptied our pharmacy to avail assistance at the police station because the Red Cross had very little. At the same time those who were treated needed transportation back because they could not walk freely in town, so we had to take them back once they are treated.

When IRC arrived I helped in the distribution of the food. We got doctors from MAP who were working with the Kijabe Mission Hospital who came during the week to help with treatment and nursing of the wounded. Towards the end of the week on a Friday evening, we also got Doctors Without Borders and discussed about sanitation in terms of toilets. It is only after the volunteer doctors came that we were able to work out the logistics of getting toilets on the ground and by Saturday, they were able to put up the first toilets and bathrooms at the police station. There was a lot of suffering as food and other resources were minimal. There was no shelter and the displaced were sleeping in the cold and children stayed without food. The situation was almost unbearable. I visited the IDPs in the camps every day for a period of two weeks even as fighting went on.

We also started working out logistics for conducting post mortems on those who had died which was very difficult. We had to mobilize resources from as far as Nairobi, including inviting a pathologist to come and carry out post mortems here. Being a member of a disadvantaged group we also workedg closely with the chairperson, Councilor Rahab. We wanted those who had lost their loved ones to help in the process of identifying the bodies of those who had died during the violence before they relocated to safer grounds as they had made it very clear during the several meetings we had, with them and the DC that they wanted to relocate to safer areas despite the government's stand that they didn't want to relocate people to other areas. We worked closely with Red Cross officials who assisted a lot in transportation of the bodies. The mortuary was terrible with the stench of the decomposing bodies. It has a capacity of about 18 bodies but it had more than 50 bodies lying there. We ensured that all the identified bodies were transported and given decent burials in their ancestral lands. The other task was to assist those who were stranded and wanted to go back home. We also worked very closely with Catholic Diocese of Nakuru in ensuring that we got food supplies and humanitarian services delivered from the diocese.

People have also been concerned with the issues of gender violence and whether we were able to identify them. My response is that we did not have enough time to get to that level. When dealing with a crisis like that, it is difficult to get to certain levels because you are dealing with such a huge group in dire need. Unless somebody seeks your help because they were sexually abused, it is hard not know. People kept quite about it because what they wanted was s to relocate to a safer place first. They could not even have time to establish rapport with any counselor at the time to disclose such information. Even if somebody had been wounded, all they were concerned about was the physical wound not the emotional. The operations were at that level.

I am a Christian, a religious woman and a catholic nun called to serve everybody, anywhere in this country and around the world. My faith knows no political background or ethnic boundaries. I am above tribal politics as a Christian and this is part of my Christian values. It is because of those values that I cherish so much thatI gave up my own life to live as a nun. To me all ethnic groups form part of the Christian congregation: the Luos, the Luhyas, Kalenjins, Kambas, Kikuyus; they all form the family of God. So if we also see each other as brothers and sisters, children of God then we will not have those differences that make us fight on the basis of ethnicity. Personally I felt compelled by my own faith, and Christian values to go out to help. I intervened when the Kikuyus relocated from Maai Mahiu and encountered hostility at the police station because the Luos and the Kalenjins were still camping there and when they saw this lorry full of Kikuyus coming in, I knew it was going to turn to a nasty situation. I was certain that Kikuyus had not intended to come to camp in the same police station with the Luos because these were two rival communities. I diverted them to the stadium camp and told them they were in the wrong place. We also did visit them at the stadium to establish what their needs were. I operate beyond ethnic boundaries and that is one of the reasons why I helped these people.

Of course by doing this I risked my own life because as I said earlier, I was confronted by two members of the militia who threatened to kill me and set my car ablaze if I was assisting the Luos. I also knew there was a lot of talking and questioning why we were assisting the Luos to an extent that people threatened to invade the Catholic Church for hosting some Luos who were employees in the parish. I remember one Monday morning, some youths threatened to attack the parish if they discovered we were hosting Luos. At one instance as I was bringing trucks to fetch water we were warned not collect water from the parish borehole to take to the camps. They questioned why we were helping the Luos and I responded that Luos are human beings just like any other person from a different ethnic community. I said even if it was the Kikuyus or others, I would still help them. I was not helping because they were Luos but because they are human beings.

I have no regrets of what I did and I would still do it again and again. I have even gone to the camp at the stadium where people are still camping although the government has officially closed all camps. There are still people here in Naivasha who are still suffering. They have been coming for treatment from visiting doctors from Joliet, USA who are treating people here at the catholic diocese. I have treated more than 10 patients who are still camping at the stadium here in Naivasha without any charges. They could not pay because they have no source of income. We have attended to a man who had his hand broken in January 2008 during the violence in Narok. All he had was a cast and he needed surgery because the bones could not join to have pins put in his bones. For the last eight months he has been in agony and we have managed to get this man's hand fixed. We paid for his bill which was more than Kshs. 30,000 at St. Mary's hospital in Elementaita. So as I said it is very clear I do not help on the basis of ethnicity or because I am supporting a particular political party or group. I don't have any political affiliations. I help people who are suffering. That man is a Kikuyu and as much as we helped others from other ethnic groups evicted from Naivasha, we also helped the Kikuyus who were camping here.

In addition, some of the past skirmishes (1992 and 1997 clashes) occurred in areas far from where I lived but the Catholic Church as a whole has always been involved in assisting victims of violence. For example, the Catholic Diocese of Nakuru has seen it all in Molo and Olenguruoni since 1992. Every five years the church is faced with the task of restoring peace in clash stricken regions. The Catholic Justice and Peace office has really done a lot to help people including resettling some clash victims from Molo in other areas. I was directly involved.

One thing I would like to see happen in this country, is to have our leaders establish and address the root causes of the violence because it keeps recurring. I feel we have never addressed the root causes of this problem. We always wait for it to tone down but we don't deal with the problem fully and once the violence is over we continue as if nothing happened. It has also kept on claiming lives. I have heard people talk of historic injustices but I have no clue what this means. I would like them to be defined. Let us not use jargons. Let us be told what these historical injustices are so that we can deal with them once and for all. Anyone who still holds on to a property that was not rightfully acquired should be made to return it to the owner so that we can bring about true reconciliation. We cannot afford to be covering up things. When violence breaks out we talk of forgiveness. This is just so superficial because it never addresses the problem. You cannot treat the symptom of a disease without knowing what the root cause is . Once you see the symptoms you need to find out what the root cause is so that you treat it once and for all. This is what I feel the government should be seriously address. Right now we are already talking of 2012 campaigns. We have forgotten that the people who elected these leaders are still suffering. This is an insult.

Q: What can the government do to avoid a repeat of this kind of violence come 2012?

A: They need to address this issue of historical injustices which is said to be the root cause of the violence so that politicians can stop hiding behind it. Secondly, politicians should be held accountable for their reckless utterances because they played a very key role in inciting people. Think of the chaos. We did not have it in Lavington Green where different ethnic communities occupy mansions. We did not have fighting in Muthaiga. Those people also are mixed. We did not have chaos in Spring Valley. Why? Why did we have chaos in Mathare Valley? Why did we have chaos in Kibera? Yet we did not have chaos in Karen. It is not that these areas don't have different ethnic communities coexisting. The poor are the ones fighting and killing each other because somebody incites them and promises them heaven. They are made to feel like it is this other ethnic community which has inhibited their progress or their development or they are responsible for their woes, and their suffering. This is not the truth. Also the issue of unemployment in this country. Our youths are abused by politicians who give them a few coins and incite them. Without having second thought they will take up arms in support of the politician forgetting that he/she will disappear for the next five years. The youth were supporting certain candidates who were contesting. I do not know how much they benefitted from the candidates they supported. Once elected, politicians go to parliament for their own gain.

Q: On the issue of those who were displaced or affected, has the government done enough to assist them?

A: I think what the government is doing leaves a lot to be desired. To me it is a mockery of the whole process. As I talk, here in Naivasha approximately 200 families are still homeless. It is clear that the government has done very little if anything to address the plight of the IPDs and the children who are in the camps. I have also seen many children who are not going to school. Young children as young as 2, 3, 4 years including primary school and high school going children are not able to access education yet we have leaders and a government. I feel the kind of leadership we have is wanting. It is as if people have closed their eyes and buried their heads in the sand like the proverbial ostrich. What is going to become of those children? What is their future? How are we going to curb crime? How can we talk of a decrease in HIV and AIDS infections? Children are left all day idling. How can they not be abused? They are so vulnerable. What is going to make them not be enticed with food because they are starving and lured to abuses or even to death? It as a very scary situation.

I think the government should be held accountable and taken to task so as to resettle these people. The IDPs have become beggars. They had homes and earned their living decently, but all of a sudden they have found themselves reduced to paupers over night. It was not their own making. It was due to politics and it was the politicians who caused this suffering as they contested for parliamentary seats. Immediately they get elected they go and settle up there. I think any leadership should be held accountable and any government made responsible of taking care of its citizens. It is the people who elect them and put them there, so they cannot afford to turn their backs on them when they are suffering. And Naivasha is not the only place. The story is replicated in many other areas within the Rift Valley, especially the areas where the violence was most felt.

Q: Lastly, what is your message to Kenyans on the issue of peace?

A: My appeal to all Kenyans is that we should stop being incited. We should stop listening to people who incite us against each other. Kenyans need to start thinking as a nation and not on political and ethnic basis. We need to develop patriotism. Ethnicity should not be used to divide us; it should be our cultural heritage. We see many people who come from other countries as tourists get amazed at how we live together, considering our ethnic diversity. Our cultural heritage is displayed in places like Bomas of Kenya where you find different dances from different cultures being performed as entertainment for our visitors. It shows our heritage as Kenyans.

We should be proud of our heritage and realize that we can still unite in our diversity. We can still coexist peacefully, as we have coexisted before. We have always coexisted peacefully as a nation and so we should not allow those seeking political leadership to divide us on ethnic boundaries. We have even inter-married. What I saw during the conflict were families breaking up, children becoming the victims of violence where mothers and fathers belong to different ethnic communities. Dividing or separating a family is a very sad state of affair and we need to build our nationalism. I do not know what is going to happen but I am sure as Kenyans we can come up with our own solution. We all need to do soul searching and find out whether being a member of a particular community gives us advantage over the other, or is it just by chance that we are from a particular community. And should that be a reason to hate somebody else? I think we need also to teach our children to become nationalists. We also need to change the way we talk even at family level. It will shape the thinking of our children. It will shape the way they envision themselves versus other members of other ethnic communities and also as a nation.

I WAS VIEWED AS A TRAITOR

My name is Margaret Wangui Muiruri. I live in Site estate, Naivasha town. I have been living here for seven years with my family. I work here assisting mainly those who have been sexually molested.

I have worked for the last four years helping children who have been defiled and the adults who have been raped. Those targeted are mostly the poor and when it happens, they do not know where to seek help. Therefore we found it wise together with Naivasha Disadvantaged Support Group (NADISGO) and Upendo village to assist them and offer them a shoulder to cry on. They bring their complaints to us and we take them to the hospital where they are given Post-Exposure Prophylaxis (PEP) before going to the police. If the accused is known, he is taken to court. We do this because when a poor woman is raped, a Kangaroo court is formed and no compensation is paid. The case ends up being dismissed before justice is served.

There are very many rape cases in Naivasha because there are many people from different ethnic groups working and living in the numerous flower farms. Therefore with this congestion such kind of cases occur. More so, people have grudges with others because of tribalism. Apart from people who live and work in the flower farms there are others who are in business. Some work in the jua kali sector and others in the formal sector. This has made Naivasha a cosmopolitan town with different communities such as the Luhya, Luo, Kikuyu, Maasai among other ethnic group.

During the referendum we had Orange and Banana groups whereby so many Luos and Luhyas supported the Orange and the Kikuyu and other ethnic groups like Kamba supported the Banana. This generated differences amongst those who supported Orange on one hand and those who supported Banana on the other. Enmity started developing then as people were divided along ethnic lines.

During the political campaigns, those who supported Orange joined ODM and those who supported Banana joined PNU. This meant that feelings were intense based on the groups supported. Various candidates here in Naivasha engaged in finger pointing campaigns and people started insulting one another. I was supporting PNU and fighting for my democratic right. I supported Kibaki.

On that day (*the Voting Day*) I was at Kabati polling station as an observer. The voting exercise went on well but in the evening when the votes were being counted, the situation turned nasty. Being an observer appointed by the National Constitution Executive Council (NCEC), I realized there was a hitch since the votes were not well counted. We had a lot of problems because some ballot boxes were stolen while some were not taken to the municipal council on time. That showed that there was corruption.

Later the votes were counted and some people started complaining. It was said that voting be repeated because the candidate who lost, Jane Kihara and her supporters,claimed that the votes had been stolen while John Mututho's supporters were celebrating since he had won. But later, it was announced that John Mututho had won and he is currently the Naivasha MP. The two opponents later went to court.

When the votes were counted all over the country it was announced that Kibaki had won. Violence erupted in some parts of the country. Some people claimed that the votes had been stolen since people were monitoring from the television and radios. At first, Raila was leading and the ODM supporters thought Raila would win. Later on when all the votes had been counted, it was announced that Kibaki had won. That was when violence started especially in the Western region. The Kikuyus in the Western region were attacked and people sent packing from their homes. That is the reason we have a lot of IDPs in the country.

Naivasha, being a cosmopolitan town had those who celebrated his victory, for example the Kikuyus, but the ODM supporters did not accept the defeat. On 27th January 2008 violence erupted in Naivasha. It started in town and Kabati, houses were burnt, as people from Luo community were attacked. On 28th January, the violence continued and some people went to the prison where they were given security by the police in order to go and get their properties. The people who attacked them started burning what they had left behind. It was a bad sight especially when we found burnt property strewn on the road. They did not burn the houses, instead the attackers would remove all the property in the houses, put it on the road then burn it. These included television sets, radios, refrigerators, sofa sets among many other household items. The youths who were doing this did not seem to feel as if they were doing anything wrong.

There is a man called Ndege who lost his nine children and two wives and even grandchildren. It is said that they were in the house and the attackers asked them to leave but since they were scared, they did not. I am not sure whether they poured petrol on the house but these people who attacked them lit the house with them inside. The bodies were brought to the mortuary burnt beyond recognition. Red Cross officials in conjunction with other organizations offered moral support to the victims. A lady was also burnt alive with her two children. It was a horrible sight. People were burnt in houses and I don't know if those who did that will ever clear their conscience.

Violence went on for three days and it is on the third day when government security agencies moved into action in Naivasha. There were a lot of police and Kenya army in Naivasha but still the violence continued. People from Narok and North Rift sought refuge in Naivasha. They were staying at the KANU grounds, the ACK church and later they were given some place to stay at the stadium. The Luos went to South Lake at a place called Kedong' while others went to prison, others to the police station and some to various churches. The situation was bad since there were a lot of people in very small spaces. For instance, at the police station there was no proper sanitation. The people there did not have food and only good Samaritans tried to assist them. The government also tried to help them but still there were a lot of problems due to congestion. Several organizations came up to assist the people who were affected and some helped in teaching the children. We were assisted by the Upendo village and a Police officer who told the parents that we were going to counsel them since they did not know what we wanted to do with their children. Parents and their children were traumatized and were all afraid. We prayed with them, counseled and taught them, gave them moral support and showed them that there was no difference because even all the other children were also at home and not learning.

I assisted by teaching those children. I also visited those who were in prison and gave them moral support together with sister Florence of Upendo village, Rahab Wairuri of NADISGO and the Red Cross crew. We assisted them especially when they went to identify their relatives' bodies at the mortuary because they were scared of getting in the mortuary despite the odour. We were also helped by the people from the media, in supporting them as they were going to identify the bodies. People were not able to get in because of the odour but we took courage since we knew that they were human beings like us and needed our support. They were able to identify the bodies though it was difficult for the burnt bodies. The mortuary attendants also assisted us very much by labeling those who had been identified. Working as a team, we assisted fifteen families to identify the bodies of their loved ones. The Upendo village and Nakuru Diocese bought the coffins.

We also assisted a lady whose two children perished in the same plot where Ndege's family was. She was not able to identify them due to trauma. Her relatives came from Western and identified the bodies of her husband and children and we helped them take the bodies to their rural home.

We had a difficult time because when counseling the people who were traumatized we too got traumatized because it was something we had not experienced before. We however encouraged ourselves, conducted the counseling sessions and gave them moral support. It took time because to heal that wound of knowing that the people you lost were not sick nor did they have an accident but they were burnt by someone or even killed is not easy. But finally they had strength and accepted what had happened. We stayed with them for almost two weeks; counseling them and trying to talk to them and accept that there was a problem. Eventually we ensured that they healed before they left.

We faced many challenges. For example, I remember when we were at the mortuary people from our community looked at as us traitors since we were helping the Luos. Some would ask us the kind of relationship we had with them. At the hospital, as we took the records, we were asked the same question. Some police officers would even question us as to why we were doing it. We also had financial problems because these people needed food and other things but through God's help we were able to assist them.

I assisted them because I knew that they are human beings like me. I tried to fit in their shoes and I felt as if I was the one undergoing those problems. I knew there were Kikuyus too who were facing similar problems in other parts of the country like Molo and the other places. I felt that if I was the one in Molo, I would also need assistance and therefore I tried to fit in their shoes. For example, I had neighbours who belonged to the Luo community. I did not have any enmity with them and when I needed someone to assist me, they always assisted. I remember one young Luo neighbor, his name is Ochieng'. If he had a problem he would come to me, and if I had a problem I would go to him for assistance. We have never had any disputes between us. So I pitied them and knew that they are just human beings like me.

My life was at risk because my community did not want me to assist them. Therefore I did it knowing that I was putting my life in danger but I believed that God would be on my side. My prayer is that we shall never experience such violence. But in case it does occur, I would still assist. As we were counseling the victims who lost their loved ones in the violence we asked them to forgive those who did them wrong because if they didn't then they would not move on and would never heal but if they forgave then they would get over it easily. I would like those who attacked others to ask for forgiveness and especially ask for forgiveness from God. If they don't know those they attacked but they know that they participated in the violence, they should ask for forgiveness and ask God to help the victims to forgive him.

In my opinion I think the violence in Naivasha erupted because of enmity. When a particular ethnic group is prosperous then the other one develops enmity towards this other group. The issue of land also generated hatred as some felt that Naivasha is their rural home.

Q: Do you think there were outsiders in Naivasha?

A: I would say that it is true there were some people who were ferried into Naivasha. For instance, the assailants who were burning other people's properties were unfamiliar to me and I felt that they were gangs from other places.

Q: Do you think politicians were involved?

A: I would say that politicians were involved because those in Naivasha know their constituency and they should have foreseen this and should have come in to calm down Naivasha residents. This is the reason why I would say that they participated. Politicians were not around when we had the violence. They were only heard on the radio, television and in the newspapers but did not come on the ground to see what was happening. If they were not involved, then they should have come in from the beginning to calm down the residents.

Q: Did you anticipate the violence?

A: I did not anticipate that there would be violence because it erupted on a Sunday. I was preparing myself to go to church, and when I walked out, I noticed smoke in Kabati and people were screaming and that was the time I realized that there was fighting. Earlier, in 1992 and 1997 there were tribal clashes but I did not assist in any way because it did not occur in the area around me.

Q: In your own opinion, do you think the government has done enough to assist those who were affected by this violence?

A: There are so many people who were affected, and I don't think the government has done anything to assist these people because there are so many IDPs especially in Naivasha. The government has not allocated land to them. The government is saying that it has given them Ksh. 10,000 but that is too little for someone who lost everything. I wonder how Ksh. 10,000 will assist these people yet the cost of living has really gone up. It cannot buy a piece of land, pay school fees or buy enough food for the family. This is the reason why I say the government has done nothing.

Q: In your opinion what can the government do to assist them?

A: I think the government should assist by having those with chunks of un-utilized land give the IDPs at least some place to put up a house. The government should assist the poor and know that they are human beings too. The youths must be offered employment because even when the current president was elected, he promised youths jobs. At the moment no jobs have been offered to them and the rich are growing richer day by day. So the government is not thinking of the citizens on the ground. They are just thinking about their own life and just increasing their salaries. Therefore I would request the government to know that we are all created by God and we should help one another. If it is the poor they should be considered and be helped in a way that will assist them come out of that state because poverty is a hindrance to development in the country.

Q: What is your message to fellow Kenyans in regard to peace?

A: My message to my fellow Kenyans is that we should all live in peace and love one another because what has destroyed our country is tribalism. Everybody should know that we were all created in God's image and therefore they should stop that enmity and work together as people of the same family. I would urge Kenyans to live in peace because what we saw in 2007 has led to problems that will affect our children because they now know that there is ODM and PNU. Our children will grow up by what we teach them. Therefore we should set a good example by living in peace.

ASSISTANCE IS A CALL FOR THE CHURCH

My name is Reverend Paul Matheri serving with United Methodist Church. I have lived in Naivasha since 1969, when our whole family relocated from Nairobi. Therefore I went to school here. My main ministry has been with the church where I have served as a pastor for over 30 years. I have also been involved in a lot of community and social issues.

Naivasha is inhabited by different ethnic groups. For many years we have coexisted in a way that you would not even tell where one comes from. Many residents are traders and there has been a good coexistence for so long that sometimes there is no difference in tribes or languages. Actually the main language in Naivasha has been Kiswahili. There has been an influx of many people coming from across the country since the flower farms around the lake started coming up. And therefore Naivasha has hosted almost every kind of person from all parts of Kenya.

The constitutional referendum, it just came like another process for Kenyans to move from one stage to another but with a difference. Two different parties that were pulling apart and especially when there was a 'NO' and a 'YES'; Orange and Banana respectively. Naivasha is almost a political society and therefore when these two names came up, they formed themselves as political parties and I believe that this was reflected when voting came. Reasoning was left out and it was voting based on either Banana and Orange. I think that started creating some rift between supporters of different camps. This spirit and force was carried forward to the ballot. So I think referendum was a leadership struggle.

It split Kenyans and reasoning was left out. Voters supported YES camp or NO camp on tribal lines. Actually there were rumours that when one voted for Orange which was supported here by one of the leaders in the ODM, Raila, then that person would be supporting Raila. If you say NO then you are saying NO to the incumbent president and of course people thought that was true. Some did not vote for YES because there was a need for changing the constitution but YES to supporting a particular person rather than supporting the constitution.

We realized after the referendum that campaign politics continued and never stopped. Actually for Kenya in 2007, there was no time when politicians stopped campaigning in order to talk about development. Instead they all came out in full force preparing their people for voting at the end of 2007. Therefore I believe the whole year was a year of poisoning citizens. People's minds were poisoned and divided along ethnic lines. I believe year 2007 was a very critical year. When towards the end of 2007 the voting date was announced, campaigns were in top gear and people knew how they were going to vote. At this point, it was on the basis of tribalism. People believed that if we vote and are defeated then our ethnic group will be defeated. I believe between 80% to 90% of Kenyans voted on ethnic lines.

The main christian body that is the NCCK and other bodies had programmes for civic education but were not well taken care of because of the main church leaders. When I say main, I mean people who can talk and be listened to. We have other leaders at the grass roots whose words would not be taken seriously. Most of those church leaders were looked upon by the politicians and even by part of the government to see how they were going to support the election. I believe civic education in the year 2007 was not done properly and any attempts didn't have a proper forum. I am very outspoken as both the church and members of my church will tell you. Whenever there is an issue in the country, my preachings will always be directed not only to the spiritual areas but also in trying to offer advice to the congregation. I have started introducing the debate of a new constitution to my church. I don't want a situation whereby Christians will just be moved by emotions. We should think logically.

On the Voting Day in 2007, people in Naivasha turned up in large numbers and were calm. Voting was well conducted. Though I don't have specific figures, I believe that the voter turnout of 2007 was better than previous years.

I believe that PNU won in the general elections with Kibaki as President. PNU won in Naivasha and my argument would be that the same votes probably if not all of them but over 90% of votes were for two candidates; that is PNU and KANU. I would suggest that most of those votes were for President Kibaki. There was a rumor that may be the actual figure was not given out. There were still other rumors that the returning officer could have been compromised. I am not sure if he was but after the votes were counted, there was a lot of delay in announcing the results. Usually whenever you do something like that, people will start giving their own results and I think this is why people were not sure whether the announcement and the figure was true or not. Because the returning officer delayed when he was supposed to announce the figure, he allowed people to come out with their own figures.

Then came the announcement of President Kibaki's win. There was celebration among his supporters which I witnessed. People ran along all the streets celebrating. I think it went on for over an hour. I was watching because I was standing just near one of the main bus stops in Naivasha for Nairobi bound vehicles. That is at the main street in Naivasha. People were running across the road, up and down. But this is what people do when they win. I think even in the estates, people celebrated almost up to midnight.

At that time we did not know what was taking place in other parts of the country. The announcement generated tension. The announcement and swearing in, were in the evening. Many people went back to their homes only to watch on the TVs and hear on radio that clashes had started especially in places where they were expecting announcement in favour of their party but did not. There was a lot of violence. It was no longer celebration time.

On the following day, we witnessed people coming in small and big trucks carrying nothing. They would stop in Naivasha trying to group themselves in different locations and everybody stood wondering what was happening. They said that they had been chased out, their houses burnt and even some of their family members killed.

When the first truck came in, we started calling each other as pastors and decided that we needed to do something. We met in one of the churches and said we are already in trouble. There are people coming and some of them are stranded in town. We didn't know where they could go. We said we needed to come up with a solution urgently. We sent some people to the registration office to tell them what we had decided to do and I also remember very well that we all agreed that we were going to tell people around the town that whenever they see stranded people from the clash torn areas, they should direct them to the Anglican Church ground. We thought it was much safer, as the church has a big ground and probably we could try and help them there in whatever way we could.

For almost a month we kept receiving the displaced people from the areas affected by clashes. They included children, women and old people. Many children did not have their parents and some of them did not know where their parents were. This continued until around 20th of January 2008 when there was very high tension in the town and a curfew was imposed. One could no longer be in town after 6.00 pm in the evening. Prison warders were brought in to guard the town at night. The curfew went on for about a week.

The condition of the IDPs coming in from South Rift and other parts of the country was pathetic. They came in without food, others without clothing, and they were all terrified. They were giving stories of the murder they had witnessed, houses burnt with everything in them. They said they were threatened as they came out of those places. It was not a situation or a condition you would like to be in or even continue looking at. It was very bad.

By Friday and Saturday i.e. 25th – 26th January 2008, people in Naivasha had declared that they could no longer tolerate the curfew. They said that Naivasha town was a district headquarters and people would arrive late after going out on business. The residents added that those people coming from Nairobi and alighting in Naivasha town were harassed immediately they alighted by the wardens who were in turn supposedly to guard the people and maintain safety. They would even whip them. I witnessed this because twice or thrice I came from Nairobi late. I never experienced any harassment personally but I saw it because police officers walking on the road, and especially those from the prison, would whip people on the back including those who were riding motorbikes. At one time I complained bitterly and I even told the taxi driver who rushed to pick me, I couldn't tolerate this harassment from the same people who were supposed to protect us. This is what angered Naivasha people. After everybody realized this is what was happening, people agreed and concluded that there was no conflict in Naivasha and we therefore did not need a curfew or policemen on the streets.

On Saturday night, I could hear from my home sounds of unrest. I actually called some of my friends to ask them what they were doing and where they were. They said that they were all outside. They said that they could hear the sound of pangas. Many residents were out and didn't want to be guarded by the police saying they could guard themselves.

They also feared that they might not know what would be happening if they were all inside. There were also some rumors that when people were inside at night, there were some other people who were allowed to meet in their houses. Of course it was said they were planning to attack the other tribe. So on Sunday 27th morning, I don't know how these groups had gathered because very few people knew what would happen. I remember I woke up and prepared to go to church. I was not driving my own car so I went to the bus stop and waited. As I was waiting, somebody came from the town center and asked me what I was doing and I told him I was looking for a taxi to go to town. He told me to go back home and that is when I realized that there was something wrong. He then asked me if I had heard gunshots in town and even before I could answer, there were more than a hundred gunshots. I can now differentiate the gunshots and the teargas. Gunshots were all over the town. Soon after, I saw smoke coming from different parts of the town and realized that vehicles coming from Nairobi were stopping before entering the town center. That was when I realized there were chaos in town. We started calling to get more information. Eventually I managed to come to town with an AIC pastor. There were chaos everywhere and we could not drive through. We drove through stones, went up to the police station and that is when we realized the situation was not as we had expected. There was a particular community being thrown out of their houses and were all gathered at the police station.

On that particular day, I spent almost the whole evening in town. I have a good relationship with the administration officers so I could call them directly. The OCPD and I were trying to warn them that a group of young people in town were going to attack a particular house. Because we had policemen all over, we would direct them towards the place the group was heading and if we believed there were people in a house, we would rush there to try and evacuate them. Of course we ran out of air time and we could no longer communicate and there were no shops open to buy airtime from.

Sounds of gunshots rent the air the whole night and no one could sleep because we did not know what would happen next. There were rumors all over that there were different groups gathering together to come and fight in town. It was said they wanted to fight the Kikuyus who had remained in town. It was very discouraging because rumours came in two versions: that there was one group that was going to chase away Kikuyus from Naivasha and then there was another group coming from central to beat the Kikuyus because they were not doing anything to protect their brothers against different ethnic groups who were in the town. Therefore most of the Kikuyus in Naivasha were scared because they did not know whether to run away or to stay and fight.

There was an uneasy calm on Monday. On Tuesday I was called by the then senior Districe Officer who told me that the president was coming to Naivasha and therefore I should come very early because I was going to lead prayers when the President comes. I prepared myself very early. Just like the other two days, there was no transport so I called my brother and he brought me to town.

Before we arrived at the office, we noticed that things were not normal but we managed to go to the District Officer's office. While we were there the DO asked me to try and look for my people who could speak to the youth and ask them to stop what they were doing. I agreed that we try to do what we could but after we left that place, we could not go anywhere. There were stones all over. So we only managed to move out of town and went to Caltex petrol station just outside town to see if we could gather any information from there. We stayed there for just a few hours and that is when hell almost broke loose again. We realized that there was a helicopter that moved fast across town and we realized it was flying too low. We thought the helicopter was going to land in prison. Immediately thereafter the helicopter started coming back and shooting in the air. We all tried to look for cover. The helicopter passed the first time and before it came for the second time we drove away from the petrol station to our rural home that is near Karati, about 3km from Caltex Petrol Station. We now watched and listened from that place.

After things cooled down. Between Monday, Tuesday and Wednesday one group was completely evacuated. People who were coming from Rift valley, Narok and other areas were given a place to camp at the Stadium. Those who were evacuated from Naivasha town would not mix with the other group so they were given another place near Lake Naivasha and that is where they camped. So we had two groups.

We faced challenges because the group at the stadium was actually 200 meters from the church that I serve. After visiting them and realizing that there were churches around, they would flock in the churches on Sundays and we could not just close our eyes and ears and do nothing. Therefore, we asked the people from the church to contribute whatever they had in the form of clothing, food and money; anything they could give to start supporting these people. .

But we had a bigger challenge with the other camp. These were people who came from our own town. They could not trust anybody who came from Naivasha. Eventually we tried and we managed to break through. We went to the camp and using some of their leaders and pastors they realized that we were not just an ethnic group speaking a different language but we were also people who had compassion; people who were human and that is when they allowed us to go in. We were also able to deliver whatever we had in form of clothes, food, and even funds that we had to both camps. Actually I led a group of Japanese who went to those people to get information and they accepted me. I could even go through the camp freely and I think that it was God's hand because there were some people who still wanted to know who I was but because they could see me with some of their leaders, they accepted me in that capacity.

We also noted that immediately the schools were opened, there were many students who could not go back to school and the Ministry of Education was directing students to schools within Naivasha town. They would give them letters but these students did not have any uniform, or other facilities. Most of these schools are boarding schools and they didn't have clothing of any kind so we came in to offer assistance. I know I assisted 80 students, 45 or 48 in the secondary schools and the rest in primary schools. We bought school uniforms for them and paid some fees needed at the boarding school because they would not stay in boarding schools without eating. Also while collaborating with other churches we requested for food from other Associations including NCCK and other bodies which we distributed in conjunction with Naivasha Fellowship to both camps.

Lending a hand is a call of the church. It is one of our ministries. We need to preach a gospel that redeems people from suffering, poverty and sin and this is why the church must take the lead whenever a need for serving others arises. We did it even before the clashes since we had and still have needy people around the church. It was not a new thing when the clashes erupted, only that the magnitude overwhelmed us - people came in such big numbers that we were not able to serve the way we would have wanted.

Q: *Do you think your actions put you in danger?*

A: I don't think that when you offer help especially when you give what somebody needs you would be putting your life in danger because as you do this you will be creating relationship, friendship, trust and I think this is what I have done.

One frightening incidence that comes to mind is when we had two Luo camps before they relocated to Kedong'. There were a number of them camping at the police station and there was another big number camping at the prison. I served more those who were at the prison. I went there almost everyday and in doing that I was putting myself in danger with the others in one way or another because even when I came to town, people knew me very well and they would tell me, "Reverend we know you are giving those people in prison food, and it looks like you are not feeling any pain for what they have done to us." I would just keep quiet because I did not want to argue. At one point there were rumors that there was a group that was going to attack the pastors who had been seen going to prison everyday. What we did not know was where that group was going to come from: whether they were youths from our village or people who we did not know. Of course, it scared us but there was that compassion which continued pushing us every day. We realized that we could not stop because our conscience would not let us yet by continuing to help out, we knew we were putting ourselves in danger. But our calling is to everybody.

Q: *Do you think violence could erupt again?*

A: We can't afford to sit back and see a repeat of what happened. Nobody is looking forward to another event like that one. But of course we cannot avoid it because life is full of ups and downs. We are trying to prepare our people but the worst thing is that the people we are preparing might also not have been involved in the first clash. Therefore I am not sure if the perpetrators have been reached because one of the fears is that, may be, the main problem which arose and which was just triggered by the announcement may not have been addressed. What I would say is that all bodies which can assist should always be ready to assist. I would assist in the same way I did until I am not able to do it anymore because that is my calling. Even if violence erupted again today, I would still walk in and do my part.

Naivasha chaos came up as a result of anger. People who were coming from war torn areas, Rift Valley especially, and landing in Naivasha made the people of Naivasha feel like they were also supposed to do something about what they were seeing. They acted just like the normal people they are. A person would always want to revenge when something wrong is done to him or her. I also believe people did not want to be seen as cowards and more so when it was pointed out that people from Naivasha were not doing anything. This added salt to injuries. Thus instead of solving the problem through reasoning because may be people who were much hit in Naivasha town had nothing to do with what was taking place in the Rift Valley, they became the nearest target. So whatever happened in Naivasha was as a result of revenge and anger and it was not planned beforehand. It took over a month to start; so it was a reaction to what was going on in the country.

Q: Do you agree with the rumors that there were some youths ferried in to beat the Luos and the Kalenjins?

A: I think there were. The only thing I would not be able to say is how they were ferried in and who ferried them in. Naivasha, especially the town is not too big and it is now that people are flocking in big numbers. If a number of young people gather into a group you will definitely notice and they are people whom we are familiar with. Naivasha youth are known whether they are people from the streets or people who just do small work like shoe shine or those who use donkeys to ferry water. If they were the only people in Naivasha many of us would have been able to identify that these are so and so who are doing it. Young people from Naivasha joined in and I think many people in Naivasha may have been initiated and are now a part of the group that was ferried in. I believe Naivasha is not the same today as it was.

Q: Do you think some politicians were involved in the chaos?

A: Although there were claims that some politicians and local traders were involved, I will not particularly say local traders were. Because if the issue was addressed before the end of that one month, Naivasha would still have been peaceful. But it looked like there was nothing which was being done by the government or by the security agents and whatever may have happened in Naivasha whether it involved local traders may be it may have involved a trader or as a resident just like any other because at one point or another, everyone would gather as a Naivasha resident. I believe that is what happened. Rumours that there was funding and all that could have been true. But of course if it was true funding it could only be done by people who have money and therefore it is logical to say that these were traders. But I am not defending them. I am not a trader but a pastor and I am taking it from a human point of view.

We were not aware there was going to be clashes in Naivasha. I did not expect there was going to be any clashes. There had been clashes even in the previous elections from 1992, 1997 and 2002 and our people in the Rift Valley had been affected and had even come to our homes, stayed for a while and then gone back. So even when the announcement was done in 2007 and fighting erupted, I thought this was going to end very soon and at no point did I think that Naivasha residents would react in that way. I always look at Naivasha as a place where we had so many ethnic groups that you would not know which group will fight the other. That was what I always believed in. So it was a surprise. I knew there was very high tension. I would not actually say that the politicians did not play any role. They did and this was across the country. Politicians played the greatest role and are to be blamed fully for what took place in our country.

It is worth noting that in 1992 and 1997 I assisted because there were people who came but these were family members. Apart from that, as a church we went around clash torn areas, such as Mai Mahiu and visited families that were housed by relatives and we were able to give them what we could. We also collected clothing and food and ferried them to our churches in Nakuru so that they could distribute them to people who were housed in Nakuru area. We have always assisted clash victims in Kenya.

Q: Can you forgive those who attacked each other or what would you like them to do before they are forgiven?

A: That has been my preaching. I did that a number of times in the church. I was looked at negatively because probably people were thinking about it in the context of what took place in Naivasha. I said that there was no reason as to why anybody in Naivasha was attacked. But then I would say that there are certain people even today whom the government will need to take strong measures against and these were the people who in their knowledge planned and acted. Then there were the young people who were pulled into all these wrangles in ignorance. But what I would say is that in order to deal with impunity that has dogged the country for a long time some measures must be taken.

For instance, those people who will be found to have been involved in the planning, the law should definitely take its course. I have so many victims who come to my church. I always tell them that forgiveness is the first step to their healing and urge them to start a process of forgiveness in order to heal. It might be very painful but forgiveness is the key even at the national level. It is very crucial that the perpetrators accept that what they did was wrong for them to be forgiven. It is not for me to force them to accept their guilt but if they cannot accept that they did wrong, then forgiveness might not be effective because it is good for the person who is forgiving to forgive but the person who is being forgiven needs to accept that he has done wrong. Let me put this clearly: I blame anybody who comes up with a statement that whoever fought, killed, burnt or destroyed any property that they did it in the name of democracy or they had the right to do that. I don't think anyone has any right to kill or destroy property for any reason. But forgiveness is key in our country.

Q: Coming back to the recent clashes, has the government done enough to assist the victims of the chaos?

A: That is the worst scenario. The international community thinks that the government is doing enough, but that is not the case. The government is now giving some money to those victims and I think the recent announcement was that they are building houses for them. I would challenge you to travel along the Eldoret road and see that the people who have moved out of the main camps and have gone back to their areas from where they came. They have put up other small tent sites all over. So how can the government say they have done enough? Actually I would say if the government is saying that 450,000 people were affected and they have not been able to resettle them, then the government is not doing anything towards restoring peace in this country. You cannot live in peace if there are people who are still staying outside their homes and the government is celebrating while giving actually a wrong signal.

As United Methodist Church we have an arm that gets involved with a lot of people locally and internationally called UMCO. The information they have is that they cannot continue sending any support for the IDPs because the government has taken its role; they have compensated the victims and are even constructing new houses for them now. I wish the government is doing what it is supposed to do, for example using the same churches who supported victims when they came in the first day. Why are the churches not involved particularly in Naivasha? Why isn't there someone coming in to ask or even to at least share with the pastors and others on the successes of IDPs compensation and resettlement so that they can join in celebrating government successes. Why are they doing it in secret? If these people came in Naivasha and we saw them, why are they not involving us properly when they allocate them funds and yet we still have IDPs in Naivasha? The camp is still there and when the government officials leave, they put camps along the road. So the leaders in government must pull up their socks and do something. Let them not say they have done anything.

When the founding father, Jomo Kenyatta rose to address the nation during independence, one of the things he said is that there are three enemies that must be fought. The first enemy is illiteracy, the other poverty, and the last but not least, health issues. If this government does not address these issues properly then chaos will always come back. Why are people fighting in Kenya? We are fighting for resources because we don't have enough. But Kenya is very rich. It can be able to distribute its resources to her people and actually if we can go very well by 2030 over 80% of Kenyans will be able to support themselves in their day to day lives. But as it is, it is the opposite with over 80% of Kenyans surviving, not living.

Q: Lastly, what is your message to Kenyans out there in terms of peace?

A: What I would say is that there cannot be any development in the country without peace. There cannot be peace without development. There cannot be peace and there cannot be development without people respecting each other. So my emphasis would be that we should look for that which brings peace in which I look at my neighbor as a human being and as God's creation and as God's image. When we look at each other and respect human life then we can start guarding peace because peace is always there but it is us people who move away from it. If we start guarding that peace, we can live together. All human beings are equal.

THE SCENES WERE TRAUMATIZING

My name is Alex Kamau and I am a trader. I was born here in Naivasha and I have lived here all along. It's one of the fastest growing towns with various kinds of businesses like flower farms, beer brewing and a ready market. It's between very fertile lands like Maela and Kinangop and thus most of the fresh produce is sold here. I am also a volunteer with the Kenya Red Cross Society. Red Cross has various departments but I deal with disaster management and preparedness and I am also in charge of First Aid. Disaster management deals with collecting food stuff and non-food items that we use to assist victims in cases of crisis. We are first in assisting our brothers and sisters for example in Moi Ndabi if it floods. Other tasks include community service, cleaning up and saving people involved in accidents mainly along the highway. We also have blood donation drives.

I was in Naivasha during the elections and that is the time that we saw politicians preach tribal politics when they came to their ethnic groups appealing for votes. There was the issue of Banana and Orange camps during the constitutional referendum and that was the start where people learnt to vote on ethnic lines. There were a few cases of violence and we moved in and assisted. Violence started due to the influx of IDPs who came in trucks and were dropped in Naivasha. The number was very high and the locals were angry and thus decided to revenge. There was also incitement from politicians.

In 2007 we were ready to offer services mainly during the voting day but this was overstretched. It was more than we had planned. Tension started building and soon people were flushed out from different places. We had never planned for this and we received so many people from Nyanza and parts of Rift Valley. We gave them food, tents and the non-food items that we had received from the business community and locals. The main problem was food and clothes as all their properties were torched by attackers. They also needed medication as many had wounds and various diseases. We worked in conjunction with the local hospitals and they were assisted. The largest number of IDPs were kids and women and were first hosted at the Kanu offices while others were in a church in Mai Mahiu.

I was at home when the Naivasha violence started and the Red Cross chairman called me and told me that IRC would bring in tents and we were expected to assist in pitching them in the camp. While there we received reports of violence where police were shooting in the air and hauling tear gas while the people were throwing stones and blocking roads. In the town, there were clashes with the police. People were also opposed to a curfew and wanted permission to flush out the Luos and Kalenjins as their brothers had been flushed out in other areas.

One principle of the Red Cross is alleviating human suffering and thus we came in to assist all the people who were affected in one way or the other. The traders told us not to feed the fleeing Luos with their food and we thus relied on food from IRC which we gave to the IDPs in the prison and police camp. In case of emergency we came in handy and partnered with other international organizations to assist. At the camps, hunger was the main problem as some IDPs had not eaten for over four days and some mothers could not breastfeed. It was even hard to distribute the food as they scrambled for it. Some fainted and we had to give them high energy biscuits so that they would recover. Also the IDPs were affected psychologically after seeing relatives killed, property burnt and they had many other problems. We had to hold counseling sessions in the camps.

It is true we were risking our lives but the people in the camps had so many problems and thus welcomed us. Since we had Red Cross jackets, we got no problems. Also the Kikuyus saw as if we were taking secrets to the Luos and it was hard to explain to them our situation. The DO had to call a meeting with them and they cooperated. Most of the victims didn't understand our operations. They were impatient and thus jumped queues causing confusion. The police were at times overpowered. Others insulted us in the camp but we ignored them. We had a case where one of the volunteers was kidnapped and taken to one of the big hotels. He was told that we were taking all food to the Luos and ignoring the Kikuyus in the camp. We were worried as he was off air for five hours but he later surfaced after the D.O intervened. There was a problem but we had security from the government and we were always taken home. We also had an emergency phone number.

I never knew there was going to be violence so we were caught off guard. From our investigations, we learnt that this was planned and particular communities were to be flushed out of Naivasha town. The scenes were really traumatizing. We would trace reported cases and end up finding them in the mortuary and their status would really be bad. The bodies were in bad shape and I do not think I would have what it takes to assist again. One of the cases was reported on a Tuesday as we erected tents. One Luo boy came up to us and we took him to hospital after going for a long way. The doctors were few and the injured were coming in every minute and the doctors were over worked. One man was brought in from Karagita and he was full of blood. A doctor tried to assist him by supporting his head. He had been cut on the hand and on examining him he found the injured man had a bottle lodged in his head. He died after 20 minutes and that still traumatizes me.

Some of our members at Red Cross have gone for counseling because of the trauma especially after going to the mortuary, watching mothers die and leaving behind minors and vice versa. It was so hard and it really haunted us mentally. The holding capacity for the mortuary was ten bodies but at one time there were 68 bodies and we had to seek for assistance to get body bags and protective gear to wash the bodies. Previously in 1992 and 1997 some people came from Molo and Maella and we assisted by giving them food and non food items as there were no camps like this time round. They were sheltered in the Catholic Church and we also gave them tents made from polythene papers.

Q: Can you forgive those who were involved?

A: I can forgive the perpetrators because the Bible says so but I cannot forget because of what I saw. Also those who attacked others should first admit their mistake and repent and vow that they will not repeat this.

Q: *Do you think the violence was planned?*

A: During the violence, it is true that Mungiki boys were brought in and they came to where we were Their faces were unfamiliar. Even our colleague who had been kidnapped said so and this was supported by some local youths who said that the youths had been brought in. It is reported that the violence had been planned for like two or three days but the violence in other areas was planned for a longer time according to the IDPs. The attackers had even bought weapons.

Q: *Has the government done enough to assist the IDPs?*

A: The government has done its part though it should do more because people have gone back home with Kshs. 10,000 yet they have big families. This is too little and so the government should not stop and we hope that more will be done.

Q: *What can the government do to stop this kind of violence in the future?*

A: The government has to unite Kenyans in order for them to live together and show them the negative effects of ethnic violence. The Politicians should also face the law for inciting people to fight. That can act as a lesson. Lastly, we should stop preaching ethnic hatred.

Q: *What should be done to those people who attacked others?*

A: All those involved should be arrested and face the full wrath of the law. Let them be jailed so that they can be a lesson to others.

Q: *What is your message to Kenyans?*

A: Let us live in peace and live together as this is our country and we shall not go anywhere else. We have to guard it jealously.

WE ESTABLISHED A PEACE DESK

My name is Stephen Thuo Njuguna, and I reside in Naivasha. I came to Naivasha as an employee of the Block Hotels after which I entered politics and business. Right now I am in properties and motor vehicle business.

I first came to Naivasha in 1986 as an employee and worked until 1992 when I ventured into business.

Since the referendum on the Draft Constitution in 2005, Naivasha was divided because there were those who supported and those who did not support the Draft Constitution. People were sometimes driven by party affiliations although some of us stood on our own, fighting for the new constitution. The Orange group people didn't support the constitution and mobilized supporters into a movement and later into a political party. Our view on new constitution differed and this affected us all in a way because the attitude towards those who said "Yes" to the constitution became negative. They perceived these people as people of the same thought. In addition, having been a member of NCEC, I had participated in many forums agitating for the new constitution. So I actually had to support the proposed draft constitution because that is what I had been fighting for.

For a long time I have been involved in the NCEC since the time of Professor Kivutha Kibwana. I have been the District Coordinator for the larger Nakuru District preparing our people and showing them what made Kenyans solicit for a new constitution. In my work, I interacted with a lot of groups and joined others like Kenya Human Rights Commission. I am an activist and I am also involved in NGO forums as their coordinator dealing with environmental issues such as the sustenance of Lake Naivasha and its catchment areas.

In the 2007 politics, the main fight in Naivasha was not between ODM versus PNU but KANU vs PNU because it was Jane versus Mututho. Most of the young generation (ages 40 to the voting age of 18) had a lot of support for Mututho but the older generation (45 and above) supported Jane. It was a tough competition but eventually Mututho ended up winning.

Previously, during the campaigns I can say things were normal because in every campaign there are opposing parties. I was a candidate for Hells Gate civic sit which I wanted to capture for the second time but I didn't succeed. However, I didn't witness any violence within my locality of Hell's Gate.

On the Voting Day, PNU supporters were more orderly in most polling stations. They had a say but they could not convince and control the minds of the voters because voters were decided and voted for the people they wanted. There were many coordinators who could be seen moving in and out of every polling station in Naivasha.

The election results were received with mixed reactions as all the people supporting Mututho were very happy. They said that they had made it but those supporting Jane objected and said that there were some problems in the counting and tallying of the votes. They later made a petition and filed a case in Nakuru.

Subsequently, the emotions during the announcement of the presidential vote varied. Naivasha people supporting both sides were eagerly waiting to see which presidential candidate would carry the day. But Naivasha being almost an extension of Central Province by virtue of the fact that it borders the province, expected that Kibaki would win. He won.

Naivasha was very cool after the election results. People celebrated and went back to their work and houses but after two days, an influx of IDPs moving from the inner parts of the Rift Valley started. They were coming with luggage and some with nothing. They said that their houses had been burnt and some of their relatives killed. So as a member of the Kenya human rights, I organized friendly NGOs and together, we sourced for a tent and went to the KANU Grounds where we established a peace desk where the IDPs were welcomed and comforted. The IDPs came from Rift Valley, Nyanza and other parts hit by violence. We tried to assist them in some ways since the Red Cross society had not yet arrived. We had to go all over asking residents to kindly donate some resources which we used to pay for matatu fares to connect these people with their families wherever they were in Central Province and anywhere else.

However, there were those who did not have anywhere to go and were desperate. And because we didn't have a camp to host these people, we looked for foster families who came in big numbers and accepted to take these people in and give them houses where they went with their families. We were also receiving some food from the government and well wishers which we distributed in weekly rations.

There were those who by the virtue that they were from big towns and were working, had some little money and wanted to rent houses and may be start some small *jua kali* business. We tried to assist them by getting cheap houses and some business premises. We talked to the council which at times offers exemptions on council fees for small *jua kali* people. The exemptions were granted by the council. We also assisted students who were to join schools but had nowhere to go. Through the Provincial Administration and the Education Office, we agreed that any student who was displaced must join a school near where they were being hosted. We recommended them from our peace desk by giving them letters. This helped them to be acknowledged and assisted as IDPs. Most of them got admitted to schools. We sourced for uniforms for those who did not have them.

We also mobilized well wishers to donate clothes for those who didn't have clothing because theirs were burnt. We helped with the facilitation of medical care because they did not have money to cater for their medical needs. Through the Catholic Church, the local district hospital and the provincial administration, we agreed that anybody who had a letter from the Peace desk identifying them as an IDP should be exempted from paying any fee at the district hospital and they were treated. We worked together with members of a local NGO called Bridge Partners and the Kenya Human Rights Naivasha Chapter who really helped us. These members were Benjamin Mungania, and a volunteer named Esther. We worked with The Red Cross. We distributed food while they started putting up tents for the IDPs. I can say we uplifted the hopes of the many desperate Kenyans who joined us at that time.

We assisted more than 5,000 people including children. Most of the IDPs came from Burnt Forest, Kondoo and Kamuyu areas. Others came from Londiani, Kipkelion, Eldoret, Molo, Kuresoi, Njoro and its surroundings. We also had people from as far as Kitale, Kakamega, Bungoma, Kisumu, Narok, Nandi Hills, Isebania among other areas that were affected. A lot of people came to Naivasha from very many areas.

Basically, they had the immediate need of shelter, food and water. Some had medical problems because some of them were HIV positive and they were on ARVs. We had to make immediate arrangements so that they would continue with their programmes. We also had those who had school problems so we helped them join schools. On the issue of shelter, we agreed with foster families to take them in. Some even employed them and gave them houses as well as farm work so that they could get some money for their livelihoods.

In anything that you do, the people whom you are helping should acknowledge and as far as I am concerned they were making calls to their relatives who were still stuck back home advising them that it was only in Naivasha where they could get assistance. However, we had some resistance locally because we had camped at KANU grounds. Those opposed to KANU as a party took our initiative as a party affair but we are happy that the police and the provincial administration in Naivasha saw us as peace keepers and not as KANU supporters. We were operating on that ground only because we didn't have any other open ground and there were no other facilities that we could use in the town center where these people were being dropped. But thereafter when Red Cross came in tension built up and the IDPs were very unhappy.

We started giving assistance immediately in January 2008 when the problem of IDPs started and we continued the process until mid February 2008 when Red Cross started full operations. By then, we had reduced our responsibilities to looking for foster families. We left the facilitation of medical care and school admittance to Red Cross but we were left with one problem which was that of the Intergrated IDPs. These were the IDPs not in the camps and were not receiving any help from Red Cross. So we continued sourcing for resources to help them in maintaining their weekly food rations and any immediate need they were likely to have such as children who were joining secondary and didn't have school fees. We tried to link them up with well wishers and we did this until March 2008 when we were satisfied that most of these problems around Naivasha were at least 70% - 80% settled.

There are many cases of those we helped. There was an old lady who had cancer and was suffering. She had her two daughters and grand children. We located a house for her. In conjunction with Sister Florence from the Catholic Church we arranged for her to be taken to Aga Khan Hospital Naivasha branch and she was eventually operated on there. Together with the Catholic Church through Sister Florence. We paid all her bills But she eventually succumbed to the illness after two months. We also arranged for her funeral and buried her. We persuaded the local council to employ the woman's eldest daughter on casual basis. She has now taken charge of the family.

At first there were no chaos in Naivasha but a lot of IDPs were coming here. As they started coming day after day, people started feeling touched and asked why these people were coming from these areas to seek refuge here. That is when tension started building in Naivasha and when it grew out of hand, prison wardens were sent to patrol the town. When they started doing so, there were cases of rape, arrests and beating up of the youth as they left their working places in the evening. This annoyed the residents because rumors started circulating that they wanted everybody to stay indoors so that they could be attacked. This increased tension and residents started demonstrating, demanding that the prison officers be withdrawn from the streets and taken back to the prison. Instead, there were clashes between the forces and the locals. The allegations made about the prison officers had some truth because I had been involved in the operations of IDPs at the KANU grounds and I could see people being beaten at night because they could not enter the place. We were however exempted by the police. Nobody within the Kanu ground was attacked. But outside, we saw it all. We could even send our own people for shopping to buy things to cook for the IDPs in the evening and they would come back running that they had been beaten and chased away by the prison wardens.

After January 2008, people in Naivasha felt that the ODM people were the problem so anybody who was associated with ODM in any way was to be flushed out of the area. The main targets were those who were associated with the ODM - the Luos and the Kalenjins. Therefore, when the skirmishes started, the youths went round looting all business premises and households that were owned by the two ethnic groups. I could see them move around the town because I was at the KANU ground camp. Unfortunately, I cannot tell who these people were because they were new faces. I cannot say people were ferried in or not because Naivasha is a very big town. It includes many villages so when things started getting out of hand, everybody moved from wherever they were to the town.

But the agonizing thing was the prison wardens who wanted everyone out of the streets. How do you put a curfew on people to stay indoors yet there were IPDs coming in and rumors that Naivasha was also going to be attacked? So people needed to be ready for any eventualities. In addition, I do not think that any politicians were involved here while these things were happening. The two candidates were busy: one preparing to take over and the other one preparing to go to court. So I do not think they were involved.

The victims of these chaos in Naivasha went to the police station and some went to the prison. At first we did not engage them because we would be perceived as traitors. There was a lot of hostility by the locals towards the victims or anyone offering them help until the Red Cross came. Later the victims were taken to the Kedong camp. The investors demonstrated good will because they assisted these people and saved the lives of those who could not travel to their homes immediately.

When Red Cross came we formed committees within the sitting NGOs. We went to all camps preaching peace and reconciliation and telling them that we needed each other and to stay together. We surely inspired them and some started coming to town. They even went back to their work places and gradually people started working and living together again.

As a human rights activist, and as a Christian by faith I value life and abhor human suffering. When I saw these people carrying sacks being dropped in the center of town, with nothing to eat (including the young and the old), I was touched. I asked myself why I could not lead and show others that we can assist our brothers and sisters. That is how we started. It did not matter if my life was in danger. Our aim was to save the lives of those people arriving. Some of them were ailing and others in desperate conditions needing assistance. I volunteered and considering that as a Kenya Human Rights activist, anything could happen to you (for you can be killed, you can be betrayed or even taken to police or jailed) we are always ready for any eventuality.

If the same chaos occurred again, I would still assist because I am proud that I can move around Naivasha and see those who came and settled here are happy. Grateful people with very good hearts thank us because they recognize the effort we made and the services we voluntarily offered them.

I think that the Truth, Justice and Reconciliation Committee should be formed where people will come forward and disclose who misled them, what they were told, apologize for their actions based on the misleading information because hate will never take us anywhere but will instead be detrimental to our development. As for the chaos, I would totally blame both the opposition and PNU because they both claimed they won. They would even threaten that Kenya will never be the same again if they did not get favourable results. People believed their words and took to the streets. This action sabotaged the economy of this country and the way forward because whatever had been achieved receded almost back to zero.

Investors lost part of their confidence in this nation because they saw that this nation is not stable and can burn easily. So investments slowly went down and the mood of the people towards others is also down because not everybody understands that all this was because of incitement. It will take long to heal and unless the Truth, Justice and Reconciliation Committee is put in place whereby people will be forgiven. Civil society organizations will have to create a lot of awareness to convince our people that we need to coexist. I was very proud the other day when I saw that there is an NGO in Burnt Forest that has opened an office and they have a book where people are signing apologizing for what they did and they even had a demonstration led by the two ethnic groups at the centre of the conflict. That was a good move towards reconciliation. If other parts of the country can start such programmes, then I think we will be moving towards true reconciliation.

In 1992 and 1997 I did not assist the clash victims because I was busy in Naivasha, but I was able to visit some of them in Molo area because I was in charge of NCC in the larger Nakuru District. Visiting them, talking to them and giving them hope about life was very important. However in 2007, I did not anticipate any chaos of that magnitude. What I thought was that even if there would be a repeat of chaos, it would be minimal unlike in 1997 and 2002. But this time, I think people were so mad. It was excessively done.

I think the best thing in Kenya today is to have a new constitution and change the mode of administration. I am highly opposed to the provincial kind of administration. I think the highest administration in Kenya should end at the district level so that people from the region do not team up and say we are from Western, Rift valley, Nyanza or Central. If the government can remove provincial administration it would reduce the occurrences of clashes by more than 70%. Two - and others support me in this - all ministers in government should be civil servants not politicians. This will reduce the number of people fighting to support a presidential candidate so as to be given ministerial posts. Instead the president elected should choose his administration and work with independent people who are not politicians.

The historical nature of land ownership in Kenya should also be dealt with once and for all. People coming from a particular ancestral land lay claim to it even if they do not own it legally. Other people are on that land legally because they bought it and have titles to that land. A mechanism should be put in place so that every person in this republic respects title deeds, ownership and private land. This should be done by an independent commission without any political interference.

On the issue of IDPs, I cannot say that the government has done enough. First, government worked with the Red Cross and yet the people who came with Red Cross did not understand how the situation started and what was happening on the ground. They just came and in their own "professional ways" said things should be done in a certain way and in so doing, they neglected a lot of people who were staying with families around Naivasha. Secondly, on the issue of rationing food, there were a lot of stories within the camps that even the Red Cross staff were sometimes making favors to girls and young women who did not have their husbands there and those are issues of immorality. The rations were also too small that a lot of these people at the camps especially the young generation were forced to engage in risky activities such as prostitution so as to earn money for extra food. This was another thing that was very bad because it encouraged the increase of HIV infections around the town.

I feel disappointed and up to date my opinion is that the Red Cross never helped people in catering for their needs. This was because the government gave them the sole responsibility of caring for the IDPs and that monopoly should never be repeated again. Let interested agents participate and work for the people. If it is in Naivasha district, let Kenya Human Rights Commission be involved. In Molo district, let Red Cross be there and such kinds of distribution will enhance effectiveness in the delivery of services. Another case of the government's failure is in Kitale where I visited last week and I found a lot of IDPs in tents. The IDPs had not gone back to their houses and they don't even have houses where they could go back to so they need to do a lot to resettle these people before the next general election.

Some IDP's are still in Naivasha town because their businesses were burnt down and have nowhere to go. They may not have relatives who can accommodate them and also do not have money to buy land. A few of those who were paid the Kshs. 10,000/= bought land which is 3 acres on the way to Maai Mahiu. They took the very tents from the camps to that land to serve as shelter so they are just moving out from public land and going to their now personal land. There are still many problems because there is no water, no food, nor employment. On the issue of employment, as much as some of the investors tried to accommodate the IDPs, they still have a formula that is used by those farms that doesn't favor the locals and the IDPs. The officers employ people from the region they come from. So you find that if you do an audit on these farms and where the head of the personnel department comes from Nyanza, Nyanza will have a majority of people working in that farm at the expense of the local people and the IDPs. A plan has to be put into place by the labour and the administration office in the farms whereby local people are given priority.

Some of the integrated IDPs are trying to adopt to the new kind of life under severe hardships, searching for employment or business locally so that they can earn a living. They are barely surviving because of the multitude of problems they face yet the government is not there. The Red Cross registered them and we had also registered everybody who came from the clash torn areas but they ignored our list. Red Cross was given the priority to give in the list of names yet they came in much later after the chaos had started. This means that they did not have all the names nor all the details. As the first people on the ground, we had all the details of who they were, where they were going, where they came from and where they are settled.

Q: Are there any fears of a repeat of the chaos in 2012 election period?

A: We can't categorically say yes or no but if there is no interaction and dialogue between people and the government, I am certain that chaos will be there. For example, the Kalenjin think that their boys are still in custody while the government says there are no boys in custody. So if they have to ask for their children wherever they are, the concerned people have to come out and say they are not there or where they went to. If they are in custody, let the government say how many they have. Show them by a list and where they come from so that their parents will know where their children are. Otherwise that kind of bitterness is still in their hearts. Politicians have also been accused that they have forgotten the sufferings of the IDPs and are busy aligning themselves for 2012 elections but I support those who are saying "let's first settle the IDPs, unite the country and our people then move forward and see who among us will be the next president". This is not the right time to campaign for presidency. My own observation is that people fought without knowing what they were fighting for. It was just a political influence and at the end of the day people acknowledged that the beneficiaries of the violence were the politicians. So they wonder why they fought. I do not see another situation whereby ordinary Kenyans will fight again but may be politicians will now fight in their own avenues.

Q: What should be done to those people who attacked others or the perpetrators of the violence?

A: If there is any evidence, anybody no matter which office he holds should be taken to court but not in Kenya. They should be taken to The Hague because that was massive killing of our own people. They should be taken there, prosecuted and given the toughest penalty possible.

Q: What is your message to Kenyans out there on the issue of peace and on the coming 2012 elections?

A: My message to them is that we need each other. There is no ethnic group can live in this country alone so let us unite. Let us not listen blindly to our politicians. Instead let us think about ourselves. Let us see what dangers we pose by following politicians religiously and let's focus on the development of our country by joining hands together regardless of where one comes from. Let us have one ethnic group called 'Kenya' and the other group called 'politicians'.

I Protect Human Rights

My name is Benjamin Mungania from Naivasha. I have lived here since 1978. I am a businessman and I also a human rights activist. Naivasha has a hot sunny climate with different ethnic communities. We also get people from different countries who are on transit vehicles from Mombasa going to Uganda and Rwanda. Basically Naivasha is a place that has a lot of activities. The town is mainly known for its flower farms.

During the constitutional referendum the situation changed since people became divided along ethnic lines following what their leaders were telling them. For example, those who supported the Banana wing which was for the change of constitution had enmity with those who supported the Orange wing which was against the constitutional changes. The Orange group won and the Draft Constitition was rejected. This made the communities who won feel that they had power over other communities.

During the 2007 elections we had problems because it was announced that Kibaki had won and the people who supported PNU went round the town singing and celebrating but later on Kikuyu people from Nakuru, Kitale, Eldoret and others from North Rift started streaming in to Naivasha. Earlier during the campaigns in Naivasha contestants were from PNU, KANU and NARC-Kenya. The ODM was not heard because its candidate was not vibrant. The campaign was okay but there was a time when there were chaos in Mai Mahiu when the ODM candidate went to campaign there because this was his home and area residents know him. At that time, we were monitoring campaigns and we had been assigned duties by an organization called Community Aid International. We monitored these campaigns and they were generally peaceful.

On 27th December 2007, people voted peacefully and later on we went ahead with the counting of the votes. During the tallying of votes all was peaceful though there were a few challenges at the Municipal Hall. One such challenge was when a youth wanted to steal votes using Form 16A. He had written another 16A Form and wanted to give it out as if it was the correct one. The other problem was that the returning officer made mistakes as he announced votes. We also had a problem when the returning officer stopped the counting of votes and said that he was tired. But people forced him to go on until all the votes had been tallied. There was even an attempt of switching off the lights. But the situation was contained by the police.

Later on when the results were announced at the national level and since almost all the Naivasha residents supported PNU, there was celebration in the streets. In the excitement, the ODM office was burnt down by the PNU supporters. Later on people were calm and there were no incidences of violence.

After the announcement, people started streaming in to Naivasha from other parts of the country fleeing from the areas where there was violence. Some come from Kisumu, Kakamega, Eldoret and Burnt Forest. They came in lorries. When they arrived they had a lot of problems and when I saw how the street children and other thugs were taking advantage and mistreating them, I felt that I needed to support them. We assisted them by putting a basket near Jubilee House and after two hours we had collected Kshs. 16,800 which we gave to them so that they could proceed on with their journey. From there I talked to some people and we decided to have a place where we could receive those who were coming in to avoid congestion in the town. We were able to secure KANU grounds and someone helped us with tents and that was when we set up the tents on 5th January 2008. A lot of people came in and we started dividing the ones who had somewhere to go, from those who did not have anywhere to go. For those who had nowhere to go, we would talk to friends and seek assistance. We ensured that these people did not encounter sufferings here in Naivasha since they had suffered enough.

We continued with this mission up to 20th January 2008 when the Red Cross came in. The Red Cross acted like the government and they said that the people had to be given a certain identity paper so that they could accept them. At that time we were known as Peace Net Desk Centre. We were giving the affected people a certain paper and they used to take it to the police who would record them in the Occurrence Book (OB). Then they would be taken to the tents. For those who did not have the Red Cross papers they were not given a tent there by the Red Cross. We continued until the government came in and dismissed what we were doing.

Those who came told us that the violence had started during the referendum. The Kikuyus were being called *madoadoa* (blemishes, stains) that needed to be removed and that they should go to Central Province. Therefore, even during the campaigns they knew that they would be attacked because they had been threatened that whether they won or not, they had to leave since that was not their land. They also told us that those who forced them out of their land would claim that the land belonged to them. They told us that a prominent leader was deeply involved in leading the whole operation. He would tell his people that they would own those lands the moment they threw the Kikuyus out. They also claimed that a trained militia was used in the attacks.

Although there was peace in Naivasha we received threats from other ethnic groups especially Luo and the Kalenjins. They even identified the properties that belonged to the Kikuyu and they would say that they were waiting to take over the properties. So as Naivasha continued to be peaceful, these people started bringing in arrows with the help of the person who was in charge of prison. There was a time when a vehicle carrying weapons was stopped. This angered people as their people were coming in to Naivasha with injuries. Among the injured was a man who came from Narok whose hand had been cut and one of his eyes gouged out. That is how violence started in Naivasha.

On 27th January people became angry and they started demonstrating. They wanted the person in charge of prison, the DCIO and the person in charge of Wildlife to leave because they accused them of supporting those who were threatening the communities here. Also there was anger due to the curfew as it caused a lot of problems for the Naivasha residents since the senior police officers who were in charge, armed police based on their community, i.e those from the Luo and Nandi community, while others did not carry weapons. People demonstrated and blocked the roads saying that they did not want these people there. Furthermore, they had shot down a woman and even wanted to shoot the then DC. Later on Bishop Kairu addressed the people but they did not calm down. I also tried to calm the prison warders and they left.

People started attacking the Luos as they wanted them to leave town the same way their fellow Kikuyus

A security officer helps an internally displaced child to alight from a vehicle. By Antony Gitonga

were being chased away from other places. This violence continued and it took the army three days to calm it down. Victims from Naivasha went to the nearby prison and others went to the police station. They stayed for a while before proceeding to Kedong camp, which was put up by the flower farms. This group was going to work from these camps and this angered people because they had pay slips and they are the ones who were getting all the assistance. There was a woman who brought about 400 bags of maize and all these was taken to the IDP camp in Kedong. The Naivasha DO, worked with the Red Cross to ensure that they did not help people from the other IDP camp. There were two camps, at Kedong and at the stadium, but the camp at Kedong benefited more because they got mattresses, running water, fenced area with electricity, TV and so on. In fact they enjoyed as if they were at home. These IDPs had many luxuries and some even refused to leave the camp since they were getting a lot of things for free. There was discrimination in the distribution of facilities to IDPs.

I wasn't able to assist them because they did not want to see anybody who was conversing in Kikuyu. Although I am a Meru but they saw me as a Kikuyu. There was a time I brought people from the USA who wanted to assist all the IDPs and as we wanted to get in they blocked me from entering. The Americans had to go in on their own and we were left by the roadside. The IDPs who were at the stadium needed our assistance but those at the Kedong camp did not require our assistance due to the donations they were getting from the owners of the flower farms, the Red Cross and other donors.

Q: Did you know that there would be violence in Naivasha?

A: I did not know there would be chaos in Naivasha. It was very calm and it was even mentioned on radio as one of the towns that had maintained peace. But people started bringing in weapons. For instance, inside the house of a certain man it was claimed that there were over two drums of petrol and a lot of arrows which were recovered. This was at the town center near KFA. This created a lot of anxiety.

I would say the Naivasha violence resulted from a number of things. First, it was the curfew. Secondly, people were filled with emotions due to the injured who had fled from Kisumu, Eldoret, Kitale and other places. Thirdly, it was due to people who were saying that they would take the properties that belonged to the Kikuyus in Naivasha. Fourthly, they said that they wanted to push all the Kikuyus up to a shopping centre called Flyover. Those in my view, are the things that caused violence in Naivasha.

Q: *Was the violence planned?*

A: The violence was not planned. When people started demonstrating and displacing residents of Nakuru, there was violence. The attackers said that the only place remaining for them to take over was Naivasha. Nakuru residents defended themselves and the Naivasha people knew that they were next on line of attack since that is what they were saying. The Gilgil residents joined together with the Naivasha residents in order to stop the other people from attacking them.

I can solely blame the Naivasha security agents for the chaos since they knew everything having declared a curfew which affected some people. They were informed but they did not take any action. Also they did not involve the stakeholders. For example, we had lived together for a long time and some people were now threatening to take other people's property. Intelligence was getting all this information but they did not take any action.

Q: *How will forgiveness occur?*

A: Forgiveness is given according to the situation. The government should have asked for a meeting with the two communities and talked to them so that they could give out their views. I can forgive if the offenders accept their mistakes and ask for forgiveness. The government is saying that we have forgiven each other yet people have not yet come together and talked in order to bring back the relationship they once had. The government is not handling this issue in the right way. In addition, to avoid a repeat of the violence, the government should call the leaders from the ethnic communities that were affected or had differences. For example, if it is in Kisumu they should go there and talk to Kisumu residents - both the attackers and the victims - and the people be open enough to say what led to these problems. If people dialogue openly this will lead to reconciliation and if anyone is mentioned as the one who incited, he should be brought to these community leaders to be reprimanded since the problem we have in Kenya is poor leadership and political parties.

Q: Was the government to blame?

A: I blame the government for the violence because it did not handle issues as required. They did not help in bringing people together when it was tense. They only came in when there was violence yet the Intelligence Officers would have helped them know what was being planned. The politicians should be in control of their campaigns, because of multi-partism democracy has become excess in this country. Politicians did not think of the country's laws. Their utterances were threatening people and the country and they used the freedom of expression to incite people. These politicians should know that they are Kenyans too and hence respect Kenyan laws.

Q: Should attackers get amnesty?

A: The issue of amnesty is a tricky one because those who attacked others are not known since they have not come out in the open. You cannot forgive someone who has not asked for forgiveness. The one who is saying that these people be forgiven is the one who was inciting people into violence. He promised to help them, that is the reason he is saying that they be forgiven. He should go to the law enforcers and say, "On behalf of those who committed the offence we are asking for forgiveness." If he does this, then it shows that he is the one who incited them in the first place.

Q: In your opinion how can the government assist the IDPs?

A: The government has many ways and resources to help the IDPs. One, it should get money so that these people can be employed in the town in which they are for sometime. Two, it should set systems on how they are going to resettle people and in a better way by maybe giving out land for resettlement. The Intergrated IDPs had gone to clash-torn areas to carry out businesses and their businesses were destroyed so they cannot go back. For those who were employed, their employers were also sent packing. They have nowhere to go. For example, there is a land at Moi Ndabi which is over 2000 acres, there is also a land that is over 7,000 acres that was being used by a European by the name Dick Evans. The government can take this land and give it to the IDPs and this will lead to reduction in poverty. They should also build schools for the children of IDPs.

Q: What is your message to the government and fellow Kenyans?

A: My message to the government is that it sets a committee consisting of the IDPs, the stakeholders, the NGOs, the Red Cross and churches and also the business community so that they can come up with ways of assisting the victims especially Naivasha and Nakuru. The government should not be in the committee. The president was here and he should have helped these people, but the Red Cross came in and took over. The government should stop saying that only Red Cross is capable of helping when there is a calamity in the country. This work should be delegated to several NGOs so that people can get proper assistance since people were affected in the hands of the Red Cross.

Q: What action would you recommend be taken against those who attacked others and those who incited them?

A: These people broke the law and therefore if they walk scot-free people will see them as enjoying freedom and therefore they too will feel that it is not wrong to attack, insult and kill in Kenya. They should be convicted depending on what they did. The law says that rape, murder and arson are offences. Let them face the law.

I WORK IN THE POLICE FORCE

My name is Douglas Mugira. I work in the police force and my home is in Meru. I came here from Eldoret and I have been in the force for around two and half years. I work as a dog handler though I serve all as per our motto *Utumishi kwa Wote* (Service to All). Naivasha is a good town with both positive and negative aspects just like other towns. I am a Christian and I love Jesus. I worship at Victory Outreach Church and my life and work as a Christian is through the mentorship of my pastor.

During the referendum, I was in college for further studies. Therefore I did not participate fully though I was taken to Kitui to offer security. After that I went back to college and graduated after two months. I cannot say that this is the time that ethnicity started because we were all in unity but these are the signs in the Bible that in the last days there will be hatred between brothers and bad rumors will erupt. During last year's elections there was violence which is prophesied in the Bible. We are facing so many things now like earthquakes and these are the signs of the last days. But others look at it in a worldly way such as ethnicity which is all wrong.

Campaigns were vibrant in Naivasha just like in other areas and all the political parties were in town selling their parties and policies. Supporters were shouting and singing as per the norm to win more votes. The main parties involved were ODM, PNU and ODM-K and there was no violence apart from the normal crime and accidents but this situation changed when violence erupted immediately after the general elections. I did not know of any fighting and never thought there would be any fighting. I think that is the work of the devil. People allowed the devil to have power over them and used them to fight. We always pray that it does not happen again. I am sure people will follow God's doctrines and people will thus love each other and stop the senseless killing.

On the Voting Day, I was not in Naivasha as I had gone to Baringo on the Pokot and Turgen border. I never knew what had happened. I was in an arid place where registered voters were only 128 and all was peaceful and we took the returns to Kabarnet. The following day we returned to Naivasha. Naivasha was okay but in some areas there was violence after the election results were announced. Later on a Sunday as I prepared to go to church we found that the roads had been closed. The residents were complaining of a curfew and harassment which was carried out in the nights. After that there was high tension and we went to the station. We were told of chaos at the highway and we went there to know why motorists were being robbed. There were many youths there who said that their people had been beaten and it was chaotic. Lorries carrying displaced people passed there and this incited the youth.

Naivasha became like hell because as we left Kayole, we received reports that a house had been burnt in Kabati and people killed. The area MP came there and tried to talk to the youths to stop the chaos. We thought that they could resolve the issues peacefully and we never knew it could go into the streets. The boys did not listen to him and shouted him down. We left for Kabati where another group had caused mayhem. This is where we saw the first bodies and a house which had already been burnt but we did not stay there for long. We rescued two children who were crying and a man. We went to the police station with the children and then returned to the estate later. We found women and minors who had locked themselves in houses and we first saved their lives. We later learnt that the attackers were flushing out non Kikuyus, so we had to escort them to the police station. The attackers were armed and we could not confront them. I talked with some of them because of the power of God and also prayed for His intervention. Some of the youths who knew me heard our pleas and allowed us to escort people to the police station. God was there for those who believed in Him and we managed to rescue them. After that I was attached to the IDPs for the duration that they were at the police station.

Assisting them was easy as I was assigned to guard them together with another Christian officer and I think it was God's making. I understood their predicament. We looked for ways in which we could assist and I came to know a lady called Rahab. She came to me and we became friends. We started assisting. I became a social worker – a new responsibility which I had never thought about. The victims came with nothing. They were devastated, afraid and their faces were very dry depicting hunger. There was no food and water to give them and they used the little in the station. Some parents did not know where their children were and some children had also been separated from their parents. They took refuge in churches, prison and the police station. It was a pathetic condition and I just knew things were not good. We thought of ways of assisting them with Rahab and Sister Florence. On the third day, the Red Cross came after we called them. It was hard to distribute food because a fight ensued. Though we were few, we tried to assist. Many police officers were out in the streets. We had to do our duty of providing for the victims.

We preached to the victims, counselled them and felt that we were part of them. We talked to them and told them that God was with them no matter what was going on. Even if they had lost property and loved ones, God still loved them and this would pass. Some felt better and they would come looking for us so that we could comfort them. We continued preaching and about 15 people got saved. Food started coming in regularly and flower farmers came in to assist the IDPs. Two children were born in the camp and there were all classes of people there. It was not a good situation and we relied on well-wishers. I remember one day it rained so much that everything, was soaked. As policemen, we do not have big rooms and I wondered how we could assist them and I prayed to God to intervene. It was very touching.

For those who lost their relatives, Rahab, The Red Cross and I assisted them with funds for coffins, post mortem and transport. But most of the times I stayed in the station guarding the IDPs I made a lot of friends. I became more of a social worker and we even started classes for the small ones so that the trauma could be eased off through games and books. Despite being very few, we planned for it. We got some balls and stationery. We took them to a mechanic's workshop. During the day it became a classroom and at night it became the sleeping quarters. We brought in a TV and they watched cartoons and the trauma started to ease off.

Since I got saved I am a changed man and I decided to assist those suffering. It came from deep down my heart. We are all created by God with a purpose. The feeling to assist was in me and I was not afraid since the Lord was there to protect me. I did that as I never saw the danger and the main mission was to help. Those who were involved in this chaos should repent and I am sure those who did that were forgiven by the Lord. I prayed for them to know the Lord and learn that what they did was the work of Satan. If you kill that is the devil's way as he uses his spirit to make people commit sins. The bad spirits settle in people who are not before the eyes of the Lord. It is against Gods commandment to kill and those who did that were possessed by the evil spirits. We are still praying for them so that they can be forgiven after repenting and stop these evil acts.

I pray to God that such chaos will not happen again as they were part of learning that peace comes from God. It is through God that Kofi Annan mediated for peace and answered our prayers. God loves this nation and through our prayers this kind of violence will never happen again since the Lord really loves us.

Q: What action should be taken against those who killed and organized the chaos?

A: I think the law has its part to play and it should be followed. If someone did something bad let action be taken against him and then justice will be done.

Q: What is your message to all Kenyans?

A: I would like to remind them that we are all Kenyans and God was not a fool to create different ethnic communities and put them here. God has a purpose for all of us so let us follow Him. When you kill someone it means that you do not fear the Lord the creator of all of us. We possess God's power in us and therefore we should love and respect each other.

Q: *Anything else you would like to add?*

A: I would like to appreciate the arm of the law because during the chaos God intervened and that is why the armed forces acted well. God intervened and that is why the forces had no favourism during the chaos. There were no tribal feelings amongst us and that is why we managed to put off the chaos and through God's assistance, we were able to work together. In all the security forces, there were no differences; we worked together to quell the violence. God gave them the authority to stop the killings.

•

Army Officers unblock Nairobi-Nakuru Highway. Photo by Antony Gitonga

SECTION III

NARRATIVES OF AGGRESSION

Scenes of Destruction.

Top: *A destroyed home in Maili Nne, Eldoret.*
Bottom: *Shells of burnt out vehicles at the Eldoret Weigh bridge.*
Photos by Kimeu Muindi

I Blocked Roads, Attacked and Burned Houses in Eldoret...

My name is Johnson *(not real name)*. I live in Turbo. As the campaigns went on in top gear, we had doubts whether our preferred candidate would really make it. It is always hard to compete with the incumbent. There were rumours eeh ...that the government must win whatsoever the case and they – ODM - were saying "our people, if diplomacy fails we apply violence."

This was not an open plan because nobody knew that the votes would be stolen. After the election votes were counted and announced on 30th December 2007. People started seeing PNU closing in on the gap and winning and trouble started. People started screaming and there was unrest and they started barricading the road. But fighting had not started by then. After the announcement that the government had won, people said that votes had been stolen, and started planning the attacks. They didn't plan before but after the voting. Actually, they had not planned anything prior. It was only a reaction to PNU winning the election.

There are some people who could reach certain regions so they would call a meeting where the village elders call the shots by giving the instructions, means of transport, food and also making of weapons. There were some Kalenjins who were also in PNU and the youth were being used. For example, we would identify and attack them, then bring them to the elders where they paid fines. One paid something like Kshs. 20,000. The *Wazees* (elders) used that money to look for people who knew how to make the weapons that we later used for the attacks. Even councillors participated. I know them but I can't mention their names but someone like Chep* who was a close ally of the Mheshimiwa. This person used to organize the youth and when they were arrested he used his influence to get them released since he was very powerful. Others used to give milk which was used to feed the attackers. After eating, the youth who were about 2000 would assemble and go to the highway to block the road to Turbo and attack people. The attackers would begin in one place and the others would come to help. Turbo was too chaotic. There the two major communities (the Kikuyus and the Kalenjins) were fighting. In Turbo, the population of the Kikuyus and the Nandis was leading. These are the groups which mostly attacked each other.

A prominent politician used to send resources like money. He could even call us during the meetings to ask if we had decided to go but…you see people like us who are educated at times used to ask, "What if we were arrested?" Then they would say, "No problem we are there for you, we will support you in all means to see that you are freed". That gave us the morale and encouragement. For example, during a raid, one of my friends was shot dead and Mheshimiwa gave Kshs. 50,000 to the family as consolation. This was the norm of wars. This gave most people the drive to fight on. Also in our place, they used to identify the rich people like businessmen who sell maize and they would tell them to contribute to the warriors - (youth). Some even contributed and gave out their cars and lorries which we used. We indeed used the same mode of transport to attack Eldoret town.

We got incited. The businessmen used to tell us that the way leadership of the government had been taken, we will never have opportunities again. They would tell us, "Now you see the government has gone to Central Province. We should fight to ensure that all the resources come back in accordance to our wish". The businessmen said that roads would be built in Central Province only. They said that if the ODM had won we could have received favors and develop more economically than the other regions.

This violence - especially in Turbo - started precisely on the evening of 29th December 2007. They had not even announced the results but the ranges were near each other. Then ODM leaders claimed that PNU had started stealing votes at the KICC and obviously would eventually win. We started attacking from the centre where one Kikuyu, Mzee Njonjo, had a business. In fact, the youth started from his shop where they beat up his son. That was the beginning and by 30th December all hell broke loose. This man, Njonjo, had a big business and was a staunch PNU supporter. Now people were at the market centre and heard from the radios about the turn of events. They immediately went to his shop and found his son. The son was celebrating outside. It took only one stone and the screams started from there. In Turbo, people started burning houses. By 31st December the GSU had come to save houses but the damage had already been done.

In a community like the Kalenjin once a person is circumcised, one is taught how to fight using bows and arrows. It is an ancient tradition. So when you are through with initiation you are ready for anything. That is why I am saying that they were equipped because one is taught how to attack his enemy which is normal and is there. So no one was trained during the violence. Equally no one took any oath. The only training done was during initiation. You know, when they are practicing circumcision, there are no specific oaths. No! Oaths are not just taken. One has to support his community so I was involved in the chaos. I was in the group charged with attacking, burning, and looting. You know killing cases in Turbo were not many. Personally, I did not kill anyone. I knew automatically that that was bad and I feared it. But burning, attacking, blocking the roads and others, I participated fully. Indeed, these attacks came automatically. Being a youth, I couldn't just sit back at home when my friends went to attack! It was necessary for you as a youth to go. It was only the women and the old men who remained behind.

Before a raid it is normal for Kalenjins to be given some advice and instructions by the old people. One is called in a group to be advised. If it turns out bad in the war and your colleague is hurt, they told us that it was better for all of us to be injured but never to leave any of our own behind. Then when you see your enemy you cannot just attack, there was a formula of attacking. We were organized in groups. Let's say a group of 50 would be sent to attack and another group of 30 would be sent later, so the victims would be caught in the middle.

We were not paid much. If there was something small like money, of course you were given but this happened when sponsors came. Some would give us something little for a *soda*. I remember taking home Kshs. 800 for all that trouble. When the Mheshimiwa would come, we would be many and at times the cash would not reach us at all. For example, if he gives Kshs. 20,000 we would leave the cash to the very needy amongst us. I got 800 shillings only. This depended on how much money would be donated to us and the number of people in the group. That Kshs. 800 was for one day.

After the chaos, we decided to accept these guys back through *Operation Rudi Nyumbani.* Now, the way they came, you could see how they had suffered because most of them were homeless. They had been living in tents. I really pity them but there's nothing we can do. Personally, I feel guilty. I am not amused at all. I realized it was just a reaction of expecting something to happen in a certain way but then it ends up in the opposite way. Also, the media contributed by depicting a realistic picture of how the votes were stolen and that angered us to act that way. You could hear these local stations saying things were worse. For example, KASS contributed a lot. They broadcasted that things had gotten worse and that they could not leave the government to take over easily without doing anything. You see, those are some of the small things that contributed a lot to the violence.

In 1992 I was still very young and so I did not participate, but in 1997 at least I contributed a little. In 1997 I just participated in screaming and blocking the roads. Those days you only heard noise and what would follow was to rush there and throw stones. But the latest one was terrible because it was like having all the ethnic groups against one. In 1997 the President was on our side so we didn't participate a lot.

After the clashes, I no longer trust any other group in the community. I can't go to a nightclub alone or in the company of another ethnic community even though they are my friends and we schooled together. I can't go with, let us say a group of five of them, to drink. You know if a guy was very rich before the violence, then poor after what happened, do you expect to sit together and have a good mood to enjoy the party? Like in Turbo, everyone knows his/her property. For instance, if you spot your property even if it's a bicycle and the colour has been changed, you will know it and will not feel comfortable walking with it anyway. I am always afraid, and although we have reconciled, the gap of trusting is still very wide.

In order to reconcile, the IDPs should be helped. They were stable financially but now they are poor and don't have anything. If there are organizations that can really help them recover, that will be good for them. They should be helped even to build houses. Then civic education should be conducted to enlighten people. The projects should be started especially those that will involve the communities. If these projects succeed, then they would help us go back to our normal life of trusting one another.

In our area we have seen the mistrust reducing because the IDPs have settled and started businesses. What made things worse was incitement from the leaders. We saw that the Kikuyus, the Kisiis and the Luhyas had left their provinces to come and rule over us. I feel that if it was not for the hate campaign, this violence would not have occurred. Things were pretty bad this time. You even find that if a lady was married outside the Kalenjin community, she was forced to leave her husband and come back home.

The politicians should be fully involved in the peace and reconciliation process because they are the ones who declared war. They should be the ones restoring peace. We need rehabilitation. Our people have married Kikuyus. I even had a Kikuyu girlfriend. During the elections and the chaos that followed I was with her all that time. In fact, I escorted her when people started screaming at her. People started fleeing to Western Province since we are at the border and there was a police station there. I escorted her but when I saw things turning worse, I urged her to just go. Just imagine! We are back together again and I tell her that there was nothing I could have done. Now I feel happy with her though it is painful. But she is very open. She told me Kalenjins are bad and that we betrayed the trust especially by how we treated them. I too affirmed that indeed we destroyed our image. She told me that she saw me among the attackers but I assured her that I didn't burn their house. If I had the ability, I could have prevented their house from being burnt. Yes I witnessed it being burnt but I was powerless.

The way I foresee 2012 there will be violence if people do not get civic education. You see this might become a habit for some people. People should be taught the truth and all those leaders who incited and contributed to this chaos should be arrested first to serve as a lesson to others. Sometimes you hear a drunkard shouting, "You have come eeh?" or in cases of a small disagreement someone threatens with a phrase like "it's me and you in 2012." Yesterday I was with a friend of mine and we visited a Kikuyu old man. At times, my kinsmen wonder if I am Kalenjin. During our conversation he said, "I cannot build anything permanent here. I had even decided to sell this land and settle in Nairobi. If a repeat of the same occurred in 2012 it will be really bad."

People say that the 1992 clashes were worse in that place since it is at the border. I feel that if they do not resolve the conflict, things will not be good. But if they use all means, there is nothing that can go beyond control. Even our MP who is known to be tough, for instance said during the referendum, "These guys are just one pick-up and if we decide, we can collect all of them and ferry them to where they belong." This was because when he came and held a rally here the Kikuyus just continued with their businesses. The other community should have come to the meeting. Even though the other person is talking nonsense, they should just listen to them even if they won't do a thing. After all you just go to your house at the end of it. Even if you will vote for PNU just be quiet. Don't campaign because you know you are in someone's place. You know they say that, you can do anything to a guest and the guest can never complain because they are guests. In my opinion, I want people to come and enlighten them; tell them the truth since tribalism is growing at an alarming rate. They should just be quiet and vote quietly. People should know their democratic rights; where to vote and who to vote for. People should respect one another.

Q: Will you participate again in violence if it were to re-occur?

A: I can't participate again. You know it depends. Ah! It may even not find me here because you know I may be employed by then. I will not participate because we subjected people to a lot of suffering. We didn't gain anything. At the end of it all, nobody came to pay my school fees. It has always been my parents. It's only the politicians who benefited. We are still in our old state. Nothing has changed. We fought for nothing! Had it not been for our fighting they wouldn't have gotten those posts. But right now they don't know we exist. They are enjoying alone. There are a lot of illiterate people who are being misused and if they approach you, you cannot say otherwise. The Nandi have rules which force everyone to participate. That's what drove me to it.

Q: How did the elders participate?

A: For the elders, they advised the youth on how to attack and organize people. They gave out their expertise on how to go about it. Some of the Nandis had intermarried and they would narrate stories about past days on how they used to attack. This gave us psyche to do it. They told us that if one was killed during the war, it was a good sign of how one defended their ethnic group. This made us value our community and we could do anything for it. So the old men advised us and ensured we had food. In our culture when people go to war they do not go back home but feed and stay in the forest. It was rare to meet with your family members. We could go to fight for maybe three days and on returning others would go. It was done in shifts.

The churches were no longer active in preaching since they also participated fully in the chaos. I was with a pastor's son in the violence. In those meetings, pastors were praying for God's blessings and when we went to fight they would pray for us. One pastor said that if we were fighting for our rights, that was not a sin and that God would help us succeed. What do you think if you are in a squad where a pastor has prayed for you?

The women were in charge of cooking, looking for food and screaming but they didn't participate much. In the Kalenjin community, screaming is the only alarm we have for showing that something bad has happened. Sometimes if the General Service Unit were around and for example, if you were raiding Jua Kali the women would scream. Depending on the type of scream, you would know what to do and would take cover until they pass.

Q: How can the government assist?

A: You know our government is slow in implementation. Even if they say they want to bring a solution that may happen in the vision 2050 or so. It takes a lot of time and it doesn't take issues seriously. They can even say that they have formed a commission but such a commission may not even reach the grassroots levels. That commission collects its information in a hotel in Nairobi where no chaos was witnessed. I don't know about the Kenyan government. I don't even know if it has money. It looks like they are not financially stable because they are supposed to take things seriously and come up to the village level. When you go to the village, you will meet the actual people who participated but in Nairobi one will only get con-men who will lie to you yet they didn't participate. They should come to the grass-roots and meet with the people who actively participated like me.

I was in the thick of it. I painted myself, wore war regalia like a warrior, a spear in one hand, and arrows in the other hand. I was ready for the attacks. You are fully prepared and psyched and even if you heard gunshots that did not scare you. I am glad that people have now started going to the grassroots where they will get the truth.

You have heard about the Majimbo. There is tribalism in Kenya. I don't even know why they created provinces because it brings a lot of problems. Most people migrated to these areas due to population explosion and scarcity of land. In Kenya, there is freedom of movement which people exercise. If I left Eldoret for Central, I can't go there and start saying "Ooh... I will vote for a certain politician because I support him." The best thing is to enlighten people.

Again issues of being financially broke are a contributing factor. They need to give the youth jobs. I am hustling and if you tell me that you will give me five hundred shillings by the end of the day to attack and that if am arrested, you will free me, I will not let that chance of getting the 500 Shillings go to waste, I will go. There are two things: you either die or survive. I hear that there is a Youth Fund and people get money for business. It has never reached here. But if one is busy working where will they get you? What if I will be working by 2012? If they keep people busy these wars will be no more.

The speeches that the politicians give have great impact. For example, in Kalenjin community a leader is highly recognized and valued. If he directs that a town be burnt, and razed to the ground, it will definitely happen. Just think back, the leaders are usually in Nairobi. You will hear them saying *"Gigenyi saba ...gororona saba gagoich"* (We are waiting for the branches to come). This meant that "let us wait or check on the message that has arrived.' You can't know what they mean.

The mobile phone was used to communicate and the leaders were signing treaties all over. At times, you could hear that the situation has deteriorated because some info rmation has leaked and that *Mzee* is refusing to sign, so you act in a different way. The government would just be shocked that things are deteriorating again far away from Nairobi. These were the threats they were using.

WE WERE ORGANIZED LIKE A BATTALION

My name is Danny *(not real name)* and I live here in Turbo. The way I know it from the ground, the post election violence was planned. What I am saying is that in 2005 during the referendum, one of our political leaders told us that there was a problem for we were in KANU. Then he told us that we, the Kalenjins, had been oppressed; that the Kikuyus had taken over the government and our people had been dismissed from employment. Moi had employed many of our people but the Kibaki government had sent them home. They had all come home and that was the problem. He told us to vote for Orange so that it would help us because they would take control of the government and our people will reap the fruits. They said that anybody who would not vote for Orange would be beaten and cursed by the community. He said all of us had to vote for Orange. But it happened that there were people here like the Kikuyu and others who didn't go per the expectation. So he said that those people are *"madoadoa"* (blemishes). So if these people are *madoadoa* then they should be eliminated and chased away from our land because they are not with us. Soon they would vacate our land and we will be told how this matter would be. So the rallies went on. During the actual voting, in November 2005, we voted and we won. In January 2006, there were meetings organized by the local leaders and they were convinced that they were about to take over the government and anyone who was not with us would be chased away from here. So now we asked *"Where has this come from?"* He said that the leader had said it. So we proceeded on 2006 and then 2007 when we started our campaigns. We were told ODM is the team to be in.

Business premises flattened during the post-election violence. Photo by Kimeu Muindi

Based on what I saw, I would say the leaders had planned the clashes. Especially in Rift valley it was our Kalenjin leaders and the rich businessmen who planned the violence. They were all claiming that the outsiders had come and grabbed land in Rift valley and their resources and are dominating. And so they decided to chase them away. All this was orchestrated by the political leaders who today hold offices in government. Now you know it started from them and trickled down to the local leaders. They were the ones who used to call us to the meetings to update us on the turn of events. The real planners were the political leaders, then the businessmen assisted financially and gave out their lorries. They also gave fuel for burning properties. They said they wanted Rift valley to be clean of *madoadoa*. Others went to the extent of saying they wanted Rift Valley to be a country on its own. So we confirmed it was true because of the way they were behaving which gave us the feeling and determination to do so. Now as a community, we were called to these meetings and all of us supported the plans and gave out death threats to those who could not support us. You see it was a must we had to support them because our leaders had decided. We consoled ourselves that if the leaders were supporting it, who were we to oppose the plans? We had no alternative.

In my opinion, our leaders indeed incited people because they were the ones who planned it and gave out direction on implementation. We were told to board lorries. The Kalenjins are trained as warriors ready to face anything. If anything happens, you only leave with your bow and arrow. You cannot turn back whatever the case. In my constituency I witnessed one incident just before the presidential results. There was one case of violence at Osorongai in Turbo division where the rival supporters of ODM and KANU clashed. Leader A *(name withheld)* went to a rally and got a few supporters and Leader B's *(name withheld)* group attacked Leader A's group. His supporters were mainly from the Luhya community not Kalenjins.

According to the way things had been planned, we didn't know there would be violence of such magnitude. We were caught off guard after the elections and that was when we realized that it was real. I didn't hear anything about oath taking but you know with us the Kalenjins we don't like oaths. When we are circumcised we are taught to be warriors. So most of the times in cases of any eventuality, you are ready to face it. Sincerely speaking there was no oath taking here.

When the violence started, after the elections, we were directed somewhere. After a week, we were told that there were weapons that had come from Mt. Elgon. So in some areas like Nandi and Cheptirwai some warriors were taken there to be trained on how to use guns by the retired or ex-military men. That was the only training I heard from that region. Another place I heard is in Nandi at a place called Lelmokwo. But mostly it is Cheptirwai where I got information that there were guns there where they were trained to attack Eldoret. There are some people from my area, about three, who went there for training. All of them were previously in military and they are the ones who went to train people there. What I later heard was that it was the bigwigs eh! Those people I told you earlier are the ones I heard that they did the supply from Mt. Elgon.

As I told you earlier, all the youth went there. Personally I woke up and went with bows and arrows to Turbo and started chasing people there. We were chasing the Kikuyus. We were patrolling in shifts at times. I did not harm anyone. I didn't get the chance to. The way I see it, there was nothing one could do. The way you were organized determined how it would happen. It was like an army, you had no choice but to do it if the chance arose. Others did, those who were ahead of us told us so. You know, we were organized like a battalion. In a community there are those who are sharp and they are the ones who formed the front line. And so it followed that way to the lowest level of sharpness.

During that time, for instance, I was not paid. I later heard that the organizers mostly picked the sharp guys for rewarding. So when the *Mheshimiwa* (Honorable) comes, those are the people who were paid. I heard them mention three prominent leaders and one prominent businessman. Those are the people they said had come to support the Eldoret attacks. You see it was a strong battalion. In 1992 I participated. I was still young and I had just left school. We had gone as a team although we didn't harm anyone but we evicted the Luhyas, the Kikuyus and the Kisiis. At that time they supported FORD, the original FORD. That time we were in KANU. We were backing Moi. There was a lot of destruction and lots of lives were lost. But in 1997 I didn't participate. At that time there was no violence in my area. Also in 2002 there was no violence. I have realized that most of the time it is the youth who are used by the politicians. So if we follow the politicians in the end they end up not helping us. Up to now, we have tried to form groups but help has not come our way. So we participated mostly because of poverty. Secondly, unemployment and lastly because of tribalism. We have not changed up to now. I participated in 1992 and 2007 and I didn't benefit at all. I am encouraging everyone in the Rift valley to live in unity. We should not say that Rift Valley is for Kalenjins only. There is no sense because God had put everything in place just for all of us. I don't like the idea of dividing Kenyans in provinces saying; Rift Valley is for Kalenjins, Western for Luhyas and Central for Kikuyus. People should co-exist. Personally I don't hate any community. The constitution says that we should live together in harmony.

Q: *Do you think there will be a repeat of the chaos in 2012?*

A: The way I see it, if they don't take care 2012 will just be like 2007 because those people who sponsored or funded the elections were never apprehended. They have not done any peace and reconciliation activities in Rift valley. There are no visible changes and so if they don't take care there will be a repeat of 2007 in 2012 and it can be worse, I tell you. They haven't done anything on peace and reconciliation especially on the ground. We only hear of it in newspapers. So I am seeing 2012 to be a worse year if no changes are going to be done. To avoid a repeat of 2007 chaos, there is need for thorough peace and reconciliation campaigns in the Rift Valley especially in Eldoret. And they should involve the youths mostly.

Q: *Will you participate again if it occurs in 2012?*

A: Although I have participated in the two occasions, I haven't benefitted in any way. It's only the politicians and their families who benefit. In 2012, they will not see me again, and I am ready to carry out peace and reconciliation if I am assisted financially. I am ready to approach all those who participated to foster peace in the community.

A number of people participated in the planning and execution of the violence. For instance, I was really amazed and astonished to see some church leaders especially the pastors blessing and praying for the youths before leaving for attacks. The old were advisors, they were the ones advising and organizing the youth. They used to give directions especially on where to attack and more so they are the ones who used to communicate with the politicians. Some women also participated by encouraging the youth and cooking for them. They mostly played the role of support staff. Teachers, prominent people and the civil servants provided funding mostly. The athletes also gave lorries, money etc.

Q: *Do you think Kenyans will stay peacefully?*

A: I don't think so because, you know all the top politicians who used to sponsor or finance the chaos are still in power. They have not yet resigned. It's hard for Kenyans to stay peacefully especially when those who sponsored the post election chaos are the ones who are leading. It means systems have not yet changed. There are also businessmen who are their big supporters. Yet these people have not faced any justice. What I am seeing right now is that we are headed for a tribunal. But you hear people saying that if one of us is touched, they will start chaos again. These are the big fish. It is very hard to live in peace if at all justice will not be administered.

Q: *What can people do to live in peace?*

A: People should stop tribalism. They should see themselves as Kenyans and not as ethnic groups. Secondly, people should ignore the politicians and leaders who incite. We should see each other as neighbours and friends.

Q: *What do you think the government should do to bring a lasting solution for people to live in harmony in this region?*

A: It should involve the people in peace and reconciliation activities, mostly those who participated in the chaos. The main problem here is the provincial administration who do not give information to people. Instead they take sides with the politicians. So the government has failed especially in the side of provincial administration.

Q: *What about Kenyans in general, what can they do?*

A: Kenyans should accept one another. They should accept other communities and trust one another. I also urge the government and other organizations to take seriously the issues of peace and reconciliation though it has not yet reached the grassroots level. We only hear of it in the newspapers. They should emphasize it. They should not wait too long.

They Sponsor Clashes to Protect Themselves

My name is Shadrack *(not real name)* from Iten. I blame the leaders for causing post election violence. They heightened peoples' emotions by hinting that there was something coming. In the real sense it happened like something that was carefully planned. The leaders had predicted it and so they prepared the locals on what to do at the right time. For some, it was evident because as we went to vote, they were saying, "If we are defeated there will be fighting." As the tallying was going on, we noticed varied reactions on people with some vowing not to give up if they were defeated.

That was what I saw and truly I was willing to do what the community wanted me to do. It is normally a condition that if you don't participate, you will be excommunicated as an outcast but if you went as per the expectations the community was bound to be proud of you. The reason why I say it was planned is because had they (ODM) won there could have been no violence. Rumours went round in Eldoret that their opponents had joined hands; that Kalonzo had joined ranks with Kibaki. They definitely saw something cooking and so people were encouraged to turn up in large numbers to vote. If you observed keenly the politicians had their own agents down at the grassroots. They could not be seen on the ground even when the fighting was at its peak but these politicians cooperated with key local people. It started so abruptly making it look like it was not organized initially. The attackers came from a place called "Sewer", the next day and after sometime others came from other areas. They vowed not to leave anything to chance. But they didn't know exactly when it would happen and where. It is something everybody decided from the other side. There were vehicles and people passing, others volunteered their cars to be used and others gave out food. It was terrible. They could even force individual milk suppliers to stop delivering their milk to Kenya Cooperative Creameries (KCC) and the youths would then boil and drink it all.

This was something they had thought out clearly and they had reached a state of no retreat no surrender. Even when you were doing your own activities they would summon you, tell you to be off and then allow you to continue. So it wasn't good because it affected everybody. Even the rich were not spared. They had to cooperate. It reached a time when a former Minister's cows were slaughtered by the youths. The youths did not spare anyone's property. They used anything they put their hands on; thus affecting even the MPs and also those who planned. Though at first it didn't look very organized, they later had people in place who would manage different activities and properties. But if their parties had won the violence could not have erupted. During the tallying, people started regrouping and came up with a plan. The incitements were during the campaigns. People planted negative thoughts which took root; that if they dared to vote on the other side there would be problems. But if they had followed what the inciters had directed them, then it would be peaceful.

In this area, violence broke out on the night the presidential results were announced. The fight did not start before the tallying at KICC. I had gone to Iten and when I tried to go to Fluorspar I couldn't travel since the entire place was burning. Everything was burning. So the next day, the roads were blocked and things were now turning ugly. No one wanted to be defeated. ODM believed that they were going to win and the majority of the people here believed that they were going to win and they had their own targets. So if the results could have been announced the other way, there could have been no fights at all.

The Kalenjins don't take oath. What they normally do is gather at one place before raids and may eat together before they go to attack. But on this there was no actual oath apart from the guidelines on taboos and superstitions which guided them. They could caution that if you had done something bad, or you had a bad history or sinned you were not eligible to go for the attacks. People were eliminated from that squad. Those who refused were the ones who were killed in the clashes. In a place called Sergoi athletes and the business people were told to give their vehicles. Some of those cars ferried arrows. There was this old man, the father of my friend who was killed and another old man who also lived within, both had a bad history. The first had taken somebody's land. He was told not to go and young unmarried men were not allowed either. So that is the only form of oath that I can say was taken.

There was no oath taking. They only slaughter a goat or cow when they came together as a way of union. Also when they were going to fight in the evening they had to slaughter and feast to boost their morale. It's a culture administered to morans when they want to go for fights. Personally I was forced to participate in the violence because everyone was supposed to participate in the violence. If you didn't go, your property would be destroyed completely and they would warn you that you are going against them. I was left with no choice but to join them. I was given the responsibility of monitoring the vehicles which went to collect arrows because I know Fluorspar well. That is where they manufactured the arrows. We could go there with the vehicle to buy them.

Some of the arrows were poisonous and some were not. They even made poison instantly from there. There is a formula in which they make poison purposely for a short time and use it there and then. There are a lot of ingredients they use. I don't know what they make the powerful poison with. I know of about two indigenous trees. It is a poison that you cannot stand for two minutes. It clots blood. But recently they have invented another one. They use wheat insecticide known as 72 which is mixed with another one and with the indigenous one barovin. This one causes instant paralysis and death.

I was not paid a cent. Those who went to fight were the ones who were paid and others took cows to their homes. I really felt bad during the entire season and at times I wished I was elsewhere. On the other hand it was a lesson I learnt well and I felt at times that there was a purpose for me to witness all these chaos in my lifetime, I will probably tell people in the future. Those who participated in the violence are the illiterate guys and mostly those who are not exposed. For instance, a prominent man whose stand on issues is a product of the colonial era was the one who was coordinating alongside the MPs and he gave out his vehicles.

Sometimes they used Kalenjin sayings and talked in Kalenjin, to encourage the youth. For example, the youth were told in Kalenjin "*ngot koit punye dong korengun' anangoit ko ne ya ko muregeteya,*" (no matter what happens, you have to stay in front so that if anything arises against our community you should defend it as morans). Thus for those of us who are exposed we saw it as an outdated way of life. I was not involved in 1992 because I was still in primary school and in 1997 I was doing my Kenya Certificate of Secondary Education (KCSE). I didn't involve myself in violence. Kenyans can stay in peace if the leaders are avoided and our people enlightened to use diplomacy. People have to be taught to use diplomacy and not fracas. They must be taught to accept defeat and look forward to other good things for if no one was a loser then what would happen? If you look at the destruction, it will take about ten years to recover. Our economy is in ruins because of the 2007 violence. Everybody is crying and when you cry you should ask yourself if this is what you contributed. In Kiswahili they say *"malipo ni hapa hapa"* (you get what you deserve here on earth), and *"Utavuna Ulichopanda"* (You reap what you sow). If Kenyans change and acknowledge that they are brothers and sisters, they would build this country.

Trust between communities must be encouraged. In my opinion, I trust all communities because I am an athlete. My coordinator who has been helping me is a Kikuyu and he is called Timothy *(not real his name)*. I have even trained with a Kamba and worked with a Kisii and I trust them. My view is that the person who can help you is not from your ethnic group. Previously, we used to stay with other ethnic groups and I coordinated very well with people from other communities than our own fellows. I don't know what is happening to Kenyans, but in the diaspora, we are brothers and sisters. There was no discrimination. The one who got a job for me is a Kikuyu and I work with a Kisii. In the evening we used to sit together and share the experiences of the day. That is what I want for Kenya.

Maybe in the next 10 years we will have such a generation when all the outdated leaders who plant colonial thoughts in us will be no more. Maybe one acquired two acres of land illegally during the colonial times and so he wants to protect it. Those who stole public property earlier are the ones who are sponsoring such activities so as to safeguard their corrupt gains. They will sponsor clashes so that they protect themselves and this is what is destroying Kenya. If we end ethnicity and shun incitements, we will be able to coexist well. We need to change Kenya now. We should not wait until it's too late.

I pray and believe that there will be no violence in 2012. We can avoid it by educating our people. We need to tell the truth irrespective of the outcome. I do believe if someone wants a repeat of the same clashes they will be committing suicide. We need to tell the truth even if it hurts. Corruption needs to be dealt with and all the perpetrators who fall under that category need to be punished. The government should set the pace by dealing with impunity ruthlessly.

In case violence happens again, I will not participate. I am even planning to be away in 2012 because I am now starting my training and maybe by 2012, I will be abroad. My training has been affected by these events. We are no longer living where we used to because we don't feel comfortable living with the people we tormented during the post election violence. By then people would have learnt a lesson. I was even talking with my friends the previous day and they were remorseful. They also feel lucky to have survived. With that I think by 2012 nothing will happen of that nature.

Our ladies never participated a lot because they were taking care of the children. When we went to fight, women were nowhere near the slaughtering place of cows or the goats which was done before going to war. According to the Kalenjin tradition only the *morans* were allowed there and women were not to be seen anywhere. The other people as I told you earlier who were inciting the morans were the elderly. Those whom we could listen to are ones who guided the chaos. Some were over 70 years old and had the colonial mentality. These are the people who led the youth. The church people were involved and some of them were killed and this really surprised me because it seems our people even forgot what they were preaching. Some of the church people were even on the frontline. Some pastors were also involved in the incitement.

Q: This region has been experiencing violence and has a history of violence. What can the government do?

A: In bringing peace in this area the government should initiate two processes: there are those who agree and those who don't. It's the young men who will bring change and a lasting solution. We should encourage people to move freely. For instance, I should be able to go to Nakuru or Thika and buy a piece of land and settle peacefully. But a wrong concept of ethnicity has been planted that our land had been snatched and so we need to reclaim it.

If the government seriously wants to settle these issues it needs to bring together all the stake-holders: the, local leaders, the old men, and the youths in a series of *barazas*. It should also listen to the needs, views and contributions from the community. This way the government will be able to look for a lasting solution to the problems. The government needs to do background checks by among other things: perusing the records and doing a confirmation of ownership to properties; informing the other people and telling them to look for their own property elsewhere. Secondly it needs to educate the people especially the youth because the old generation is coming to an end. The government should empower the youth by first uniting them. They should start youth groups whose members will be in percentage ratio from different ethnic groups and this will enable them to interact, educate each other, help each other and in so doing appreciate each other.

In general, we are all Kenyans and there is need for communities to accept and forgive each other first. They should also know that no matter what happens they are still Kenyans. We need to build our national identity and to accept ourselves. It is not right that the leaders give orders or advice people to forgive others because nothing will come out of it. It needs the people to come together and to discuss the way forward on how they will forgive and seek forgiveness. Forgiveness has to come from the people themselves. Some elders have learnt a lesson while others haven't. People lost their loved ones, their cars and property. If you check again those who supported ODM in this area did not lose anything. Those who supported PNU are the ones who lost their loved ones and / or their property though it was their democratic right to support whichever party they wanted.

There is no democracy here. Their democracy was snatched from them. They were not targeting leaders but against those who supported PNU. They were looking for a certain ethnic community or those seen to be supporting PNU. They didn't touch the Luhyas but some ethnic groups like the Kisiis, the Kikuyus and a few Kambas were all attacked more so at the end of the campaign when Kalonzo was seen to be pro-PNU. The Luhyas were not attacked because of Mudavadi who was in ODM. These attacks were meant to drive a point home to those who supported PNU that they didn't support the right party and individuals.

Loses were in both groups: the attackers and the victims. The farmers incurred heavy losses because they were not able to deliver their milk to KCC for two months, the Kikuyus lost their houses, maize cows, goats and even dogs and Kenyans really lost a lot such that recovering from the losses is next to impossible.

The Kiambaa incident may bring animosity among the communities. There is bitterness and I have heard people objecting the move to have a monument because many wonder that the Kalenjins also died and they did not put up a monument. How then can another community put up a monument for their dead here at Kiambaa? The government should understand and try to do something else that can be remembered without bringing back bad memories, like building a school and calling it Kiambaa or something productive in the area. But not a monument which will continue showing that there is a grudge.

The Kikuyu said they killed many Kalenjin and the Kalenjins say the same but you see like in Kiambaa, if 100 Kikuyus were killed, 20 Kalenjins were also killed so both sides were affected. Some families lost two people while the other side also lost two to three people. For example, I saw in Kimumu, the Kalenjins would attack from one side and the Kikuyus would be on the other side so whenever the Kalenjins attacked, they were also attacked. An old man's leg was chopped off and another person was slashed. The Kikuyus too had arrows and you go to hospitals you would find people with arrow wounds grotesquely swollen. In conclusion, no side can claim they won because families on either side lost loved ones. Even prominent athletes.

It was not a confrontational fighting because Kalenjin use arrows. Thus they shot from far and the Kikuyus have to come near but they too had modified the panga. It was sharpened on all sides and could cut when thrown. The Kikuyus were no match to the shot arrows and their houses were burnt down. Techniques were used whereby petrol bottles were first thrown then arrows were shot into the burning house. Some of the house blew up because they had gas cylinders.

It's an African culture of people that anyone who hides anywhere cannot be attacked. But I don't know what happened on the side of Kiambaa. People felt bad. They also say in Kalenjin culture that if someone runs into your house for refuge, no one is supposed to touch that person. I was also astonished. I think it was because some of them were illiterate and were not enlightened. So those who entered Kiambaa church had run to safeguard their dear lives. They should not have been attacked. Moreover in our culture they never used to kill women and girls but would kill boys even if they were one year olds. In case a mother is holding a small boy in her arms, that small boy cannot be killed because the mother is protecting him. The killing of women and children was not in accordance with our culture.

We used to hear rumours that there were Mungiki and I really pitied the government because policemen were taking sides. We didn't understand why some went on leave suddenly while some who were on active duty came and joined the Kalenjins in fighting. People said that some civilians were in police uniform and they were not policemen because they couldn't take up signals thus they concluded that they were *Mungiki*.

People have now started coming back in places like Chepkanga and Iten. They have even rebuilt their houses and have resumed their activities. The Kikuyus who were in the IDP camps have now resumed and our relationship is not bad according to me. There is no visible animosity. But the memories will always be there. We have to call for forgiveness and confession. If need be one can take two or three people and go mediate with the person you took the cow from. If we just stay away it will reach a time when you need help and the only helper will be that person. You see sometimes ago, a fellow runner maliciously hindered me from attaining my goals. I was helped by a Kikuyu. Although my colleagues were skeptical, this man was true to his word. He helped me. I train away from home together with the Kikuyus at Iten. We have joined the microfinance group. Nowadays, when my community members seek my help, I use the same contact person and they later inform me of their success.

Q: Do you think that the FM stations contributed to this violence?

A: The FM radio stations contributed to the violence because they broadcasted in mother tongue. They spread the message that people should be cautious with one another, a language which even the grandmother understood. Once an old person accepts something it becomes hard to change his/her mind. It's like the local stations fueled the violence. They reached out to a wider audience, even the grandmothers used to carry their radios just to listen to politics. The FM stations contributed about 70% of the chaos and most people young and old still listen to the same stations today!

Q: Is there anything you would like to add?

A: I believe that it's not the politicians who will change this country and the youth should not depend on leaders but forge ahead. The youth should not place themselves in situations that can lead them to problems. Instead they should choose ways that are free from problems. As of now we are in a ditch. We have to look for ways of coming out of the ditch instead of just crying about being in the ditch without making headway out of it. We need to come out of the problem, then checkout where we went wrong and correct it.

We cannot talk of tribunals now because some people are still suffering in IDP camps and people lost property and relatives. The government should solve this immediate problem then later think of tribunals and the Hague. Even if the top leaders say they have been forgiven and they have not come to the grassroots to meet the people they really hurt, then that is not reconciliation. Raila and Kibaki can help those who are suffering because they have the power, land and resources to compensate the victims. People need to act and not just talk. There is no need for people to harm each other.

One needs to think on matters that can benefit him because if Raila, Uhuru, or Kalonzo became the next president and people have been killed, who will they lead here in Kenya? Some leaders just get voted into parliament then they move to Nairobi and never look back, leaving their people dying of hunger. They never take the initiative even to contribute their salaries for just one month. Moi was the president and his people never benefited but are being given relief food. Kibaki is the president and his people have not benefited. Instead they have jiggers. So it is only the leaders who are benefiting. The man at the grassroots just wants to carry out his activities peacefully. As long as he has enough to eat and a place to sleep, he does not care about who gets which leadership role.

The young people need to come together in a forum which they can use for development. A centre can be set up at a neutral place like the equator which can link up young people from many provinces. At this centre, the youths can see that there are other important ways of making a livelihood. Instead of just relying on land they can make innovations and educate others. It can also become a tourist centre, a business centre, an educational centre and these young people can come from different places like Moiben, Ndhiwa, Tinderet, Baringo, Pokot, Marakwet or even Kitale and if those ten youths educate ten others then those too educate others, this can make changes and we can start other centres.

Saying people can live anywhere is a lie...

My name is Jeremiah *(not real name)*. I was born in 1948 in South Nyanza, a place called Gwasi. When I grew up, I went to school up to standard four. I later came to Kericho Township where I finished my primary education. I went to Thika Technical School for secondary education. I came to Kunyak Settlement Scheme in 1970 and lived there until 1992. During this time, clashes started because of land and multipartism. The fighting started from Miteitei then it spread to Kunyak on 3rd November 1992. Kikuyu houses were burnt including those of Luos and Kisiis as well as other communities who were there. This was because of multipartism and mainly because of land bitterness as one could get land here even if he was coming from Kikuyuland. So these people from other parts of Kenya were chased away. Now in 2002 we were not so much affected but in 1992, all of us were affected though we were chasing those other people.

In 2007 the clashes were very serious. In that year I vied on a KANU ticket as a councillor. I never got it. It was very clear, even a small child could tell that ODM was a strong party. Even I in KANU knew that ODM would win the election. It was amazing after we had finished elections that the ODM MP had been elected. Even the civic seat was taken by ODM. What remained was the presidential seat. When presidential results delayed and people were watching on TV what was going on at KICC, we were expecting that Raila would win. Even if you were to guess, it was obvious he was ahead by a big margin. It was shocking to hear that Kivuitu had disappeared and he was said to have gone to State House and announced that Kibaki had won. War was started immediately by people who were listening to radios and those watching TVs. War started from nowhere. Nobody could tell who started this war. No one actually planned for this war because everybody was planning to celebrate. There was no plan even here in Kunyak. The bad thing which was there is that the PNU supporters had said, "Whether you like it or not we are going to take it". That is what brought bitterness. When Kivuitu announced shakily, he sounded like he was forced to announce. People were prepared to celebrate if ODM was to be announced the winner but it turned into cries.

If the truth be told, though Ruto was making his own things, I was watching on my TV, the person who was pestering Kivuitu was Kalonzo and the government knows exactly who did what. The reason why people fought was because of Kivuitu. After that, fighting started seriously. Our youths chased everyone they suspected to be a PNU supporter. The Luos were doing the same on the other side. With us 'old men' we were surprised how organized these young men were and how they were working in precision. Sometimes, they could stop but may be at night you could see them with torches moving around. We could not do anything, we usually blamed the Nairobi people. At first, it was only burning of houses. Our youth never killed anybody. When everyone had gone to the refugee camp, our boys moved around and burnt the standing houses.

Then the government came. The first person to be killed was a Luo. We heard from home that a Luo had been killed. We stayed for some time, then there was war at Lelu and our youth went there. On arriving at the enemy's' territory our boys were killed – four of them, no they were five. One of them was found later killed and thrown into a hole. The government shot and killed four of them and we came here to Kunyak. One person was killed in the hospital by a police officer who is well known. By now the number of our people who had been killed was six. The other house (community) not even one of them was killed. We kept calm. When the time came for us to ask questions about the killing, I asked one of the two DOs who had come why they were silent and yet people were being killed. They just said, "You go and report at the police station". I asked him how can we go and report to the police and yet they are the same people who killed? After all reporting is just a matter of writing. We argued until I told him that it was not fair. We stayed for long until when the clashes subsided. And then the government took IDP's to Nakuru and others to Koru. A small number remained in the camps and others in the school. When schools were about to open, we requested the DO for the school to be opened as well. The few who remained were moved to the next church. Recently, there was a plan to return them to their farms. The way they were brought back! Nobody can lie to me. They were brought back by force.

We were asked if we were ready to receive them. But how are we to receive them yet we have not settled our recent differences? The DC and the government brought them back. Shortly, they were given iron sheets and other items. But you see there has never been any discussion. A few people were selected and called peace builders and so on. Another mistake is to select the IDP representatives without any representative from the host community. The other day during Kenyatta Day, I asked the DO why they were sitting with only one community and yet we also had problems. How would he know our problems? For instance, the other day someone was cut. He should have called us for a meeting. We went to Ngirimori and the DO was not there. But we had a meeting and we sent one of the Kikuyu who was there to go and tell their people to identify the person who cut that person. We were cheated that the person had been arrested. The destruction that was there was that the youth destroyed coffee bushes by cutting them down. The following day, the DC, DO and everybody had come. What happened is that these people had some connections with senior people in Nairobi. We didn't know as our people do not get newspapers. They are doing this to us and when we react they victimize us.

On the distribution of food, when the conflict started it affected both sides. In Kipsigis culture, when there is war they do not go to the camp. I expect even in Kipkelion if there was one he must have been a bad man. Our people do not go to the camp but usually they go to their relatives. We have people who were affected but they went to their relatives. The government cannot believe this! What they know is that a Kisii or a Kikuyu moved. I am sure the government does not have any record of our people who were affected in one way or another. What I can comment is that the government never beat us in our villages unlike the chaos of 1992. They beat and killed people in the villages. They killed a Luo, but it was a directive telling a police officer to shoot him. In the recent one (2007), the police killed because of a certain Kikuyu who is a teacher who told the officer to shoot.

We recently talked to the DC, though he was talking harshly. I think he was intimidating us. I responded to him when he enquired why the trees were cut down. I replied by asking him why someone was cut in the first place? Do you first ask about cut trees or a person who is cut? I was not afraid of him. I told him on his face that the government is terrorizing people (us). We are not unified. What we don't want is this person (the Kikuyu) looking down on us.

Secondly, these people don't want to know that we exist though they have been given land. When they are living with us they should know that we belong here. We are the indigenous people and they are the visitors. We cannot let them lead us. The government employed a Kikuyu as a chief in Kapkoros location leaving behind several of our people. The government we have is based on the old system. Most of the people in Kunyak are Kalenjin. Therefore they are the ones who should be made chiefs. I had told them to forget the issue of administration and politics until another time in the future but now we still have the Kikuyu and the Kalenjin. They should stay around and do business. And when they have money I become their slave. The Kikuyus are very lucky to possess that gift.

The other thing is land. The person who started giving out land was Kenyatta. He brought Kikuyus from Central province to Chepseon and others from Nyeri calling them Mau Mau etc. When he did that, he never picked some people (Kalenjin) from here to Central province. People should be taken to Nyeri, Mombasa etc so that we can know that our people also are there. But there is nobody living there. The pain we have is that when we are traveling towards those sides we see large pieces of land. Who are they preserving this land for? Rift Valley is now having many communities.

The policy of saying people can live anywhere in this country is a lie as our population was still very low and Kenyatta wanted to bring his people here. A time has now come for somebody to either go away or adopt our way of life. That is why there is this saying, "when you go to Rome do as Romans do." The ones who want to live with us, should change completely.

Recently, there were rumors that there were Mungiki around. They have always been threatening people claiming that our arrows cannot do anything to them. The problem with these people is that they never want to adopt our culture. They should not show us that they like Kiambu. It is like somebody saying he likes Belgut and he lives here. That person has to leave. They should accept what we do. You can't do your things inside the territory of the majority. We know there is democracy. You vote the way you want, but what about the majority? We want to teach our people that we are not as wild as it is said. It has reached a time when living is not equal. If Kenya is equal, why not in Kiambu, why not Nyeri? Before I finish, one may ask who cheated you. Kenyatta brought people and Moi never took us to the Kiambu system.

Q: Like the way you were taken to Gwasi?

A: After the creation of KANU and KADU, the Kipsigis called us back after Jaramogi joined hands with this other one and Moi remained with Ngala and we were brought back. What we want is peace but the behavior of these people (the Kikuyu) is provocative.

I Participated in Attacking People

My name is Philip *(not real name)*. I am a resident of Manyatta and I like the place despite having problems of water shortage and the fact that these houses were built in 1968. We are tenants here as well as businessmen. People of diverse ethnic background live here.

Truly life before 2007 was superb and not as bad as we are experiencing right now. Initially, one could buy bread and sugar with a hundred shillings. But things have changed, it's not possible to do the same with that amount of money. We used to relate well with the Kisiis and the Luhyas who were our neighbors. Personally, I have married a Luhya and my immediate neighbour is a Kikuyu. All was well until 30th December 2007 when violence broke out after the announcement of the presidential poll results. After Kibaki was declared winner, I really felt bad. I didn't believe it and being an ODM security agent it didn't go down well with me. I heard my child shouting that Kibaki had won the elections. I can't say that the 2007 violence was planned. My wife had gone home and I was left behind to take care of the house as I prepared to join them later on 1st January 2008. Nothing was planned by anyone because we voted knowing that Raila would win but the results were contrary to our expectations. People felt agitated because they believed that they had been robbed off their victory. This was the main cause of all the confusion.

Being a security agent for Raila, I was sure that if he assumed leadership, I would automatically get a job. This really motivated me and the rest of the youth especially in this area. So when we realized that our hopes had been dashed, we resorted to violence. We lit bonfires on roads. Indeed, I participated fully in attacking people of other ethnic communities who were thought to have voted against the will of the locals. The situation got out of hand. As a result, everyone stayed indoors most of the time because chaos had engulfed the entire Kisumu. People had money but they could not buy food because all the food inlets were blocked by rowdy youths. There was only one source of food and that was Mamboleo Junction. One could not even communicate despite having money because buying a scratch card was a nightmare.

I am ready to live with the people I attacked; I fully understand that we are human beings who need each other. After all, I am a driver of public service vehicles and it's the Kikuyus who own most of the vehicles around. I am ready to be employed by them as I was before the post election violence. I cannot set any conditions for them but fully accept that we have really messed up our lives. I need to feed my children and lead a normal life like before.

Q: There were chaos in 1992 and 1997, did you also participate?

A: In 1992 I was still in school and in 1997 I had just married. During that year (1997) we were involved in heckling when people were demanding to be given another constitution.

Q: What do you think the government can do to promote peace?

A: The government should go ahead and implement what they had promised people earlier. They should compensate everyone who was affected by the violence. The government should not compensate a particular ethnic community and leave out the rest. All of us were affected by the same violence. The relationship between those who fled and those who were left behind is that while the former lost property and maybe loved ones, the latter could not access basic needs especially food.

Q: As an individual, what can you do to promote peace?

A: People should forget what happened; we need to forgive one another. We need to reconcile and live just like we did before the post election violence. When peace prevails, life becomes easy.

Q: Is it possible for people to forget that easily, how can that be done?

A: People will need to undergo counseling in order to overcome whatever they encountered. The leaders in government told people to fill forms at the District Commissioner's office for them to be compensated. That has not been effected yet. Lastly, the government should subsidize the price of foodstuff so that many people can afford food. They also promised free education but that is not the case, there is a fee of Kshs. 2,000 being paid to schools. Therefore, how free is free? Lastly, we need to preach peace. Peace is a major contributing factor to good living.

I DID THIS TO EXPRESS MY VOICE

My name is Kevin *(not real name)* and I am a resident of Kondele. There are many people of diverse ethnic backgrounds who live here. We have Kisiis, Luos, Nandis and Kikuyus. Some of these people rent houses while others live in their own houses. Personally, I am a tenant.

Before 2007, life was amazingly good. After the announcement of the presidential poll results, violence broke out. All the major roads to Kisumu were barricaded with stones. The situation was growing worse day after day because basic necessities like food and other commodities were scarce. It is so unfortunate that the youth here participated in the violence. I was involved in the violence because I am one of them. I belong to that age bracket.

The violence was never planned. I was just defending my rights and so that is why I participated. I did this to express my voice and that of the common man. I wanted the government to hear our cry; we had to disapprove theft of votes.

I was not involved in 1992 and 1997 violence because I was young and still in school. The Kikuyus were attacked because Kibaki is a Kikuyu. The Kambas also felt the wrath because Kivuitu was the Chairman of ECK and Kalonzo had conceded defeat by saying it was free and fair. The Kisiis were victimized because Nyachae was talking too much. Several cars belonging to a 'Kalasinga' (Singh) were burnt because he had employed members of the Kikuyu community only. Violence erupted as soon as Kivuitu announced the presidential results three days after we had voted. We had been pushed to the wall and that is why we had to do it. No one organized the violence; it was just a coincidence that all of us had a common goal. Nonetheless, I have no problem living with those I attacked. If I continue to hold a grudge, they will have no place to live. We are Kenyans and we need each other especially during this period when the economy is bad. I cannot put up any conditions for them I just urge all Kenyans to love one another. People should shun tribalism because it was the main cause of this violence. But this will have to start with them (Kikuyu) because they had vowed earlier that a Luo will never ever lead this country. I think people should avoid tribalism and live as brothers and sisters because we are more than 42 tribes in Kenya.

Q: What do you think the government can do to promote peace?

A: I think people should work together in unity, especially here in Kisumu. Secondly, if the youths are employed this problem will become a thing of the past. We should stop associating people with where they come from. Instead let us promote brotherhood in anything we do. On employment, people should be employed based on merit.

Q: What can you do to promote peace as an individual?

A: We should live in unity now that we have learnt a lesson.

I WAS WORKING AT A CONSTRUCTION SITE...

My name is Delvis *(not real name)* and I was brought up in Naivasha. I went to school here but despite performing well in national examinations I could not continue with education beyond class eight. I had to drop out of school because my parents were poor. Now I work in construction sites as a casual labourer and also do other manual jobs.

There are many ethnic groups living in Naivasha but the Kikuyus are the majority. The second largest community is the Luos; there are also Luhyas, Maasais and Kisiis. Majority of them work in the flower farms. During the referendum for a new constitution, I did not vote because I did not have a voter's card. However, the Kikuyus supported teh draft constitution symbolized by the Banana while other ethnic groups and mainly the Luo supported the Orange which symbolized the refusal of the draft constitution. This is where hatred and tension started. The Luos started bragging that if Orange won, then the Kikuyus would be in trouble and would have to shift from Naivasha. The Orange won and tension reigned in the area and sadness as we watched as the Luos brag in town that they had won.

In 2007 I was in Naivasha and this time round I voted as I had a voting card. However, after voting we waited anxiously for the results and we celebrated after Mwai Kibaki was announced the winner. Our neighbors the Luos and the rest on the other hand were not comfortable with the win and this brought hatred. Previously during the electioneering period, I was fully involved in the campaigns and the politicians would collect us in the morning. We would "eat" their money, move around campaigning for them and in the end get paid Kshs. 100 per day. During the campaign period there was no chaos apart from the tension and hatred generated from the referendum time.

The voting was okay and people turned out in large numbers. I had voted by 7.30 am *(laughs)* and then we waited for results without any worry. We were following the election reports and results from the television and from our point of view things were not all that bad. After the ECK announced that Kibaki had won the elections it was dance and joy in Naivasha and people celebrated making some roads impassable. The celebrations went on till late into the night with some people celebrating until 11.00 pm and 12.00 midnight. Reports started arriving that violence had broken out in parts of Western and Rift Valley provinces and people were being killed in churches and homes torched. We could not take this any longer so we decided to evict outsiders from Naivasha so that our people who were fleeing could occupy their houses.

Those people who were fleeing had so many problems with no food and clothes as they fled using transit lorries and camped at the KANU Grounds. We took it upon ourselves to feed them using the little money we got by buying them things like milk for the young ones. They came in large lorries which dropped them in town and abandoned them there. They were assisted by everybody and even the churches came in. Anybody who had clothes that were no longer in use brought them to the victims. This heightened tension in the town with the locals deciding that the Luos and Kalenjins had to move out of the houses for the incoming IDPs.

There was rising tension within the town as police and prison wardens introduced a curfew. All shops were to be closed by 7.00 pm and everyone was to be home. This did not augur well and locals clashed with the officers. The main complaint was the harassment by the warders who even robbed those getting home late. The people could no longer take it and on one Saturday in January 2008, people decided to hold a demonstration on the following day to oppose the curfew. They at the same time decided to evict outsiders from the houses in various Estates by blocking roads and flushing them from the houses until they left. I was fully involved and I was in the midst of the attacks as I could not watch as our brothers who had fled continue to suffer. We moved in groups and evicted those who had refused to move out and burnt their property before moving to the next house. The Luos, as they were many, were the main target. We flushed them all out. There were many groups in Kabati, Kihooto, Council and Lake View estates and we communicated through mobile phones to plan and attack.

We would communicate through phones and tell our colleagues in Kabati Estate to attack and all the police officers would move there and leave other Estates unmanned and then we would attack. Many people were involved and it is true that some senior people funded the youths to buy weapons and petrol to burn property. There were claims that Mungiki were involved but I don't know how members of the Mungiki look like. However, on that particular day there were so many unfamiliar faces and I am sure they could have been some of them.

It is possible for people to forgive but first those who stole from others must return the stolen goods as it would be painful to see your neighbour using your property such as roofing sheets yet you are staying in a tent. Let people return the stolen property first. I can live peacefully with both Luos and Kalenjins. I don't have any problem with them since we are all Kenyans and we should live together as brothers. Those who fled from Naivasha can come back but they should stop bragging and talking negatively about us. Unemployment among the youths was one of the main causes of the violence in Naivasha. Many youth are idle and spend most of their time loitering. In the end they joined those groups which attacked other communities.

Q: If such chaos were to re-occur again, would you participate?

A: It all depends because if people try to attack us, we would be ready to defend ourselves but we hope that we shall not have such chaos again.

Q: From the chaos did you learn anything or did it act as a lesson to you?

A: Yes, it was a lesson. I have learnt that there are some areas one cannot buy land. It is also wise to be prepared for any eventuality.

Q: What can the government do for people to live in peace?

A: Our leaders should preach to all the need to live in peace and to co-exist like brothers and sisters.

Q: What message would you like to pass to your fellow youths on violence?

A: I would like to say that violence is not good as many people are injured and property lost. The best thing is to live peacefully. We should all learn that we are Kenyans and nobody has his own country. We should therefore love each other as we love ourselves so that we can live in peace.

THEY REFUSED TO ACCEPT THE RESULTS...

My name is Kim *(not real name)* and I was born and brought up in Naivasha. After completing a certificate in computer management, I was unable to get a job. I went back to college for accounts and dropped out halfway. I started hawking within the town centre and during the post election violence, I was among those involved in burning property belonging to the fleeing families.

Naivasha is best known for tourism due to various tourists' destination sites and many flower farms which have employed hundreds of people. There is also small scale trade, vegetable and fruit farming. During the referendum on the draft constitution, I was in Naivasha. Two groups emerged; one supporting (Banana) and the other one against it (Orange). The Orange supporters claimed that the constitution was meant to benefit the Kikuyus as they would continue owning huge tracks of land and thus it had to be dropped. This is when hatred and mistrust started with talks of "majimbo" arising. I did not know what majimbo was by then.

The referendum divided people along tribal lines. There was hatred, tension and fear. The referendum came and went after those who did not want the proposed constitution won. We accepted the results of the referendum and life continued as usual though the element of mistrust never ended.

2007 was a very busy year with many political parties coming up. Campaigns became the order of the day. The main parties were the ODM and PNU and the campaigns took the referendum angle with the Orange and Banana issues cropping up again; splitting the electorate further. ODM said that the elections would be a replica of the referendum vote. Again voting was on tribal lines. I was fully involved in the campaign just like during the referendum and this time I was supporting PNU just like my fellow Kikuyus. We supported Mwai Kibaki for the presidency against Raila who was in ODM. The campaign was very peaceful with no reported cases of violence though as it is normal in campaigns, harsh words were exchanged but people later on voted peacefully.

On the voting day there was a large turnout never witnessed before. By 5.00 am there were long queues in many polling centers. We voted well and headed home to await the results which took long to be announced. The day that brought tension was a Saturday. That was on the eve of the election results announcements by the ECK. On Sunday the 30th December 2007 results were announced that Kibaki had won and ODM supporters refused to accept the results as it had earlier appeared like they would win. This is when chaos and tension started. Naivasha was however quiet that night until the following day when reports of chaos emerged from Molo, Eldoret and Kisumu.

There were celebrations and people were jubilant over Kibaki's win. People from all walks of lives flooded the streets on foot, motorcycles and vehicles with song and dance; some roads became impassable. However, the ODM supporters retreated back to their houses while others escaped from Naivasha fearing for their lives. Nothing was burnt during the celebrations and people went back to their homes though reports started coming in of violence in ODM strongholds.

Soon after people mainly the Kikuyus fleeing from the clash torn areas started coming in large numbers to Naivasha town. They had all kinds of problems and we assisted them with food, clothes and shelter. Some came without shoes; some were injured with no food and had trekked for long distances. The situation was bad. They told us that they had been flushed out of those areas as the ODM supporters didn't agree with the outcome of the elections and regarded the Kikuyus as traitors. They were thus kicked out. Because of this tension started building up in Naivasha. People started meeting in bus-stops and markets over the increasing number of IDPs. It was in these meetings that it was decided that the Luos and Kalenjins had to leave to give space to the incoming

Kikuyus. People argued that since Kikuyus had been attacked by Luos and Kalenjins, then the same should befall the two communities in Naivasha.

In the morning of 27th January 2008 we started flushing them out of the houses but amongst us were strangers who we later learnt were members of the Mungiki sect. Chaos reigned for the better part of the day. There was looting, killing and burning of property all in the name of revenge. I was involved in one way or the other in flushing the Luos from their houses, burning their property and sending them away so that the fleeing Kikuyus could occupy their houses. It was not a good day for visitors as people were butchered, property burnt, others looted and a lot of damage was done. A really bad day. The chaos went on for around three days then the government came in. The army was sent and peace and calm prevailed. However, many people fled from the area after the attacks.

The chaos were not planned at all but it was more of revenge for the incoming Kikuyus who were evicted from parts of Rift Valley and Nyanza. In fact, during the chaos, the IDPs who had camped in Naivasha were the most active in the attacks. They blocked the roads and burnt property because they were hurting after being attacked where they had come from. The police came in with the army using helicopters on the third day. But on the first day, there were no police officers as they were overworked and overwhelmed by the magnitude of the attackers.

There was a curfew and prison wardens were called in but they ended up beating people, arresting, robbing from them and even raping women in the name of curfew. It was a very bad time for the locals. The curfew assisted in a way as tension was high especially at night where Luos were the most targeted. The influx of IDPs mainly from parts of South Rift caused emotions to rise among the people of Naivasha. They became angry and were pained after hearing what the IDPs had gone through in places like Eldoret, Molo and Nyanza. This made them seek revenge on behalf of the fleeing IDPs.

Q: In case there is a repeat of the violence, would you participate in it again?

A: What we saw was really bad. There were huge losses, businesses collapsed and all kind of jobs were affected. As a hawker I deal with people from different the communities and with the chaos, many went away and my work was adversely affected. I don't want this to happen again and if it ever does, I will be in the forefront to stop it.

Q: *Were politicians involved?*

A: I cannot say they were directly involved as they did not give funds. Their biggest mistake was keeping quiet as people were being killed and did nothing to stop the chaos.

Q: *What could they have done?*

A: Well, they should have talked to their supporters to stop the violence and work together as the campaign was over.

Q: *Is it true that members of the Mungiki sect were ferried in?*

A: I am not sure but there were so many strangers at the forefront of the chaos. I was born and brought up here so I know many faces but there were lots of strangers and as a hawker I noticed that I had never seen them before and they talked in refined Kikuyu just like the Mungiki.

Q: *What is your message to Kenyans on the need for peace?*

A: After seeing what happened, I now know that peace is very precious and we should live peacefully. For those who have lost in elections, just give in and life should go on but we should ignore taking tribal inclinations. The law has always been there over those destroying other people's properties and it should be followed to the letter. However new laws against discrimination on tribal grounds should be introduced and stiff penalties issued for those breaking it. The ECK should have more powers to bar any politician campaigning on tribal lines.

EVERY SIDE WAS CONFIDENT OF TAKING THE PRESIDENCY...

My name is Daudi *(not real name)* and I was born in Nairobi but shifted to Naivasha at a tender aged of six years. I have grown up in Naivasha, gone to school here and learnt everything that I know in this town. Naivasha is like Kenya because since my childhood, I have met all the ethnic groups in the country and even outsiders.

Because of its nearness to Central province and the fact that three sides of Naivasha border the province, Kikuyus are the majority. There are also many flower farms and for this reason there are a lot of Luhyas and other communities who work in the farms. They are preferred because they have no problem with the low wages. Therefore you will find that many of the people working in the farms are from Western Kenya while many Kikuyus who live in the town shun the jobs in preference for other jobs mainly in business.

When the election day neared at the end of 2007, there were talks of Majimbo and people in Naivasha were confused as they knew nothing about it or how the town would be divided. So people had to tell each other the truth that was, "you either vote with us so that we can live harmoniously or you move out." In the flower farms where the opposition has the largest numbers of supporters they believed that they would win and in the town centre where pro-government supporters were many, they also believed in a win and this is how the war started.

Before the polling day, campaigns were peacefully conducted but a PNU supporter would not campaign in an ODM stronghold and vice versa but there was also exchange of harsh words as is normal during campaigns.

The voting day was perfect; voters woke up early in the morning to vote and if there were any problems, maybe in very few polling stations. Later in the night, it was counting of the votes and waiting for the results. As the Naivasha results were delayed a little bit, tension started building up. After one or two days, what surprised many is that when the presidential results were announced and my preferred candidate Mwai Kibaki had won, many took to the streets with dance and song in celebration but in other towns violence started with the people saying that Kibaki had rigged the elections.

I remember that is where the problem started because the results were announced on a Sunday evening at around 6.30pm and violence erupted in other towns. This was being aired on TV as what was happening in other towns with the locals attacking Kikuyus saying that Kibaki had not won but had rigged the elections. And through the TV sets, tension became very high as people watched Kikuyus being killed in other towns and this is when it was decided that since they were sending Kikuyus away, then we should also send away their kinsmen too.

Looking at it in details and from a distance and though I was not fully involved in planning, I can say that the government security agencies were caught napping. The violence started on a Sunday morning and two days earlier, there were reports that the Mungiki boys would be brought in to show us how to flush out people purported to be outsiders. Also from rumours going around this was meant to act as a lesson to other ethnic groups that the Kikuyus too could defend themselves. Thus, when the violence started on Sunday morning, stones were thrown on the road and bonfires lit just as it had been planned the previous day. Many who did not know what was going on woke up as usual but by 8.00am all the roads within the town and estates were impassable due to the stones used in blocking them.

The main target were the Luos and Nandis and they were also caught unawares as I believe that if they knew of the attack, no one would have waited for death. But maybe because of the secrecy and the belief that neighbors could not turn against each other they were not prepared for the attacks.

Because of the tension in the country, it had been decided that Naivasha was to act as the benchmark and for us who participated in the chaos, it never hit us that the chaos would be this serious or that they could go on for over two days. Before the army helicopters came in, we did a lot of anarchy and we were forced to do some things because we were told that any non-Kikuyu had to be flushed out of the town. We even went to their houses and burnt their property and to show how angry we were, we took knives and killed them.

Before the army came in we thought calm would return, but mob psychology set in and it became hard to tell your colleagues that they were doing wrong and some of those who had hidden the victims had to throw them out as chaos prevailed. From the first day, things got out of hand and despite the presence of police, roads were blocked and since the police who came to bring back order were new they could not contain the marauding youths who were also opposed to some police officers who came from other ethnic groups. It thus became hard to contain the violence and come the second day, the violence continued with more property being burnt in the town before we moved out to surrounding areas like Karate, Karagita, DCK and the only place the fleeing families could run to was the police station.

Then on the third day, sense prevailed and since we are all human beings we were touched on hearing who had died, who had lost what and as we contemplated on this. Some people who had fled to prison grounds decided to come and revenge by burning a house in Site Estate. This was the reason why so much property was burnt as the first days it was just killing and beating the Luos and Nandis but the attempt to torch the house cost them their property and the destruction.

I believe that the Naivasha violence started as revenge to show other people that we could also fight and defend our own. In addition, Naivasha being the gateway to Rift Valley and having the main highway it was believed that if it was closed down, people would recognize that we were also men who could act and revenge.

I believe the chaos were planned. How come there was food and drinks issued every day after the attacks? I believe that some people started and planned the whole thing. I also believe people were ferried into town because locals could not just wake up and start killing the same people whom they had lived with for years. And when the Mungiki boys came, they spread the spirit to kill and the local youths took over. I don't have any problem with other communities and to be sincere we have been friends since childhood and to meet them now is hard because how can you convince them that you were not involved in the chaos where they lost property and relatives? Any way some times it's shameful meeting them.

Q: *In 2012 there will be elections. What is your advice so as to avoid a repeat of such violence?*

A: In my view we should first forget about the elections and in the next five years deal with peace, justice and reconciliation. Things might get out of hand if we have another referendum at such a time which will end up complicating things. As a result, this will bring more animosity as those who have returned back will be forced to flee come election time and we wonder what will happen if this time round they win. So let us first heal the nation through truth and reconciliation and think as Kenyans and not on tribal grounds.

My appeal to fellow Kenyans is this: Let us be patriotic. Let us forget our tribes and work as Kenyans for the benefit of our country and if possible get rid of old leaders and elect youth who can lead us well.

Q: Taking you back, are you able to talk or even face those people you attacked?

A: The truth is that we speak but on tense grounds as you are not sure whether he is trying to trap you because they have developed mistrust. On the other hand, there is also the shame; fear of whether he knows you participated in the killing and looting. Since we all have rented houses, we also took their houses and their property was burnt but not ours.

Q: What is your message to Kenyans?

A: Let us first of all be proud to be Kenyans and let us stand above tribal leadership. Let us respect human lives.

IT WAS THE CURFEW THAT MADE US ANGRY...

My name is Peter *(not real name)* and I live in Karagita Estate which is a slum area and has all the tribes who mainly work in the flower farms and in construction sites.

An officer tries to calm down the youth protesting over an imposed night curfew in Naivasha. Photo by Antony Gitonga

Before the 2007 violence, Karagita Estate was good and the only politics in this area was related to the campaign between the two main parties, PNU and ODM. We mingled with other communities and even played football with them but things were to change later on when some people started bringing in hate speech. They argued that if ODM won we would have to leave the town as Kikuyus belonged to Central province and not Rift Valley. This caused anxiety because Kikuyus had built houses and invested in the town. As Kikuyus, we did not take this lightly. We started arming ourselves in case ODM won as the party was getting popular in the country. Our area was safe, campaigns were perfect and people conducted them in a mature way. As for me, I campaigned for one of the councilors and since many of the people work in flower farms, the campaigns started after five when you would hear songs and dances as they campaigned. As is the norm in the country, the campaigns were marked with insults and name calling. In Naivasha the main parties were PNU and ODM.

On the Election Day, people voted well and in large numbers. Later in the evening, we started getting reports of results through the press and ODM was leading at the time. The ODM supporters started hauling abuses at PNU supporters saying that they would leave town since ODM was winning; yet all votes had not been counted. The people from Nyanza, Western and even Kalenjins openly told us this and we did not take it well.

Things were normal in Naivasha even after the presidential results were announced and business was back to normal though there was tension and anxiety. Then we started getting reports of violence in Eldoret, Kisumu and other parts of Rift Valley where the Kikuyus who had invested in those areas were attacked and killed. During the whole month of January, they fled to Naivasha and came in transit lorries and told shocking stories of how they had suffered. We assisted them with shelter, food and clothing. But the Luos started enjoying themselves as the Kikuyus fled saying that this happened because Kibaki rigged the elections and ODM had won. We could not take it any longer. We decided that we should evict the Luos and Kalenjins from the houses in Naivasha so that the fleeing Kikuyus could occupy them.

In Naivasha, violence did not start right away. I remember that on the 26th of January 2008 a curfew was introduced and we had to be in the house by 7.00 pm. There was football going on and many youth thus failed to get a chance to watch the matches. The curfew made us angry. On 27th of January we came together as youth and decided to go to Naivasha police station and establish why there was a curfew in the town but police dispersed us using tear gas. We therefore decided to attack the Luos who had made us to be beaten by the police. Our main aim was for the fleeing Kikuyus to live in their houses.

After being chased by police we moved to Kabati Estate where we flushed out the Luos and closed all the roads and the two main highways passing through the town. We decided that no non-Kikuyu would use the road apart from those who supported PNU. In Kabati we evicted the Luos. Some people lost their lives but we have no regrets as our kinsmen were also killed in parts of Nyanza and North Rift. People became beasts and decided to revenge. We were not prepared as such but some youth from outside Naivasha came and said that every home had to produce a man who would be involved in the violence. So I had no otherwise but to join them and we moved from one Estate to the other beating and killing them. We wanted to show them that we also had rights just like any other Kenyan. Consequently, we did this because we were angry at what was happening to our kinsmen. We thus decided to burn their property and evict them from the houses.

At first, it was free for all but later when the Mungiki came we were split into groups of 30 youth and we were told where to attack and when. Afterwards, we would meet after 20 minutes and decide where next and how to avoid the police officers who were on patrol. I was born and brought up in Naivasha hence I know all the corners and streets of the town. As a result, we managed to evade the police easily as we attacked non-Kikuyus. With this knowledge, I showed my colleagues which houses to attack and which ones to leave. We only targeted the Luo and Kalenjin houses and what we did was to get the property out and burn them as the buildings belonged to the Kikuyus. We would then move to where the IDPs were camping and take them inside the abandoned houses. I don't have any real problems with other ethnic groups but the issue comes with their attitude. For example, when we invest and improve our lives, the Luos say that we have robbed other people yet like me I have a loan from Equity Bank. They only want what is ready and are not ready to work for it. But the Luos and the Kalenjins rely on assistance and if they want us to live in harmony, they should be prepared to respect us and stop accusing us of stealing because we really work hard for what we have. We are now living together. For instance, the plot where I live, we have two Luos and we also play football with them and stay together as brothers because we have forgiven each other. There is however one ethnic group that we have problems with as they evicted our kinsmen from North Rift but for the Luos we have no problem with them and they have gone back to the flower farms.

Q: You have said that you have a problem with people from North Rift. What would you like them to do before you forgive them?

A: They should allow our kin in IDP camps to go back to their farms and they should come and apologize to us and assist those they evicted by reconstructing their houses and giving a promise that such attacks should not happen again. If they don't do that, then I foresee a problem as we have never voted together with them and there is no trust among us.

Q: What can the government do to avoid a repeat of the violence and for Kenyans to live peacefully?

A: The biggest problem is unemployment which has seen many youth engage in drugs and taking illicit brews. The government should come up with programmes to assist the youth earn a living and let the youth from different parts of the country interact. The government should offer them jobs.

Q: What is your message to Kenyans on peace?

A: Let us live as brothers and sisters peacefully. A lot of blood was shed during the fight for independence and there is no need to shed more blood. We have 42 ethnic groups in Kenya and only two or three of them are fighting. I urge the government to look for ways so that people can stay peacefully, be patriotic and know that we are living in the 21st century where ethnicity should be a thing of the past.

I AM A TOUT...

My name is Sam *(not real name)* and I was born and brought up in Naivasha. I dropped out of school in Form Four and later became a tout.

I know there are many kinds of businesses but I prefer my job as a tout as I have survived in it for around ten years now. I was here in Naivasha when the Banana and Orange thing came and I was supporting the Banana though we lost to the Orange people as they were many. People from Western Kenya were voting for Orange and we and people from Central Kenya were voting for the Banana. Orange won in the referendum and we accepted the loss.

It is after the referendum when trouble started as the Luos who were supporting the Orange started bragging that they would win in the general election just as they had won in the referendum. Things went back to normal although the Luos and those supporting the Orange kept to themselves and started organizing how to attack us and that is how the violence started. We just ignored them and this is where tension started to rise between members of the two communities. We are very good people and we didn't take any action and even when the chaos started countrywide, the last place to be hit was Naivasha.

The campaign period was okay and even the ODM people campaigned freely with people from other parties like NARC-K. We mingled and we were well paid by politicians after campaigning for them. We woke up by 5.00 am to vote and it was not until 10.00 am that we voted. Voting was very peaceful and after voting we headed back to our house to listen to results.

When Mwai Kibaki was declared the winner, we celebrated. Our celebrations were very peaceful and no shop was broken into or any property destroyed. But on the following day violence in some parts of the country were reported especially in Kisumu and Rift Valley. We started seeing Kikuyus fleeing to Naivasha. People from Western Kenya retreated back to their houses and we later came to learn that they were planning to attack us. The IDPs in Naivasha told us to be ready and that is how we attacked the outsiders.

The fleeing IDPs had many problems as they came from different parts like Eldoret, Kitale, Narok, Molo and Kisumu and they came in trucks. They told of terrible stories and we assisted them in every possible way. They informed us how their houses were burnt and looted and we could no longer bear that pain. The violence in Naivasha was due to the pain of seeing and hearing sad stories from the incoming IDPs. The Naivasha violence did good for the country as things cooled down after the chaos. I remember the chaos started on a Sunday morning after we decided that the Luos had to move out. They were not paying any rent and our people were suffering and we decided to flush them out. We moved from Kihoto, Council, Site and Kabati Estates. We were communicating through mobile phones on where to attack and we evicted them and flushed them from our houses. The chaos went on for three days before army helicopters were sent in and calm returned. I am however happy as other people saw what we did and this brought peace to the country. And we also decided amongst ourselves to stop the chaos. We were never organized by anybody. We just decided that all men had to get out of their houses and leave women behind.

Q: Who were you targeting in you attacks?

A: We mainly targeted the Luos and Kalenjins because we felt that our kinsmen had been attacked and killed by them in parts of Rift Valley.

Q: Do you still hate Luos and Kalenjins?

A: The hatred was there but things have now changed and we have no problem with them as of now.

Q: And when the chaos reigned, where did the Luos and Kalenjins run to?

A: Some escaped to the prison, others to the police station and others went to the flower farms where they were locked in by the flower farmers.

Q: And is it true that the prison guards harassed locals?

A: It is true that the people from prison instead of maintaining peace went ahead to rob the youth by stealing their mobile phones, clothes, and cash.

Q: When you say people from prison, who do you mean in particular?

A: It is the prison warders.

Q: Is it true that members of Mungiki were ferried to this town?

A: The truth is that I did not see any Mungiki and those that I saw were people I know very well.

Q: And were politicians involved in the violence?

A: They were doing their things quietly and we did not know if they were involved or not.

Q: If there was a repeat of such violence, would you attack other tribes?

A: We would not like such violence again as we have learnt a lot.

Q: Are you ready to live with the people that you flushed out?

A: I have no problem with them and I consider them as my brothers despite what happened.

Q: What would you like them to do first so that you can live with them peacefully?

A: We have no issues with them as long as they live peacefully like human beings.

Q: In 2012 there will be another election, do you foresee such violence?

A: For me I would not like to see such violence again as lives were lost, property burnt and businesses affected and we should avoid another war.

Q: And is it true that some politicians were involved?

A: It is true and I would like to warn my fellow youths to shun the politicians that use us and dump us to suffer with no jobs or means of survival.

Breinigsville, PA USA
28 April 2010
237040BV00002B/3/P